TABLOID MAN
& the Baffling Chair of Death

—•••—

REVEALED:
Shocking Secrets of the Scandal Sheets

PAUL BANNISTER

TABLOID MAN
& the Baffling Chair of Death

PAUL BANNISTER

Cover design: *Kim McGovern*
Chair image: *Robert Williams*

Dedication

For Jennie, my steadfast star on this absorbing journey, and for our daughters Claire and Rachel, who have enriched and enlivened every step of the way.

Acknowledgements

I'm deeply grateful for the clear-sighted editorial assessments and ideas of Rachel Williams, my publishing professional daughter, whose input made this product considerably less tedious. Book editor Jeff Bolkan's shrewd advice and my longtime friends Christine and Joe Mullins' manuscript review also truly helped shape things, while designer Kim McGovern's talents captured the look I wanted before I knew what it was. Thank you, all of you.

CONTENTS

A would-be satirist, a hired buffoon,
A monthly scribbler of some low Lampoon,
Condemn'd to drudge, the meanest of the mean,
And furbish falsehoods for a magazine.

—LORD BYRON, 1809

PAPER CHASE

Chair of Death and My Life

Locals said the Baffling Chair of Death carried a deadly curse, and it certainly hexed me.

Because of it, I strapped into a series of tourist-class chairs in the air and travelled the world, reporting for supermarket tabloids whose editors sent me to be groomed by a gorilla, to work with the CIA's psychic spies and to talk to ghosts. The Baffling Chair, which was supposed to cause swift death to all who sat in it, led to an exercise guru in sparkly underpants prancing on my desk, exposed me to the wrath of movie stars and presidents, dumped me into a hurricane and made me suffer the mysterious revenge of a Brazilian witch doctor. And, I'd only looked at the fatal furniture. Thank goodness I never sat in the thing.

I was a British newspaper reporter when the Baffling Chair came into my life, and my trade had already exposed me to some interesting, unlikely and follicle-elevating moments. I'd shared a sardine with a man who was a prince, an earl and a duke twice over. I'd been shot at by the Irish Republican Army, spat on by a kangaroo and threatened with violence by one of the world's greatest soccer players, just before he ran away. On that day when I first faced the Baffling Chair, I was mercifully unaware of what was yet to come...

The Chair, reputed instrument of the supernatural, stood in a Yorkshire pub's store room. Locals said it caused all who sat in it to die within three days. This had all the ingredients of a good yarn, so I suggested it to an American supermarket tabloid. After all, like many of their stories, this tale had at least one small fingerhold on fact. Many people who'd sat in the Baffling Chair were now dead. Given that this particular piece of furniture had reportedly been around for 300 years or so, and few of us pass the four score mark, the high ratio of chair sitters to dead wasn't too surprising.

My problem was that eager editors in faraway Florida wanted a Hey Martha out of it, a story that would make the reader turn to his wife and call on her to listen to this one, Honey. They wanted a gripping chronicle of how every soul who'd parked his bottom on that worn elm seat had died, swiftly and dramatically. They wanted a piece to make magazines fly from the racks, something to send shivers down readers' spines. They would headline it as The Baffling Chair of Death, on the front page of their weekly disbursement of Untold Stories as they sought to make it more famous than the papal throne, more perilous than any Siege at King Arthur's Round Table. All I had to do was gather and write the facts and send them to the National Enquirer at its very own zip code in Lantana, Florida. That's 33464, USA.

I wondered how I'd come to this. A working class boy, battered into some sort of shape by the Christian Brothers in industrial Lancashire, I was one of a cadre of British newsmen who learned their trade covering local court sessions and council meetings. My journo-generation didn't attend university, and remained happily innocent of academic certification except that provided by the National Council for the Training of Journalists. College courses in medieval husbandry or the meanings of Renaissance quatrains were not for us. We studied subjects like shorthand, local government, law and the essentials of page makeup, and we did it in the evenings, after a working day. We were reasonably literate, became street-savvy with a little help and were drawn into newspapers because they seemed to offer an interesting time and fair rewards. The only qualities essential for real success in the trade, Nicholas

Tomalin famously wrote, were 'rat-like cunning, a plausible manner and a little literary ability.' He later admitted he stole the phrase from a colleague, which neatly supported the premise.

Few of us seemed to have a burning desire to evangelize for social betterment or high-minded action, but we thrived on competitive cut and thrust, for in almost all UK towns there were several competing daily or weekly papers, plus a half-dozen nationals. Like many others, I'd been recruited into newspapers by chance. A sports writer on a local weekly who'd been receiving my cycling club reports called to tell me they were looking for a junior reporter. Was I interested? Was I? This teenager almost fell over in excitement. An escape from my stultifying life as a management trainee at a giant electrical corporation was most welcome. I still relish the memory from my second day at the Eccles Journal, of walking alone to the town hall to record the rulings of the magistrates' court. Unfettered and relatively unsupervised, I'd found my dream job. Go and ask questions, write it, just do it without some prodnose peering over your shoulder.

The weekly paper job led to a progression of others, working for an evening daily, freelancing for a cycling magazine, taking a staff job in faraway London. There, I lived, breathed and wrote about bicycle racing and, an elite cyclist, was for a time probably one of the fittest people on Fleet Street, the epicenter of UK newspapers. When, for example, a Midlands cycling club asked for a Cycling Magazine editor to address their annual awards dinner, I didn't consider it unusual to ride the 120 miles each way to give my little speech. I just left after work on a Friday evening and pedaled back on Sunday.

The job even equipped me with a wife, who's still tolerating me after 40-plus years, as I met her while working at the 1966 Earl's Court Cycle Show. Jennie and I married a year later, and I turned away from bike racing and my slender Olympic hopes and went north to a morning paper in Sheffield. From there it was a short step to a national newspaper, where I found myself a member of a sort of club of jovial cut throats. We were a clan of rival reporters who'd remove the diaphragm from a public telephone to disable it so a competitor couldn't file copy (we learned to carry a spare) but we often worked cooperatively. After all, today's rival might well be tomorrow's colleague, when you switched newspaper jobs.

Back Door to Truth

So it was that I'd fallen in with a onetime colleague now working for the National Enquirer, had sent them freelance offerings and was on the verge of going to Florida and the sandy, sleepy coastal town of Lantana. This whistle-stop settlement was the unlikely Ground Zero for tabloids. The genius and drive of a single man, Generoso Paul Pope Jr., changed newspaper culture for decades. His influence caused newspapers and magazines to slide from the sober to the sensational in a shift that colors the news media today. His drive was responsible for changing the very philosophy of newsgathering, at least as it relates to reporting the posturings and doings of the famous. In the old Hollywood system, stars under contract to the studios made a handful of movies each year, and the world was fed a diet of fact and fiction to keep their names bright. Those old-school actors were fewer, but had lengthy careers and an adoring, uncritical public. Pope changed that. His willingness to pay sources let him floodlight the famous, often revealing foibles and flaws the studios had kept hidden. Celebrities, whether of the Hollywood or District of Columbia variety, quickly retreated behind ramparts of privacy. At roughly the same time, the long-term contract system died, actors' longevity of career vanished, and although one could make literally millions of dollars in just a year or two at the top of the movie tree, it was easy to fade into relative obscurity again. No celeb wanted negative publicity to taint such a short career, so spokespeople who once welcomed publicity became protective guardians of the gates of silence, while celebrities' lawyers acted as attack dogs to savage any intruders who evaded the gatekeepers.

The result of the new gloves-off approach between celebrity magazines and the famous they covered was that the magazines saw little point in hiding the grubby secrets they unearthed. Once, in the cosier studio-press relationship, a reporter wouldn't publish, say, some male heart throb's homosexual tendencies because the actor would later cooperate over other gossip, as payback. Under the changed relationship, with no cooperation likely, the tabloids could treat the famous without respect. They lampooned and exaggerated, embellished and fleshed out stories around the bare bones of information they'd been leaked, had bought from their tipster sources, or had gleaned from stakeouts and stalking. In time, the adversarial relationship and pressure to unearth lucrative gossip led to illegal wiretaps, invasions of privacy and other underhand methods. Legitimate newsgathering was undermined, but the tabloids actually got closer to true and accurate coverage of Hollywood or Washington by these backdoor means than ever they could expect from taking the respectable route. That orthodox way, face to face with the public relations hacks, spokesmen and other mouthpieces hired to protect their clients' privacy, became a dead end. I encountered it often enough. Celebs were so wary of my ilk they wouldn't take any chances. In a typical example, I was once turfed out of a San Francisco hotel after being formally invited to a press junket weekend.

I'd rolled up, attended the preview of the forgettable movie, been wined and dined with a busload of other hacks and spent the night in my freebie, upscale hotel room. The next afternoon I was to get my interviews. It didn't happen. Once the actress Phoebe Cates realized that her reps had invited a reporter for the Sunday magazine of a London mass-market newspaper, I was swiftly disinvited. A pleasant PR woman explained that the actress had been burned by the London tabloids and would I leave, please? Miss Cates wanted no truck with me, however innocent my purpose. For the record, the woman who once said "In this business, a girl has to be willing to strip," was announcing an end to her on-screen nudity. My story, that Cates' career had been a mix of nudity and Shakespeare, was hardly a secret, but she had an axe to grind. Leave, leper, was the message. It smarted a bit, but it fit the pattern. Just because actors become rich and famous from the public who hand over their dollars at the box office doesn't mean they'll respect those who put them there. There's little loyalty in ingrate Tinseltown. Once actors are famous, they turn away from the people who made them so. Until, that is, the star dims and they need to regain center stage. That's when the striptease begins over, with the media as voyeur and pimp, and the star revealing something, for publicity. Small wonder I didn't like to do celeb stories, no large wonder that the tabs turned to the guerilla tactics that get them closer to accurate reporting than you'd guess was likely. Remember the OJ Simpson affair, or the politico John Edwards' bust? They were major stories the respectable press could never have unearthed, with straight-shooter tactics, but more on the down and dirty ways the tabs get the truth, later.

Pope of The Enquirer

Before I breeze off into my own adventures, it's useful to know a little about the tabloid of record that became my employer. Come and meet the National Enquirer and its purposeful publisher.

The paper was launched in 1952, on the back of a $75,000 loan to Gene Pope, a New Jerseyite Italian-American who was the son of a quarry millionaire. He created a gory New York tabloid that specialized in traffic accident and murder photographs, under headlines like "I Used My Dead Baby's Face For An Ashtray" and ran circulation up to around a million before it stalled. For reasons that also will be explained later, Pope relocated the Enquirer from New York to Florida in 1971 and changed it into a tool to examine the underbelly of Hollywood. "If it's nice, it ain't news," was his philosophy on covering celebs. The credo worked and in its heyday the paper was selling around five million copies a week. Much of that success came from Pope's own clear vision and focus, and as an autocrat and sole proprietor, he was able to crush opposing views, to do it his way. He was also a famous ball-buster who didn't care for familiarity. A security guard who'd been warned not to chat to him once said: "Good evening Mr Pope, how are you doing?" Pope ordered the man fired. "It was the 'How're you doing?' that got you the sack," the personnel officer explained to him.

Tall, stiff-shouldered and with a shark grin, GP looked like the janitor as he wandered the offices adjusting the thermostats to 78 degrees. He smoked like a test chimpanzee for the National Cancer Institute, he ran celeb dirt, and he liked to publish hokey stories. "More people eat corn than caviar," he reasoned. GP had a weakness for Miracle Cures and New Proof of Life After Death and a quiver full of schmaltzy, circulation-boosting weaponry including reader contests (someone, somewhere, must still wear giveaway 'I'm a National Enquirer TV Blooper Spotter' tee shirts) and Lucky, a rescued dog we photographed with celebrities. Pope also loved tear-jerking stories and would send his favorite rewrite girl, beautiful Minnesota honey blonde Marsha May, back to her desk six or seven times to re-jig a story he liked. "Make me cry, Marsha," he'd tell her, an admonition with which most of the male reporters heartily concurred. Crying or not, Pope was hated by Hollywood and reviled by the establishment media, who called him The High Priest of Low Brow, but the readers got what they wanted, and his formula worked.

We all knew that The Boss had small regard for the corporate bottom line, but we didn't quite realize just how little he cared for it, plowing back the income into the product. Later, it turned out that Pope made an annual profit from the Enquirer of about $19 million. After his death, the new owners made a few changes and cleared $70 million almost at once.

Under GP's rule, in late 1973, I was the sixth reporter taken on staff, and eventually we'd have 80 or so of us, plus a dozen photographers and several hundred freelancers. We worked in teams of about eight under editors whose aim was to appease the publisher, for Pope liked to divide and conquer. The teams' production was monitored, under-producers were put on a month's notice and every group worked alone, so it was not uncommon to bump into office colleagues even in remote places, where rival editors from the Enquirer had independently sent reporters. Once, a reporter and photographer team who'd taken a week to reach a mining camp in the Guatemalan jungle were told excitedly of two other gringos in the same village. They went to share a beer and found themselves facing another Enquirer team working on the very same story. It wouldn't have been so bad, but the two reporters were personal enemies. For several days, the bemused miners were treated to the sight of two sets of gringos doing the exact same interviews and pictures without speaking to each other.

Seeking Utopia

At least, they were working as a team of two, unlike the man sent in 1973 on the Enquirer's most famous assignment. John Harris, a rangy, drawling wit of a man from North Carolina, is forever enshrined in media lore as The Man Who Searched for Utopia.

It was publisher Pope's idea, scrawled on a lead sheet and dropped on John's desk. The brief: "Is there really a Utopia left in this world?

What's it really like to live in Tahiti and those other pipe-dream paradises? Let's write a series." Harris, a painstaking and conscientious man, gathered up his corporate Amex card, a sheaf of traveler's cheques and his Tiffany-blue Olivetti portable typewriter. He began the search that would become newspaper legend, on the shores of the Caribbean. The region looked promising, but John had to report that there was poverty and some litter in the Bahamas, and crime in Jamaica was endemic. Pope scratched those islands off the list.

The Windward, Turks, Antilles and Leeward islands all had minor flaws and while the Caymans were very attractive, the publisher knew of the financial centers there, and business, he ruled, had no place in Paradise. John moved on to Europe, and the Greek isles. Too many European tourists. He visited castles in Spain (too ruined) and examined misty isles in Scotland (too damp.) Every week or so, he'd file a story about another wonderland. Each time, the publisher found fault with the spot, pointing out some small flaw that was enough to spoil paradise. In four and a half months, John went through Central and South America, Asia, Africa and even took a peek at Antarctica. He checked remote islands and filed report after report. Every time his dispatch revealed something the publisher considered unsuitable for Utopia. Molokai was too accessible to North America. Bali had tourists, Sri Lanka was politically uncertain, the Seychelles were too remote, Mauritius wasn't friendly enough. Nowhere met Pope's near-impossible standards. Tension mounted. Over the months of John's global wanderings, two of his editors were fired and the third was fearing for his job. Harris had become a journalistic Flying Dutchman, condemned to travel forever. Later he'd say he didn't mind. "I got that around-the-world, all-expense-paid assignment to search for Utopia," he said. "It was probably the greatest assignment a reporter anywhere could ever get."

Diligent John journeyed on, and reported back. Tahiti was scratched off the list of contenders because its capital had a rush hour and parking meters. Bora Bora had too many hotels, American Samoa was too unkempt. The world's most wonderful places just weren't good enough. Then, in mid-Pacific, journeying John visited Upolu, a Western Samoan island of glorious beaches, lush rainforest, dramatic waterfalls and volcanic scenery. The place was an uncluttered confection of swaying palms and gentle trade breezes. There was no crime in this heaven of white sand, warm blue ocean and plentiful resources. John sighed, from both relief and sadness. He knew he'd found The Place, and his long and wonderful journey was ending. He'd triumphed by finding paradise, but he'd come to the end of a glorious experience. Paradise was no longer lost, Harris wrote. He typed his report and called it in to the office. Publisher Pope got the news. Our man had found Utopia. Pope read the dispatch and cracked his rare and mako-like smile at editor Maury Brecher. "That's good, Maury, very good," he said. Brecher backed out, bowing, practically sobbing with relief. At his desk, the phone rang. The publisher had a question. "How'd Harris get this to you?" "He phoned it over, and my assistant typed it, Mr Pope," said the editor. "Phoned? You mean they've got phones on this island? If there's a phone there, it ain't Utopia," said Pope. "Bring him back."

The $200,000 odyssey was over, and Pope never printed a single word about it. "There is no paradise on Earth," he'd declare. He knew, he'd had it checked.

First Chair, Local News

GP knew a lot. He understood that readers wanted variety, and the 60-plus stories in the magazine each week ranged across a spectrum of medical breakthroughs, human interest stories, how-to's, and a panorama of 'talkers,' or stories that would tempt readers into discussion of the subject.

One of those areas was the occult, an area at that time rarely addressed in the regular media. When a Scots editor called Icepick for his near-bloodless disposal of rivals wrote a lengthy series recounting the doubtful triumphs of the Washington seer Jeane Dixon, circulation soared. Jeane's was the voice in the silence, declaring "I predicted it," when John F. Kennedy was assassinated, and a shocked America bought the claim. All she actually said ahead of time was that she saw 'a dark cloud over the presidency.'

Jeane explained after that day in Dallas that she'd known everything all along, but she couldn't actually change events, fate was fate and all that. Sorry. Gullible America gasped at her 'gift' and she became a modern Merlin to several presidents and First Ladies, all of whom kept discreetly quiet about the relationship, but Jeane's name sold papers. Enquirer editors paid attention and looked around the newsroom. Someone recalled my Baffling Chair of Death credential, and I found myself propelled into the role of the paper's senior reporter on matters psychic.

But I'm getting ahead of myself, and the chronology. A year or so previously, while I was working for a British national paper, I'd sent the tale of the Chair of Death to the Enquirer in Florida as a freelance idea. An editor had bitten on it and the call came in its usual thrilling way. A young Texan woman exotically named Rose Aleta, who was equipped with an accent so honeyed you wanted to spread it on bread, was calling on our home phone and as usual I was struggling to comprehend what she was saying. Finally, she handed me over to her boss, a Scot named Bruce, whose brogue was marginally more intelligible, and I understood I was to go at once and give oxygen to the tale of the Baffling Chair of Death.

Boots on the ground, off I went to find the Busby Stoop Inn between the Romans' Great North Road and the ancient market town of Thirsk in Yorkshire. At first sight, the deadly chair looked safe enough. It was stored where nobody could sit on it, because landlord Tony Earnshaw had locked the aggressive antique away in an old coach house at the back of the pub. Several empty wooden crates for beer bottles were stacked on it. Earnshaw cautiously moved them for me, taking care not to stumble into the chair's possibly fatal embrace. The thing, a sturdy high-backed Windsor-style piece with turned ash back spindles, baluster legs, and scooped elm seat, had the rub of years of use. It looked ordinary, if old. The landlord, who'd taken over the pub in 1966, said he was a believer in the legend, which was reasonable enough given that the murderous seat could bring coach loads of the curious to his hostelry. He solemnly told me: "Nobody is going to sit in that chair again. It's too dangerous and I want no more deaths on my conscience." I scribbled the telling phrase into my notebook, in my own version of Pitman shorthand, mentally saying 'No thanks, I won't sit down.'

Earnshaw obligingly outlined the story. In the first years of the 18th century, in the sleepy hamlet of Sandhutton, a burly local bully named Thomas Busby would claim the fireside chair as his own whenever he arrived at the tavern for a drink. Locals aware of

Busby's violent temper ceded the armchair to the big man, who was a coiner, a criminal who clipped money to make forgeries of his own with the skimmed silver. On a June night in 1702, when he arrived at the tavern with his father in law, Daniel Auty, even the kowtow of the ceded chair and a skinful of ale didn't mellow him. Busby quarreled with Auty, and killed him with a spade.

Arrested and swiftly tried, he was sentenced to be hanged on the gibbet, or stoop, at the crossroads outside the inn. Busby took his final drink, which in the custom of the time was probably drugged by the hangman to keep him calm, and took his last steps to the scaffold. As he left the tavern, he promised death to anyone who used 'his' chair. Over time, the tavern took on its current name, the Busby Stoop, and the legend of the chair and its curse endured down the years. "In the six years I've owned the pub," said Earnshaw, "seven people have died after sitting in that chair, and the last two were friends of mine. I've put the chair away."

Back in my home office, I relayed the news to the Enquirer in Florida. "Seven? Not enough. It's been killing for centuries. We need more. Focus, we don't need anything else, just a graveyard full of chair victims," they said. And, they added, get it fast. I thought out my options. As a freelance, I was paid by the story. If they didn't like the tale, I wouldn't be paid. It seemed they had their own ideas of what the facts should be, not simply to report what was there. I didn't know it then, but that's the pattern of the naughty tabloids. Later, I'd discover that tabloid editors, for all their protestations of fairness and accuracy, often decide ahead of time what the story will be. The reporter's job, by the editors' definition, is to find facts that shore up the boss' preconceived notions. The articles editors were quaking and faking, to save their jobs. We reporters were more insulated from the wrath of the publisher, and tried to tell the tale without just making it up. Editors might need to stretch it in the interests of self-preservation, but the reporter, less at risk and with greater respect for information, usually tried to bring a semblance of truth into the tale.

An innocent in those days in the art of custom-bending stories, I knew only that it was time to shore things up a little. I had to go back to Yorkshire, reflecting that the picky Americans unexpectedly wanted the facts to be malleable. Worse, they didn't praise my copy.

It was a bit of a knock to my ego, as my life on local papers had a cosy quality of being well-accepted. At my first weekly paper, where I was trusted with my own key to the office—a useful thing for a teenager eager to impress girls—I was received generously as 'The lad from the Journal' or, less tactfully, 'Lad from the local rag' by people who liked to see their names in the paper. Some were even more welcoming. On my way to work each day, my duties included stops at the local fire, police and ambulance stations to gather overnight news, and nutrition. The police were a bit stingy, but the fire and ambulance men usually treated me to my second and third breakfasts, provisions gratefully accepted by an always-hungry youth whose rounds were made by bicycle.

Lowry Links

Local people welcomed the stories that were printed, and about the most criticism I got was when the famous industrial artist L.S. Lowry visited my home town, and described our redbrick Victorian town hall as 'the second ugliest in Lancashire.' A source had tattled it to me, and I diligently reported the critique to the largely-indifferent readers of the Eccles Journal. Previously the town had been notable for three things: as the source of Eccles Cakes, a raisin-filled pastry confection; for a bawdy fete which included contests for wooden-legged women, and as the place where world's first railway fatality, died in 1830, after he misjudged a oncoming train's staggeringly-swift 15 mph.

The local librarian, who'd invited Lowry, was indignant about my ugly town hall tale, saying he feared the great man could be offended that his confidences had been betrayed. I was learning something of the minefield a journalist traverses when he gathers material from sources. Happily the great artist was unbothered, and I was able to renew contact with him when I crossed his tracks twice more. Lowry had lived on Station Road, Swinton, just a few houses along from the local doctor, a Kenya-born Indian. Dr. Rahimtulla Bhanji had married an English fashion model and was the father of actor Sir Ben Kingsley, whose stage name was inspired by his spice-trading grandfather's nickname: 'The Clove King.' Lowry vaguely recalled visiting Swinton in the mid-1950s and seeing the neighbor boy who would be filmdom's Mahatma Gandhi and Sexy Beast, walking home from school in a purple Manchester Grammar School blazer and short trousers.

Another Lowry link surfaced when I was working as a clueless financial public relations hack for a textile company client. The bustling and extremely shrewd Persian businessman who headed the company was busy buying up cotton mills as the industry died. He earned his knighthood selling worn-out Victorian machinery to Third World countries where it would be resurrected and kept running with baling wire, oilcans and elbow grease. Along the way, he displayed an amazing skill at extracting every penny from the real estate where the machinery had done its work for generations of clog-wearing millgirls. He even garnered three Lowry paintings for the cost of a used car. The man had bought a Lancashire conglomerate which included several old cotton mills that had failed through the incompetence of the company's senior management. They'd been running the business along lines that went out with the Edwardians, and were minnows in the shark jaws of my client. He toured the factory sites, viewed the central Manchester offices, studied the books and bought the company. I'll probably never know his exact maneuvers, but I was told he took the outgoing owner for a celebratory dinner on the last evening of the man's ownership, and kept him there very late. The clock turned midnight, and just moments into the day he took possession, my man drove up to the offices as the new proprietor.

He was in time to find a taxi sitting outside, its driver waiting while the outgoing CEO emptied his office. It was a bit of unfinished business that I suspect my client already knew about. The new owner strode in and caught his dinner companion in the act of removing from his wall three Lowry paintings of the conglomerate's cotton mills. The artist had been commissioned to paint the factories some time in the 1930s and had been paid the then-handsome sum of £5,000 for the three masterworks. "Those paintings," said my client to the befuddled and now-former company owner, "belong to the company, and I own it. Leave them where they are." The man protested he'd personally commissioned the paintings, oh, 40 years ago, and he'd happily hand over a cheque right now for the £5,000. "Those paintings are on the company books, they are a corporate asset and I own them," said my client. "Goodbye."

As the new proprietor, my client's first act that morning was to write his own personal cheque for £5,000 to his company. Then he took the three paintings home with him. They were probably worth several hundred thousand pounds at that time, and are almost certainly worth much more than a couple of million now.

Slips of the Type

The art treasures incident was a scary and impressive display of focus and competence, something rarely seen among the news reporters with whom I was accustomed to working. To be fair, those reporters did have an eye for something: other people's errors. I walked into our office once to find them busy celebrating our fashion editor's newest gaffe. She'd visited a local stately home and described its charms, gushing: "then we came to the Great Hall where Sir Geoffrey holds his balls and dances." We didn't hear from Sir Geoffrey, but for much of the next week, poor Sylvia had to endure the sight of her raucous colleagues dancing graphically whenever she walked into the newsroom.

Something similar happened to a friend who started as a sub editor on a national newspaper. On his first night in the new job, the chief sub gave him a story about HM the Queen visiting TreeTops, the big game lodge in Kenya where the accommodations are on stilt-like structures so the wildlife can be safely viewed from above. Her Majesty enjoyed the visit and attended a service in the lodge's small chapel. Peter put up the headline "Queen Goes to Church on Stilts." It went on the office wall alongside the classic Guardian newspaper headline about Sir Vivian Fuchs' Antarctic expedition: "Sir Vivian Fuchs Off To The Antarctic." That subeditor, we all understood, had survived a furious chief sub's tongue-lashing after the first edition was printed with that headline, and had submitted a rewritten version. He mistakenly thought the original was under fire for being too long, and came up with a second try: "Sir Vivian Fuchs Off." It was one of those classics like "Iraqi Head Seeks Arms," "Red Tape Holds Up New Bridge," "Stolen Painting Found by Tree," "Drunk Gets Nine Months in Violin Case," and "Hospitals Are Sued by Seven Foot Doctors."

The sub-written headlines all reinforced what we reporters knew and yarned about in the pub. Photographers, we said, were monkeys with cameras. Subs were well, sub as in sub normal, sub human, sub editor. Their job was to get a sufficient quota of mistakes into your copy, putting in the errors you'd have put in yourself if you'd had time. Sometimes their devil's playmates, the printers, whom we disparagingly called Inkies, did it for them. "Our relationship with subs and Inkies is based on trust and understanding," said my colleague Tim Brown. "We don't trust them and they don't understand us. We don't pick their brains, because they're not ripe."

So an error was not unexpected when I opened the Daily Mail one morning to view the story I'd filed the previous night. One wet Sunday afternoon, I'd been dispatched by my future Enquirer colleague Joe Mullins, then Daily Mail night news editor, to interview the pop singer Lulu, at a nightclub in Lancashire. The news for us was that she was in process of breaking up with her Bee Gee songwriter husband Maurice Gibb. I arrived at the Preston venue to find a mob of rival reporters on scene, and they told me gloomily that Lulu wasn't going to talk that day, or any day soon. We all hung around for an hour or two, then I went to the nearest telephone and called the office. Mullins, a canny Yorkshireman, had a plan for me. Back with the mob, I said my goodbyes, and announced that the news desk had told me not to waste more time, but to pull out. As Joe had calculated, once the news went around that the Mail was pulling out, everyone else decided it was a forlorn hope, and called their respective desks, who of course agreed with the men on the ground. Within a half hour, almost all the opposition had departed. I emerged from hiding to find just one rival, a female reporter from a Sunday paper. She posed no threat because she couldn't publish before we did. I approached Lulu's roadie, told her the scene was now no long a pack event and persuaded her to wheel out the singer for a couple of minutes' chat.

Lulu, that delightful Scotswoman, obliged us, said a few words, then went off to prepare for her show. I had time before I needed to file copy, so slipped into the audience to monitor proceedings and make sure she didn't say anything else about the breakup. To my deep joy, she opened her act with "Killing Me Softly with His Song." Killing me, leaving him, songbird and songwriter, a seamless match, I felt. I scribbled my story, found a urine-scented telephone box (they all were, in those days) and dictated my copy down the phone. For once, the surly, insensitive copy taker didn't sigh loudly and interrupt after two paragraphs to utter the copytakers' war cry: "Is there much more of this?" Instead, the lout just grunted as he typed it out, triple-spaced, 14 lines to the page. "Bannister, staff," I dictated. "Intro begins: 'I love Maurice, but I'm leaving him,' a broken-hearted Lulu sobbed to the Daily Mail last night. Stop. Then she went on stage and sang, poignantly: 'He's Killing Me Softly with His Song.' Stop."

Lovely line, I thought again, wallowing in it a bit. Songwriter, singer, broken heart. I think I even got 'poignantly' right. More copy followed, along similar lines. A trite job, but well done, I patted myself on the back. The next morning, I looked for my piece. There it was on the front page, with just the one typo, but cruel enough to make me sigh. Once again, printers had persecuted me. Maurice, delighted readers learned, was killing Lulu softly with his dong.

The Prince and the Sardine

Those pre-Enquirer days were cheerful times, with a collection of inventive rogues as colleagues. We were paid well for using some initiative and being lucky, even if the quality of the writing was patchy. The jobs were interesting, we were kept busy and even the moon wasn't off limits. When the Americans landed on the lunar surface, my paper sent me off to the radio telescope at Jodrell Bank in Cheshire, to cover events. I think the news editor had an idea that it was an optical instrument, and the telescope boffins would stand aside every now and then so I could peek at space-suited astronauts stumbling stickily through a landscape of green cheese.

Instead, as I'd stopped en route to cover another story, I got there too late for the press conference and had to crib my piece from a friendly, so-called rival. Then I raced back to the office to take turns with another reporter at sitting in front of the office TV and scribbling shorthand notes of what we imagined we heard in the radioed squawks and "Houston, auto sequencer, data relay, EVA, attitude control, retro burn" jargon. After each viewing session, we'd run out into the newsroom, try to decipher what we'd written and type it up on an old upright Imperial, taking two carbon copies, or 'blacks.' The best part was bellowing importantly for a copy boy to run every take over to the subs' desk, because we were right up against deadline. It was hardly enterprising, but I got to type "The Eagle has landed" as the world and I heard it, from a man standing on the surface of something other than Earth. Watching the broadcast got the story done, and although my humble view of history overshadowed my next assignment in importance, it didn't yield as good a yarn.

Here's the boast: once, I shared a scrap of toast and a very small sardine with Prince Charles. That dining delight came about when His Royal Highness was visiting sites of Britain's power sources: a coal mine in Nottinghamshire, a power plant somewhere in Lincolnshire, an oil rig in the North Sea. It was all part of his royal education. Your Correspondent was employed on the Morning Telegraph, Sheffield, and was sent by its late news editor, a Geordie named Mike Corner, to cover HRH's visit to the Sea Quest oil rig, in the North Sea, off Dogger Bank. Mike might have harbored hopes I'd fall in, or that the helicopter might crash and give him a real story, or maybe he just wanted me out from under his feet for a couple of days. "Gan awa and hoo," he said, or something similar, as he briefed me to observe and file. Not easy to get a story, he warned, as the prince tended to murmur near-inaudible questions from the back of his throat. "Blaydon races, heavy laden," said Mike, "Send mah piece hin. An eager nation waits." That's what he might have said, I think.

I was up before dawn, in the chopper at Tetney airfield and 80 miles out over the North Sea long before the prince showed up at lunchtime. He toured the rig, chatted to the deep sea diver who was a vital part of the maintenance crew, nodded a bit, clasped his hands behind his back, and tried to look interested as he was ushered to the wardroom by a slick of petroleum company directors. I slapped together a story about the prince in the polka dot tie and what he said to the undersea mechanic, phoned it in and hurried to the wardroom to monitor matters. HRH was standing in a circle of suits, holding a glass of white wine and making polite noises. A steward was sea-gulling around the circumference of the gathering with a plate of very small canapes. I'd been up for hours, and was starving, so I grabbed a handful of snacks and elbowed into the group alongside the prince, sputtering bits of soggy bread along with my insincere apologies. British Petroleum's well-tailored directors eyed my scruffy self with contempt and haw-haw'ed at HRH who, like me was 30 years younger than they and who seemed royally bored with it all. The steward put an almost-empty plate down on a table behind me. The dish held one undersized sardine, reposing on a solitary strip of toast, maybe two inches long. Food. I swapped my wine to my left hand and stealthily reached back with my right to snag the morsel. It didn't release. Must be stuck to the plate. I gave a small tug, and astonishingly, it tugged back. My head swiveled in perfectly-synchronized unison with that of HRH. He had hold of the other end of the scrap of toast. Unsure if stealing a snack from a future king would get me banged up in the Tower of London, I let go. "After you, sir," I said, smiling ingratiatingly to display a mouthful of half-chewed mush. "No, old boy," he coughed. "Tell you what, we'll share it."

Charles Philip Arthur George, Prince of Wales, Duke of Cornwall, Duke of Rothesay, Earl of Carrick, Baron Renfrew, Lord of the Isles, and Great Steward of Scotland, did his stewardly duty and tore the morsel in half with his fingers. I didn't protest that his bit looked bigger. I didn't ask if he'd washed his hands. Instead, I shared that sardine with my future king while the elegantly-groomed hair of the assembled board of British Petroleum directors went vertical. So much for my entry to the circles of power. I knew I wouldn't be invited back, but I very much doubted if Charles would ever share a sardine with anyone else, either, even if his motto, 'Ich Dien,' means 'I Serve.' It's a small fry claim to fame, this fish story, but it's likely a world first. I'm the Man Who Shared a Sardine with the Prince of Whales, er, Wales.

Pubs, Expenses and Reporters

My story got its expected round of laughter from the reporters gathered for lunch in the Dove and Rainbow pub, watering hole of the staff of the Morning Telegraph, Sheffield. Pubs were an important part of a reporter's life. They provided warmth and food, a drink or two, and a chance to cash a cheque in pre-ATM days. Then there was contact with colleagues and rivals who could be helpful with information, job possibilities or story sources, and most important in the days before mobile phones, an unvandalised telephone for calls back to the news desk.

Some pubs had their own newspaper nicknames, their official monikers long forgotten. "See you in the Iron Lung" or "I'll be down at Death in the Afternoon" marked destinations known only to newsroom staff. Such was the Stab in the Back, the London Daily Mirror's smoky watering hole where office politics were bloodily executed. Journalists who hardly knew that the pub's real name was the White Hart would slurp down astonishing quantities of Scotch and soda, and effortlessly turn from intelligent conversationalists into spectacularly truculent drunks. The usual results were inept fist fights or, if the drinkers were of Gael or Celtic persuasion, a decline into morose gloom and grumbled complaints about the TSARs at the Telegraph—Those Shits Across the Road—because they got better expenses.

Pubs local to the newspaper office were regarded as a workplace annex and photographers and reporters not actively employed on a story would spend hours there, ready and varyingly able to respond to a call back to duty from the news desk secretary, who always had a radar-like ability to track them down. On Fleet Street, London's newspaper boulevard, The King and Keys, for example, was an Express pub, while El Vino's attracted the Observer and Financial Times types, one of whom, my good friend Terry Dodsworth, passed out in the men's room after mixing sherry and antibiotics. He woke up in a toilet stall around 8pm to find the place shuttered and silent, and had to call the police to let him out, a story they viewed with suspicion. The irony was that of the 80 or so gin-soaked journos in the place that lunch time, Dodsworth was the only almost-teeto-taller. He'd had an unaccustomed schooner of sherry because he was lunching some city banker for a story. "Serves him right," said an old hack who claimed to have been on more doorsteps than a bottle of milk. "They let anybody into the job these days. It's like having a hitman from Mothercare."

Daily Mirror types also liked the Cheshire Cheese, or the Mitre, off Holborn Circus, because the land belonged to the distant Bishopric of Ely and obeyed curious opening times that let canny Mirrormen drink when other pubs were closed. One bear of a photographer who was a Mitre regular was noted for his bad temper, but always treated the art editor with respect. When that editor was asked why, he smiled. "He's been devoted to me, ever since the day I removed a thorn from his paw."

On a story in an unfamiliar place, the local pub was a good starting point, as a helpful landlord or barmaid often knew someone who knew someone, and with a little encouragement could persuade the someone who knew something about the story to be interviewed. The pubs were like the newspaper offices, in another way, too. They were invariably thick with tobacco smoke. At the end of a shift in office and pub, your clothes reeked, and your throat was sore, even if you'd never smoked a cigarette in your life. When I once asked a colleague about his deep, hacking roar—the one that sounded as if he was kick-starting a 650cc Norton motorcycle, but which he didn't associate in any way with his 40-a-day habit, he growled: "There's many in the church yard would be glad of a cough like mine."

Revisited and Recruited

I thought of that church yard as I drove back to Yorkshire to revisit the Busby Stoop and oxygenate my story of the Baffling Chair of Death. Maybe some of the local headstones carried a clue that "here lies a victim of the Chair?" It seemed worth a look. As I drove, I mused about the person who'd started me on this errand, Harold Lewis, a former Mirror reporter popularly known as the Laziest Man in the Office. Soon after exiting cloudy Manchester and the Daily Mirror, Harry showed up again. No clouds in his life any more, I thought. He was suntanned and glowing as he strode into the Swan with Two Necks pub on a gloomy November afternoon. Harry was a dazzling vision in white suit, open-necked white silk shirt, a panama hat balanced jauntily on his head and, I swear, white buckskin brothel creepers on his feet. He looked like Bing Crosby in an old musical. "Working for an American paper in Florida," he confided. "Big salary, unlimited ex'es." My ears jerked upright. Expenses were the heart's blood of journalists. Do a story well and the news editor would quietly tell you to put a drink on your ex'es. You could easily double or treble your salary, untaxed, with creative claims, and the more outrageous, the better. One friend always added a few pounds every week 'for maintenance and feet.' It was never queried, which was as well, he confessed, because he had no idea what he meant by it. Mirror staffers regarded expense payments as drinking vouchers and called their 10th-floor accounts office The Bank in the Sky. (The Holborn building, like the industry, has been demolished. Sainsbury's supermarket chain's HQ now stands on the spot.)

Harry outlined his new life at the Enquirer. "Drive to work under the palm trees in a top-down convertible muscle car, swim in the warm ocean, travel the world, no time pressure, no need to call the office every hour or two, and every American thinks you're Alistair Cooke." I was hooked. "Why don't you join in?" asked Harry. "I'll send you a stringer sheet." This, I learned contained instructions for a freelancer, someone who'd send ideas to the paper, then obtain the stories they wanted from the list. It was Harry's meal ticket for some outrageous entertainment expenses, I found later. He charged a handful of expensive dinners to recruiting me, none of which I saw, and I think I even paid for his drinks that lunchtime.

I continued my daily newspaper life, confronting Manchester United's legendary footballer George Best in his boutique just off Deansgate after one of his long nights out. "Hello, George, I'm from the Daily Mail," I told him as he emerged from the back of the shop. "Feck off out of here or I'll drop ye!" was his immediate effort at diplomacy. Well, I'm a rugby prop forward, and I thought this claim from a skinny Ulsterman was most unlikely, so I politely suggested he try his namesake best. With a turn of the elusive speed that made him such a star athlete, he was in the back of the shop before I could say 'Nod the ball in." Years later, when George was playing for the San Jose Earthquakes in California, I met him again and reminded him of his Ulster finishing school ways. "Ahh, I wiz just joshin' yer," he charmed me. "I'd not have hurt ye."

That tale went down as well as the one about the kangaroo I transported to a press charities ball, an event co-sponsored by the Australian wine industry. I had the creature on loan from a zoo and was taking it in a large wire-sided crate that just fitted into a borrowed van, so long as the passenger seat was removed. Half way through our journey, the 'roo crawled to the front of the crate and eyed me from close range. I turned my head and made some encouraging sound, perhaps humming a bit of 'Waltzing Matilda' to make the beast feel at home. Experts say kangaroos don't do this, or at least not often, but that animal spat full in my eye. I expect it was some editorial comment, it was certainly another one for the notebook.

Back to work, where I continued to send ideas to Florida, and the Enquirer picked up on a couple of them. I wrote a medical story about the wives of working men being more susceptible to cervical cancer. It died when an American editor probing the cause concluded that blue collar men were less hygienic than others, and that was not going to please Enquirer readers. Next up was an amiable psychic who got me very drunk while telling how he foresaw a MidEast war but no, he could not say just when, or actually, where. It too was spiked. Then there was a UFO story from a 13 years old boy who claimed a spacecraft the size of two football fields had descended right behind their garden shed. I killed that one myself.

Revealed: The Truth About the Chair

The following project was to bolster the tale of the Baffling Chair of Death. My second foray to the Busby Stoop inn was more purposeful than the first, and I took closer note of the chair's history. Before relegating the chair to the coach house, the landlord had kept it in the lounge bar for several years with a framed account of its legend. He'd even put a rope across it, to deter inadvertent seating.

The very placement of the pub reinforced the legend. In WW2, the Vale of York was packed with the airfields of bomber squadrons, and the Royal Air Force acquired farmland in Sandhutton parish to extend its Skipton-on-Swale station. The airfield perimeter was bounded on the southeast by the A61 Ripon to Thirsk road, which itself crosses the A167 Northallerton road, on the old field's east side. The Busby Stoop stands at that road junction, where the cross-roads have been replaced with a roundabout. It's just a short walk south of Sandhutton, and was the RAF station's most convenient watering hole. The tavern was a landmark, right under the flight path of the 1400 yards long 9/27 runway used by the three Royal Canadian Air Force squadrons of Wellingtons and Halifaxes, and later in the war, the twin-finned A.V. Roe Lancaster bombers that did such damage to Germany's industrial Ruhr. The damage wasn't one-sided. Ninety-eight of the aircraft that flew out of Skipton never returned to base, and legend holds that some of those doomed air crews had enjoyed the hospitality of the Busby Stoop and jauntily defied its deadly chair. Local people believed that Busby's chair took toll and certainly, more than 500 brave young men left on their last-ever flight out of RAF Skipton. We'll never know if a curse was responsible for those tragic deaths, but the legend grew with time.

Landlord Tony Earnshaw welcomed me back, and detailed other fatalities: a teenage bricklayer who fell from scaffolding a few hours after taking a dare to sit in the chair, and an army sergeant from Catterick camp who had a terminal heart attack three days after scoffing at the legend. Then there was Tony's 42 years old friend who'd 'dropped dead in Ripon market place,' a day after taking the fatal seat, as well as the death of a workman making repairs to the roof of a nearby garage. He scoffed at the legend and sat in the chair. That afternoon, the roof collapsed under him and he was killed. A chat with the local clergyman put the seal on things. The Rev Joseph Mainwaring-Taylor, a no-nonsense ex-Army padre, was vicar of St Mary the Virgin parish. "I have tried to exorcize the evil that is around that chair, without result. I believe it should be soaked in petrol and burned," he told me.

A photograph of the vicar, a picture of a very nice old lady in the churchyard, smiling as she told of her friends buried there, and the job was done like dinner. The Enquirer ran the story as the page one lead and sent me a bonus. The facts were all there, as Tony told them. Later, when I came to investigate the chair more thoroughly and with information from other sources, the legend of the Chair of Death looked a lot like many other tabloid stories—very shaky.

I hadn't done any deliberate falsifications, as some reporters did, I'd just done the required fast job. I'd not misrepresented myself to the story subjects, as other reporters sometimes did. One of my friends kept a 'Doctor on Call' placard and stethoscope in full view on the dashboard, or wore a green suit with brass buttons and fake pilot's wings that looked like an Aer Lingus pilot's uniform, to get him into places. He even kept an old pair of crutches in the back of his car, to gain sympathy as he hobbled to a doorstep from which his rivals had been shoo'ed away.

So, a few months later, when the Enquirer was recruiting and I was being interviewed, I had a clear conscience when I pointed casually to the headline on a sample of the paper. I said: "I did that." It got me a trial for a staff job. If I'd had the time to dig deeper and not quickly skim off the story the Enquirer wanted, I could have told the editor who interviewed me that the Chair of Death story had some major flaws.

The murder part of the story was copper-bottomed. The 'History of York' of 1858 records the 1702 murder of Dan Awety, (sometimes spelled Auty) of Danoty Hall (more spelling choices, here) by his son in law, Thomas Busby. Auty or Awety was either killed with a hammer, a spade or by strangulation after he threatened to take his daughter Elizabeth away from Busby, and the two men quarrelled. Parish records suggest that Busby had an accomplice in the killing, as Christopher Shaws was hung in August 1702 for the murder of a D. Notty. It's also true that Busby was hung in chains at the crossroads, after his body had been dipped in pitch, to preserve it as an example of justice served. The serious flaw in the story of the Baffling Chair of Death, however, is that Busby didn't curse it. He never saw it, and could never have sat in it, because the chair wasn't made until more than a century after his demise. Furniture historians say the chair is a distinctive Caistor Bobbin Chair that was created by John Shadford, of Caistor, Lincolnshire, between 1843 and 1881. In that time, Shadford's small factory turned out scores of the highly-stylized Windsor chairs as fireside seats or rockers, and the pieces are noted as unique to the region. So, if the man who is reputed to have cursed the chair could never have even seen it because it wasn't made until 150 years after his death, where did the legend of the curse come from? "Probably from a publican," said Thirsk museum curator Cooper Harding.

Nobody knows just when it all began, and even the commonest theory, that the deaths of WW2 aircrew sparked the legend, isn't accurate. Milly Ingham, the wartime landlady of the Busby Stoop, was adamant that the chair wasn't in the pub then, and she knew nothing of any curse. It seems it was all just a hoax by a post-war landlord of the pub. Whatever, the tabloid editors shrugged. They didn't care. It was a Baffling Chair, and they uncritically used the tale a couple more times. They stayed true to their principles, and didn't let the facts stand in the way of a good story.

IN THE NEW WORLD

Brave New Florida

I arrived in oceanside Lantana, Florida to find the Enquirer was housed in a long, single-storey tilt-up, glass and concrete building, set in lush subtropical gardens. The structure was edged with a border of bleached-white large gravel like that found on gravesites and the Bermuda grass lawns were kept to an exact three-inch trim. The newsroom was large and open-plan with a handful of glass mini offices in the center and around a couple of sides where an inventory of stories was lodged, and layout, art, photo and other editors worked. Article editors and their assistants occupied desks out on the office floor and the reporters were crammed into a double row of open telephone mini-booths where it was impossible to conduct phone interviews without overhearing those around you. Publisher Pope believed reporters should be out on the road, doing whatever they do, and he seemed to have no intention of making life comfortable when we were working in the office. Significantly, there were only 16 or so phone booths for 80-plus reporters. Further down the building was a sort of nunnery for the mostly-female researchers whose job it was to ensure that the stories contained no factual errors, plus offices for accounts, PR, legal and other ancillary services overseen by a trusted pair of longstanding Pope consiglieri. The publisher himself had a spacious office overlooking the gardens, and rumor was that the windows were bulletproof. Certainly, his security guys would check under his car with a stick-mounted mirror before he left for home each day.

Six weeks in America flashed by. The Enquirer had a tryout system —more on this later—and would-be staff reporters were plunged in at once, and sent around the nation gathering stories. I learned the mundane: how to open a US mailbox that didn't have a letters slot (the lid is hinged) and that US police cars were actually black and white. I'd always half-assumed the cop cars in the movie chases were Hollywood inventions. Also: don't rent a vast 10-passenger station wagon (an 'estate car' in English) in San Francisco, where the steep street intersections mean you can't see over the sky-pointing hood/ bonnet until you're halfway into cross-traffic, unsighted. I also learned, but not from the onetime London photo assistant who was now an out-of-his-depth senior editor, that writing concise, British-style news stories wasn't the way the Enquirer wanted things. After I'd filed a dozen or so tautly-written pieces, that editor got his third promotion in as many weeks and shed his staff. I was handed over to another paper-shuffler, who quickly enlightened me. The editors didn't want me to write the final version of the story, they wanted a fat file of facts that the rewrite team would turn into tabloid prose.

I noted sourly that the rewriters seemed to have a limited supply of adjectives, ranging from 'mind-boggling' to 'incredible' but obediently set about filling in the blanks. It wasn't enough that I'd interviewed some doctor in his office where his patients waited. I had to provide the details of where he'd been educated, where he'd served his internship and whether he was an associate or assistant professor of medicine at X university. None of that made the final write, but it kept the lawyers happy to know the doc was genuine. It didn't matter that the story was phoney. Maybe the doctor's tale was that mushrooms cure arthritis, and 50 of his colleagues derided it. If the doctor said it, and we found a couple of others to say it could be real, that was good enough. We wouldn't confuse the reader with opposing views, we'd just find facts to fit the headline. But, the facts we found should be verifiable. No fake doctor, just a misleading story, and in this bizarre Emperor Has No Clothes system, where editors solemnly offered up nonsense stories, the magazine didn't trust even its own reporters.

It was in absolute contrast to the system I'd learned, where the reporter was believed. Get it wrong, and you're fired. At the Enquirer, the reporter wasn't credible. He had to back up his every word. So I did it, and passed my tryout, when much more talented journalists were failing theirs. Back in the UK with a job offer, I bade the Daily Mail goodbye with a pang or two of regret for the warmth and fun I'd had with those lively colleagues. I was off to a more sober place of richer rewards and a more ruthless approach to the publishing business. My wife Jennie rounded up our two toddler girls, we packed up, rented out our house and we moved on, planning a 24-month stay that so far has taken 37 years.

We arrived in Florida in a tropical storm that was thrashing the coconut palms and stayed at an oceanfront motel with salt and freshwater swimming pools. It was a truly novel New World. We found the Americans warm, gullible and interested. Several times a day we said, no, we weren't Australian, we were English. Not Irish, English. Equally often we heard how our interrogator was half Irish, half Scaaatch, three parts Polish, half Italian, and was born in Detroit. These multi-persons' grandparents had been immigrants to America, but they still thought of themselves as half-Scaaatch-Irish, part Polish etc. They believed us when we said yes, we all had butlers and castles back in England and that Robin Hood's grandson still roamed the woods of Notting-ham-shire, a place close to Bucking-ham Palace. We coped with wrong-side driving, mosquitoes and humidity. It was a startling experience for someone from northern England to walk out of the accustomed cool of an air-conditioned cinema into a warm, cricket-chirping night. After a childhood where the seaside meant shivering and stepping carefully across hard-rippled sand that hurt your feet, where beaches were a place of windbreaks, hot Oxo from a vacuum flask, and numbed whitened fingers, the Florida oceanside was a delight. Sunny, bright and sub-tropical, it was a paradise.

We were part of a colony of expatriates, English, Aussies, the occasional South African, a handful of Canadians, several wild-eyed Irish, and a cabal of Scots who seemed to be constantly jostling to knife each other, preferably in the back. After work, the reporters gathered at one of several watering holes where the single guys, headed by Filthy Phil and the Granny Groper, hit on the swarm of females intrigued by these foreigners. On any typical night, one or two alcohol-fuelled clowns attempted to Pearl Harbor each other with blindside punches. Late in the evening, the drunken dregs would swarm The Duke bar, affectionately known as The Last Chance Ranch because it was populated by blue-rinsed widows eager to recapture their pasts. The Granny Groper loved it, and had a well-practiced line of patter designed to get him into their mobile homes, their beds and their reportedly-voluminous knickers, then back into his car as quickly as possible. "I always give 'em a good one, because it might be the last they ever get," he cheerfully told us from time to time.

My closest pal at the Enquirer was medical correspondent Lee Harrison, a fellow Brit from Liverpool. Lee and I were on an editorial team headed by a diminutive Tennessee country boy who had stumbled into the Enquirer all unknowing. His homely aphorisms ("I'll be on that quicker'n a frog on a June bug" and "Nervous as a long-tailed cat in a room full of rocking chairs") amused us, but Lee cracked us up most with stories of his newspaperman father, George, whom I knew from the Liverpool Echo newspaper. George had been to the US on the famous 1964 Beatles' tour, covering the Fab Four's triumphant progress for their local paper, and went home thoroughly fed up about his much-reduced wardrobe. "Silly bugger," Lee explained. "He used his own name, and kept getting his underpants nicked from the hotel laundries. The fans thought that the washing marked 'George Harrison' belonged to the Beatle and couldn't work out why such a nice young man would wear such old-fashioned keks!"

Our team was in competition with the other eight or nine editorial teams, and we had a winning formula that earned us plenty of page one headlines. Arthritis, heart disease, predictions and UFOs were best-selling words in the Franklin Gothic headlines of the page one splash. The readers ate up spooky stories, and soon I was the Jeane Dixon Correspondent, cranking out predictions, visions and tales of people the Washington psychic had saved from danger by warning them to miss that flight, have the brakes checked or whatever. Her forecasts made regular best sellers when displayed on the paper's front page, too. The tough part was easing her away from 'a famous person will fall ill' type of prediction and edging her more towards claims that the editors liked, such as "Doris Day will have her thighs eaten by a pack of wild dogs."

Pope attached enough importance to the psychics' circulation enhancers that I was given wide range. Safely married, I raised some envy among my single male colleagues because I often worked with the paper's best rewriter, my dishy blonde tennis pal Marsha May, on lengthy horoscopes as well as the predictions. We went to Hollywood to create a series with celeb astrologer Carroll Righter, we worked on the pyschics' issues poolside at my home, not an unpleasant task. There, we created forecasts—with the psychics' telepathic approval, of course—like the one that the Saudis would tow an iceberg to their desert as a source of fresh water, and be astounded when it melted to reveal the remains of an alien space expedition. Our work was to make the predictions an entertaining read, but every year jealous and underpaid local newsmen would predictably and sneeringly analyze how accurate the forecasts were (answer: not much) and report that in their tedious tales. We had the last laugh. We were selling millions of copies a week—over seven million the week Elvis died—and they weren't, and we and they knew it.

Even our readers did a fine job of forecasting the future. Every January, we invited them to send in five predictions each for the coming year, and stowed them away in the vault of the First State Bank of Lantana. At the next New Year, accompanied by a cadre of local news media, I'd go down to the bank, extract the bags of letters from their repose, and invite local reporters to examine some. The predictions varied, but after we'd sifted through the 5,000 or so letters we could usually find a handful who'd actually got five right. Of course, the more specific the correct prediction, the better, and the winner got a prize that was usually about $1,000. We never knew if we discovered any natural psychic talent. Nobody won twice, and we never heard of any reader going on to make a living foretelling the future, but I did get useful ideas for Jeane Dixon's or the other professional psychics' use.

Jeane's Blues

Creating circulation-boosting predictions was just one duty. I also had to separate Jeane's semi-religious 'visions' from her sometimes highly-accurate forecasts about the futures of her political friends. Jeane was an astute and political businesswoman, operating in her husband Jimmy's Washington DC real estate business, where she burnished a wide network of contacts. She was a professional Southern Belle from Georgia, and I wrote a book for her once, cranking out 80,000 words of some Jesuit's view of astrology, God's meanings and theology without understanding any of it. The joke was on me. I'd mentioned to my Appalachian editor that Jeane had a book to deliver to a major publishing house and was a year late with it. It would be an astrology book and she wanted me to ghost write it for her. I had the idea of writing, then serializing the thing in 12 monthly episodes in the Enquirer. Jeane kindly offered me a few percentage of the advance as a payoff for my work, but the halfwit hillbilly brushed the offer aside, saying "Oh no, Mrs Dixon, Paul's getting his salary to do this." I was still kicking him furiously under the table when Jeane swiftly murmured acceptance of the freebie, dashing my hopes of reward. Anyway, the book got written, and when we came to print the first segment in the magazine, the Appalachian editor got an urgent call from its publishers. "You'll owe us royalties," they said. "We'd paid for it. The book wasn't Jeane's to give away." Some negotiator, some deal. Not only did I write a book for free, we had to pay for the privilege of publicizing it.

But that wasn't my best Jeane story. That came a few months later and it was all about how I saved her psychic bones when Star Trek's William Shatner came calling. Mrs D. had given me chapter and verse on her latest vision, which involved some fanciful tale about going up in a UFO and seeing God's creation from the starry depths of space. I'd laced it with religious meaning and seen it appear on the Enquirer's front page as another circulation enhancer. Several weeks after the story ran, Jeane was on the phone to me in Florida, a nervous note in her voice. Mr Shatner and a film crew would be at her office the next day. They were making a movie about flying saucers and she'd agreed to discuss her UFO ride, she explained. Clearing her throat just as she did when she'd take a teaspoonful of my lunchtime Scotch to 'see just what it tastes like,' she said she wanted to get the facts straight, but couldn't quite remember every single detail of her vision. I was on the next morning's 7.25am Delta flight out of Palm Beach International and in her office on Connecticut Avenue NW before lunch.

We had a briefing, the film crew showed up and Shatner lighted up the place with his incandescent charm. All was very relaxed, but whenever he asked Jeane a question, she'd forget what she'd said in print. Give the actor his due, he knew how to save the situation. He'd ask the question on camera, then call for a halt. I'd tell Jeane: "You told me that ... the dashboard of the UFO was perfectly smooth," or whatever. She'd nod, and practice the response. Shatner would call for the camera to roll, Jeane would parrot it back, and everything was fine. As the crew packed up and I made my goodbyes, Shatner got in the parting shot. We shook hands. "Thank you, Miz Dixon," he said, looking right at me.

Travels With an Astronaut

Some of the parapsychology stories I did for the Enquirer had more heft. Astronaut Edgar Mitchell, lunar lander pilot and sixth man to walk on the moon, dragged me along in his slipstream for several months while we visited his contacts in the field of psychic research. Ed had a Road to Tarsus experience aboard Apollo 14, when he carried out some telepathy experiments with Chicago psychic Olof Johnson, and it inspired him to found the Institute of Noetic Sciences, a consciousness-exploring group in California. He told me of seeing a film of a frisbee-sized UFO circling a rocket at the White Sands testing ground as it was being readied for launch. "There was a high-speed camera trained on the bird, a UFO appeared and started circling up it like a humming bird going up and around a telegraph pole. Someone had the sense to roll the camera. I saw the movie a few days later, then it vanished from the archive. It was a rare capture on film of something of huge interest, but that film never existed, the brass said."

I enjoyed our time together, hearing how the blastoff of the big Saturn V moon rocket delivered a bruising kick to the astronauts' backsides, how they'd all urinated on the tire of the bus that took

them to the launch pad, as both a (possibly last) dog-like territorial marking and a pressure-reliever ("All they ask me is how do
you go to the bathroom in space," Ed grumbled) and how it was
to look down on an Earth rise. We went together to places like the
Menninger Clinic to meet Ed's contacts, but their work was largely
too esoteric for the Enquirer, except in one spectacular area. Ed's
intrigue with psi research led him—and me—to an involvement with
two Stanford Research Institute physicists who'd spent six weeks
testing Israeli psychic Uri Geller. By the end, the duo felt they'd
witnessed extraordinary phenomena, but never under sufficiently
controlled conditions.

These researchers were no amateur hobbyists. Harold 'Hal' Puthoff
was a full Stanford University professor, his colleague Russell Targ
was a laser physicist. They employed scientific protocols for their
tests, but Geller tantalized them, and they never could define what
they'd seen as proven psychic functioning. Russell, for example, told
me of leaving Geller's apartment in Palo Alto, California after an
evening's spoon bending and finding the stop sign at the end of the
driveway had been bent into three perfect loops. He never found
out if it was coincidence or just some prankster with heavy equipment. When they gave Geller an unopened deck of cards, he opened
and shuffled them under observation, then dropped them onto a
tabletop. The cards appeared to penetrate the table. On examina-
tion, five of the cards were found to have a missing diagonal slice.
Another time, as Geller and the two researchers were leaving the SRI
building, they saw a group working to test an X-ray-like soundwave
system. Geller held up his fist and shouted "Up, down! Up, down!"
The image on the monitor obeyed him. Once, Geller was trying to
move a light beam by mind power alone. Instead, the pen of the
chart recorder moved untouched across the paper. It never moved
again: its preamplifiers were both burned out. Later, I'd work with
Uri on a handful of experiments for the Enquirer. Typically, at a
specific time, readers would put a key or a broken watch or appli-
ance on a picture in the Enquirer of the super-psychic, and urge the
objects to bend or be repaired. Uri said he could trigger the readers'
powers, and it would be they, not he, who caused the psychic events.
We did one such experiment in 1979, while Uri was living in Mexico
City, where he was close to then-president Jose Lopez Portillo. Geller

came to my hotel room for the trial, arriving in a small convoy of limos with five security men around him. He shed them in the lobby, and casually came up to my room with the photogger and myself. I admit I was a bit alarmed that he felt the need for the heavies, but Uri was cool.

He bent my house front door key around the top of his forefinger, seeming just to stroke the metal, did a few telepathy tricks to amuse the photographer, concentrated for several minutes and announced that the experiment was over. No drama. Back in Florida, we got 1,100 reader responses in the mail. Some people mistook the date and did the experiment days early or late. It didn't seem to matter. As Geller had suggested, the readers, not him, seemed to be the ones affecting the objects. About 150 said nothing had happened and it was all a fraud, the rest reported incidents they were adamant they'd witnessed. An indignant woman from Los Angeles called to protest that three valued topaz rings had shattered inside, though the outside was unmarked. Her puzzled jeweler confirmed it to me when I called. "They looked to have been smashed with a hammer, but the outside was perfectly unmarked," he said. A contractor in Pekin, Illinois found his home's broken intercom not only started working again but the volume increased as he walked past it, and the solenoids on his fridge cracked loudly whenever he went near. A merry group of nine in Hiram, Ohio had spoons and keys bend for them, but took fright when a metal teapot hurdled objects on the table. A New York rabbi was called home by his wife, who'd watched astounded as spoons bent on Uri's image in the Enquirer. He swore to me that as he arrived, his garage door went up and down by itself even after he unplugged the power cord. The phenomenon lasted, he said, for three hours. I spent a week telephoning these and other readers and came away convinced: not all of them could be lying. I knew something else, too: my now-unbent front door key didn't work any more.

The CIA's Psi Spies

Uri Geller left the SRI researchers Targ and Puthoff with inconclusive results, but they had other vineyards of the psychic in which to toil, and fruitfully. The duo landed a nine-year, $1.1million annual grant from the Central Intelligence Agency to investigate the possibility of psychic spying and I did a series that were my most important stories for the Enquirer. Targ and Puthoff theorized that you could send your mind to view something without physically going there. They explained their technique. An 'outbound observer' would physically visit a target site at a given time, and stay alert to his surroundings. Back at their laboratory in Palo Alto, California, the test subject would first (and importantly) be assured that it was not wrong to succeed in this experiment, which was to see if he could home in on the observer's impressions. He was also told not to attempt to interpret what his mind's eye saw, just to record it faithfully. If he saw something bushy and green, report that, not try to see if it was an oak tree.

Targ, by the way, was married to the sister of a world chess champion. Joan Targ's proud boast was that she taught Bobby Fischer to play chess, adding only later that she was nine years old at the time, and he was, well, five.

In the SRI lab, usually comfortably sprawled on the suite's imitation-leather, orange couch, the test subject would be told when to start recording his impressions. Artists were valued test subjects, as they could sketch the scene as well as describe it verbally. The experiments and their results are described in detail in Targ's books 'Mind Race' and 'Mind Reach.'

It's enough here to say the SRI team had spectacular success, accurately producing in the lab descriptions and even drawings—often from a bird's eye view—of the target. In one series of experiments, using silver prices as the 'target' they even said they'd managed to forecast the future, and make a $140,000 profit for their investor. The team tested their psychic spies, whom they called 'remote viewers' with sets of map coordinates, asking them to describe what was at a specific longitude and latitude anywhere in the world. It's a task few geographers could perform, but the best viewers were claimed to be scoring in the 70th percentile, or about five times better than chance, and they described or drew things that were often not marked on maps. In one test, viewer Ingo Swann, a New York artist, described and sketched what was at a set of coordinates. It was a French meteorological station on the sub-Antarctic island of Kerguelan. Swann not only accurately drew the coastline and

mapped the island's sole mountain, he pinpointed the only population center, and its airstrip. Then, he outlined the layout of the
settlement's buildings, sketched the white cylinders that held fuel
oil, and drew the radio mast. One thing puzzled the researchers.
Swann described an orange shape in the view, but the meteorolo-
gists on the island who responded to the post-test request for data
didn't mention it. The mystery was explained later. At the exact time
Swann was describing the island from the SRI couch, someone half
a world away had erected a temporary, orange-colored fabric windbreak to protect equipment from a storm. The windbreak was in
place only for several days, but somehow Swann had 'seen' it and its
surroundings at that exact time.

Hexed in Brazil

Stories like these took me in the 1970s from Iceland to Brazil, for the
Enquirer. Close to the Arctic Circle, I met Einar Einarsson, a psychic
healer who claimed to channel the ghost of a dead doctor and who
had some jaw-droppingly successful medical successes to his credit
although he was a sheep farmer totally without medical training. In
the southern hemisphere's teeming city of Sao Paulo, it was a young
artist, Luis-Antonio Gasparetto, whose mysterious abilities puzzled
the world. I did his story, of channeling dead artists and, before
credible witnesses including a BBC crew with cameras rolling, he
painted rapid-fire in the exact styles of artists from Renoir to Dali.
I saw it myself, I can't explain it. Somehow, eyes evidently closed,
and in double-quick time, Gasparetto could whip out an original
painting in the exact style of any of a dozen or more artists. In
Brazil, it wasn't regarded as any truly mysterious manifestation, but
just another facet of fascinating life. I visited a huge college where
tutors instructed students in the art of psychic healing. I found that
small shops selling black magic supplies were commonplace. I also
discovered the Brazilian's love for midnight dinners, midday siestas
and evening classes that were hardly academic, but more like social
events that could carry on for years. On the trip, I covered other
stories, including a report of a haunted house in Mogi das Cruces,
where apparitions of people and illusions of fire had puzzled even
the local police chief. He told me of holding a banknote up into

the flames that seemed to be coming from a blank plaster wall. No heat, no damage to the note. The flames were an illusion he couldn't explain.

My Portuguese interpreter explained that the haunted house had been hex'ed by a magician and the family had brought in another macumbeira to detoxify the place. I should, he said, interview the magician, who'd performed the successful exorcism, as he wanted some international credit. I declined. The day was sticky, I was hot and dusty, I didn't feel he'd add any credibility to my story, I was ready to go home, my laundry had run out, yada yada yada. What happened over the next several days I could never explain, though I suspect it was a demonstration of the magician's ability to tap into energy we do not understand. Various physicists and others have explained that we don't know everything. They tell us that the seemingly-solid wooden desk we see is actually a collection of particles of matter held in place by energy. Every atom is made of electrons that dance in a preset pattern around a nucleus of protons and neutrons. Some energy dictates that dance and its pattern. If you could affect that energy, you should be able to change the 'solid' object's shape, or at least its properties. Maybe, as Jonathan Livingston Seagull proposed, we can sink through the land and walk on water just by thinking it. After all, everything we know about electricity came about in the past couple of centuries. Before that, all we had was lightning, and we certainly didn't have wall switches to turn that on and off. What if there are other forms of energy in our vast universe? I think now that the unnamed, unsung wizard in Sao Paolo, the man I never met and to whom I apologize today, had a grip on a little of that energy.

Here's what happened after I opted not to interview the man who lifted a curse on a Sao Paolo family. I went for dinner in the dining room of my hotel, the Brasilton, and ordered a chicken pie. The pastry was fluffy, the meat delicious. Then I crunched on a small cube of glass, of the size and color of a piece that would come from a car's shattered windshield of safety glass. The head waiter was apologetic, the pie was not made on the premises, the caterer would hear of this, the dinner was complimentary, sir. The next night, I was in Rio de Janeiro, overnighting before my Miami flight. In an hotel bar, I ordered a mixed drink. In among the ice, I crunched down on another glass cube. The bartender was apologetic, my glass was unchipped, the barman showed me the rubber-tipped glass-washing device designed to prevent such a thing. Senor, the drink is on us, please have another. It has never happened before... The third night, I was home in Boynton Beach, Florida. Maybe my subconscious made me get a glass before I took that cold Coca Cola from the fridge. I do know that as I poured the drink from can to glass, I heard a clink. For the third time, on a near-exact 24-hour cycle, I'd found a cube of clear glass in my food. This one came right out of an unopened can of Coke. Nobody ever explained it, I never got a dream visit from a gent in feathers and monkey bones, I was never harmed. Like the story of a ghostly encounter, it's most convincing when you experience it yourself. I know what happened, and it truly happened as I've described it. I think that Brazilian backstreet macumbeira sent me a harmless but effective message to tell me: "Respect is cheap, and there are stranger things in this world than you know." I take off my hat to him. I still sometimes drink directly from a can. He didn't frighten me, as I'm sure he never intended that.

Talking Cat, Signing Gorilla

Not all my assignments involved matters psychic. The paper sent me to cover news stories and human interest pieces, to get celebrity stories and cover natural disasters. And they sent me to interview a talking cat. It was a logical choice, as the Enquirer was noted for its taste for the bizarre. When those Pascagoula fishermen claimed to have been abducted by lobster-clawed space aliens, we nodded agreement and gave them polygraph tests and told their story. Other stories were just as bizarre. During the Abscam bribery scandal, the paper sent a craggy Canadian reporter to Washington in kamees robe and burnoos head dress to see if congressmen would fawn over a mega-wealthy oil sheik or if they'd scurry away, fearing the taint of corruption. The rush to grab theirs was most unseemly, and reporter Brian Hogan had a splendid time promising them all kinds of things while the elected representatives fawned over him. The readers loved it, we looked for more odd stories.

In Ecuador, photographer Jimmy Sutherland and I climbed mountains and forded rivers for two days to find the world's oldest couple, a brother and sister who were supposed to be 140 and 129 years old. We wanted the secrets of long life. They said it was their generous daily ration of rum and cigarettes, a recipe which failed to earn American Medical Association approval. Then there was the dog that refused to die. In Hannibal, Missouri, we met a mutt that had survived being chained to a tree for weeks by eating the bark. Animal control officers took it to the pound, where it was unclaimed, so the vet gave it a fatal injection. The dog survived. They doubled the dose. The dog wouldn't die. Four attempts to kill it failed. We hauled the unkillable canine back to Florida and ran an appeal for a loving family to adopt it. Tens of thousands of readers responded and an ideal family was chosen. Within a week, they were on the phone. The dog had chewed the legs off the dining room table and two chairs and was now working on an antique sideboard. A reporter was quietly sent to retrieve the dog, and even more quietly have it put to sleep.

The paper hadn't exactly run the tale of the chicken that could do calculus, but it would have liked to, so when reader Nellie Frerking wrote to us about her chatty catty, I was on a plane to Knob Noster, Missouri, or as near as I could get to that small town. The memory fades, but I recall meeting Mrs Frerking, who seemed totally unsurprised that a magazine would fly a reporter all that way to see her cat, Maisie. "Come and say hello to the nice gentleman, Maisie," she purred. I half expected the cat to speak, but she only did what cats do, rubbed against my leg. "You say, er, Maisie can talk, Mrs Frerking?" "Oh yes, darlin'," said that nice southern lady. "Say something, Maisie!" I turned on my tape recorder, self conscious but thrilled. A speechified feline! I was going to be the one who introduced it to the waiting world! This wasn't going to be like the woman who'd called to say she had a space alien in her kitchen was it? The duty reporter, John South, said to put him on the phone. The woman came back to tell Southie: "He says he won't speak to the National Enquirer."

However, Mrs Frerking's Maisie looked comfortable with the idea of being a tabloid tabby, and took very little persuading to display her vocal skills. When Mrs Frerking opened a can of cat food, Maisie revealed her total command of English. She opened her little pink mouth and said it all. One word. "Mawwwmeee," she said. That was it. A one-word story. No thanks, not even for the Enquirer. Not all animal stories flopped like that, though. When Penny Patterson taught her mountain gorilla Koko to use American Sign Language, editors at the Enquirer perked up. Koko, born on July 4th and whose name is an abbreviation of 'fireworks child' in Japanese, had more weight than a talking cat. By 1980, when I went to see her, my family and I had moved across country to Palo Alto, California, and Koko was a near neighbor in a woodsy compound in the Santa Cruz Mountains. At that time, Koko was nine years old, 55 inches tall and weighed 170 lbs. She also had a vocabulary of 1,000 ASL words and comprehension of 2,000 spoken words. She had an IQ of about 95, had typing skills and photographed her own self-portrait, which made the cover of National Geographic.

She had a doll called Underarm, a taste for swearing, and a liking for human nipples that led to a sex harassment case from Gorilla Foundation females who said they were coerced into flashing the ape or being fired. On the swearing front, Koko's 'human friend' Patterson reported that the gorilla called her 'Penny toilet dirty devil' in sign language and used 'rotten stink' and 'obnoxious' to staff she didn't like. I thought being sworn at was less dangerous than the Chair of Death, and went to see Koko, who described herself as 'Fine animal gorilla' at a Woodside, California compound. Fresh from her 14-hour night's sleep, she had her raisin and rice bread breakfast with milk and fruit, helped clean her room, then ripped the sponge to pieces when she'd finished. She underwent a half hour lesson in auditory English, rough and tumbled with her gorilla friend Michael, had some sign language instruction and met the Press. We shook hands, her hard, black, banana-sized fingers holding mine gently. She sniffed me and ran her hands inside my jacket. She plucked at my shirt, then combed her fingers through my hair, grooming me gently, before turning her back on me to be groomed in turn. I got on with the task, not hoping to find a louse or anything, but acutely aware that a gorilla can pull your arm off and beat you to death with it if you displease her.

"Koko is a gentle soul, and she's conscious of her public image, isn't she?" I asked Patterson, nervously. She reassured me, and told of a visiting child who'd warned her mother not to bring the baby too close in case Koko bit him. Later, the researcher asked Koko how the visit went. "Frown. Frown. Teeth, me good," signed the gorilla. "Weren't the people good?" "Bad insult gorilla, frown" she signed. "Insult teeth me." It seemed safer to ask Koko about the previous day's earthquake, and if she'd felt it. "Darn darn floor bad bite," she signed. "Trouble." I was impressed, and after our interview sent Koko a flower arrangement that included her favorite apples. "She ate the flowers first," reported Patterson. Back in the office, I mentioned the gorilla with the Geographic cover. "Nothing new," sniffed a reporter colleague. "Snappers—they're all just monkeys with cameras."

Enquiring Truths

One of the quirks of the Enquirer, whose reporting staff largely came from Fleet Street because the publisher Gene Pope wanted competitive, tabloid-savvy journos, was its try-out system. It didn't matter who you were, Pulitzer-winner or pop music writer, if you were interested and the paper thought you might be useful, you had undergo a try-out. They'd fly you to Florida, install you in a beachfront motel for a month and put you to work for a decent paycheck. At month's end, almost all were turned down and sent home. The deskbound article editors had the worst of it. Tryouts and established staffers could be seen bustling into the local newspaper store around dawn to buy armfuls of journals not usually seen in the sleepy retirement town of Lantana. The AE's would scour the publications for ideas, looking through stories from around the globe, tearing out cuttings, scribbling thoughts and transferring their gleanings onto bundles of 'lead sheets' for senior editors to approve, or not. It was a sort of Hell Month for tryout AE's, and the fallout rate was very high, but the survivors, who might not always have been the best or brightest talents, understood a couple of things. First was, they wanted, they really wanted, the well-paid job. Next, they had to be willing to throw away any high-minded principles of truth and accuracy. If they had a story idea approved, then they'd best get that particular story in. It wouldn't do to come up with a similar, even better story. They had to deliver that original idea, as specified.

Ruled as they were by fear—more on this later—the successful ones didn't really care about telling the real Untold Story. They just wanted to survive for another week, month or whatever and keep the paychecks coming. They were well aware that the publisher kept a league table on the notice board that spelled out the stats of who was succeeding and who was on the slippery skids. So, if it meant bending the story to get it into the magazine, and then bent the story would be. It's a measure of how desperate some of those editors were, and we all knew about the mini-pharmacies in their desk drawers, that one tryout called Elliott fast became the envy of all the others suffering through their hell weeks. He had great idea after great idea accepted, and then delivered the stories, complete with the authenticating quotes the publisher demanded from worthies like priests, police officers, judges and local politicians.

Elliott must have known it would happen, but desperate men do desperate things. For weeks, he rode the crest of success. Then he hit the beach with a thud. When photographers were dispatched, as the last phase of the story-gathering process, to capture the images of the witnessing priests, police, et alia, they found themselves confronting some puzzled people who had never been interviewed... Elliott's efforts were fake. The paper would tolerate, even encourage, bending and twisting the tale, but to invent the 'money quotes' as the editors cutely called them, was breaching the Unwritten Rules of getting that Untold Story. Reporters and photographers on the other hand had an easier time. They were given the assignments and had the escape clause if truly needed of calling back to the office to say it was totally phoney. But, should there be a grain of truth in the story idea, the reporter would be pressured by his editor to make the thing stand up. It was a cause of much heartburn to many reporters, especially among the American contingent brought up to regard newspapers as vessels of truth and light and the job of a journalist as a near-holy profession. The Brits were more pragmatic. It was about them that Humbert Wolfe had penned the 1930 doggerel: "You cannot hope/to bribe or twist/thank God! The British journalist./ But, seeing what/the man will do/unbribed, there's/no occasion to."

Our American colleagues were in a constant fret of conscience over the lowering of their standards for the mighty dollar. It was Church Lady turned hooker. They knew that their onetime comrades on the dailies in Chicago or St. Louis both envied them for their huge paychecks and despised them for selling out. When directed, they had to swallow hard, blink and bribe people with access to hospital, hotel or credit card records to gather information on their latest quarry. Sometimes, the tabloid staffers would illicitly obtain old criminal records of her prostitution arrests and put them before an actress, as leverage to cooperate on stories about herself or her fellow stars. After all, as Enquirer editor David Perel wrote in the Wall Street Journal: "The id of the tabloid media drives it to cover scandal in any form." He didn't add that it's also usually done ruthlessly.

One American woman, a freelance who'd done a decade or more of accurate medical reporting for the Enquirer, was axed when the paper was financially pruned. She told me of her attempts to re-enter journalism. "I tried to get staff or freelance jobs with any number of daily or weekly newspapers across the States," she said, bitterly. "Nobody would even talk to me after they found out I'd worked for the tabloids. If I'd been a whore I would have been better received." A tabloid editor who saw the writing on the wall as the tabs began to fail, landed a job on a paper in Texas. He'd been a cordial colleague when I worked stories like the JonBenet murder case, or the Chandra Levy disappearance and, as an editor, had often given me whispered directions on what spin the magazine wanted, and to disregard the facts. When he went to Texas, I sent him an email of congratulations and questions about his new role, expecting a friendly response. Instead I got back a stiff reply that he no longer wanted to be associated with the tabloids or their employees, he was now doing some Serious Journalism. I smirked at the idea of him painting me as the leper. He was the one who'd been indicted for criminal extortion and bribery in the JonBenet case. It took a $100,000 donation from Globe to the University of Colorado J-school to get those charges dropped.

Back to the Enquirer in Florida in the 1970s. Reporters travelled a lot because the publisher thought that was the way reporters should get stories, and he never considered cost. One example: the paper sent photographer Vince Eckersley to take some exclusive pictures of quintuplets in Capetown, South Africa. The contract gave the Enquirer world rights, meaning nobody else could have them first. Publisher Pope didn't want to wait. He wanted the photographs in Florida within a couple of days. Waiting a week to publish wasn't his style. The photo editor explained that there was no easy way to courier them direct from South Africa to Florida, they'd have to go via London. "Charter a plane," said Pope. "Fly them direct." "It would take a big plane to fly direct from Capetown, Mr Pope," said the photo ed. "Boeing make big planes," said GP. "The boss wanted to charter a 747 just to fly six rolls of film," the photo editor marveled later, in the Nostalgia pub. In the end, a sensitive, nicely-suited Scots reporter who made a niche career of being a courier carried them onto Concord and the deadline was met.

Travel Perqs

We all travelled widely and often. It was fine for a couple of years, because, out of the office and away from supervisory eyes, you were judged only on results, not the appearance of industry. Some reporters really delighted in travelling the world on the paper's credit cards. I found out that I enjoyed the first five or six days on the road, then began to plot ways to cut my assignments shorter. It was pleasant to be empowered to charter a helicopter if you wanted, no questions asked, and once in a while, I'd take an unauthorized commercial flight from, say, New York where I was working to Chicago, to spend a weekend with friends. The office didn't care, and in the days before mobile phones, it was easy to sidestep annoying queries from editors. The let-the-paper-pay attitude was pleasant, too. If you wished to dine at the Georges Cinq in Paris (or the Tour d'Argent or other Michelin-starred establishment) you could usually find an interview subject eager to talk over the steak poivre and a couple of bottles of something dusty from the cellar, and if you couldn't, you didn't deserve a good dinner, anyway. In retrospect, the travel was sometimes stressful, but good. Iceland, Brazil, Alaska, it was all interesting and flavorful. I sampled octopus in the Canaries, prosciutto in Rome, snake meat in Guatemala and duck in Hong Kong. I drank Chinese beer on a Mexican pyramid, schnapps in a Munich beer hall, moonshine in Ontario and champagne in Monaco.

On assignment in Europe, I found I had seven different currencies in my wallet – Dutch guilders and French francs, German D-marks and Italian lire, Danish kronen, British pounds and Spanish pesetas, because my current wanderings had taken me through all those countries, and I wasn't finished yet. I've a wonderful kaleidoscope of memories of travel, some exotic, some mundane, but all more interesting than life as a deskbound, paper-shuffler. I recall struggling through the skirts of a hurricane that battered Central America, of a 28-hour drive to get to the disaster site. There was the idyllic canoe trip on a summer's-end-warm Minnesota lake as I interviewed a psychic, and the horrors of stacked corpses being burned after a flood disaster in Honduras. I recall clambering through the rubble left by a massive tornado that had devastated Wichita Falls, Texas, and, a few months later, wondering if I could survive the minus-50 degree freeze in Timmins, Ontario if my rental car died in the lonely woods.

There were the ridiculous times, too: standing with five solemn psychics around the Declaration of Independence in the National Archives, trying to sense 'what the signers really felt,' or being groomed in my armpits by a chimp in Washington state who communicated in American Sign Language. There was the time I brought back Cuban cigars for the company treasurer and a friendly customs officer in New York loaned me his pocket knife to remove the bands, so nobody would know they were contraband. But, as I missed years of my wife's and young daughters' birthdays and other milestones, the travel became less attractive, even on the occasions when I could take my wife along. There was always the fret about leaving her while I went off to gather material, and the stricture of being back at the hotel at a given time, when I might be following a trail that could add a few more hours onto the search. It was an extra layer of stress and just never worked well for either of us, and we quickly agreed that travel together was only for when I wasn't working.

Sex and a Serial Killer

For overseas journalists, especially Brits and Australians, the Enquirer was a source of a paid vacation. They got the word about the paper's tryout system and came for the month's trial, travel and pay, with little intention of taking a job if it was offered. One such was Sandy Fawkes, a flame-haired Fleet Street fashionista who was found as a baby floating like Moses in an English canal, and who came closer to violent death than anyone could have imagined during her Enquirer stint.

Sandy had done it all. She'd covered the Yom Kippur war for the Express, drawn fashion for Vanity Fair, written books, and done the impossible interviews. She was sent to get a talk with Oliver Reed, at the height of his glamor and pride. Reed was notorious for dispatching journos foolish enough even to try for an interview, so the features staff shook their heads. Sandy was back the next noon triumphant and obviously still wearing yesterday's dress. "How was he, Sandy?" the others asked, meekly. "A thousand pounds of gelignite," she said, "with a one-inch fuse."

Cut to fashionable Georgetown, District of Columbia. My wife and I wandered into a bar there one sunny November afternoon. I was in the nation's capital working on a book for psychic Jeane Dixon, and had taken a chance to travel en famille without the stress of deadlines or unexpected researches. At the bar, customary Scotch in one hand, Gitane in the other, was flame-haired Sandy in her trademark, smoke-bronzed fur hat, which resembled a cat curled on top of her head. She hadn't seen me. I persuaded my wife, whom she didn't know, to approach and ask for an autograph. Jennie did it beautifully. "Aren't you Sandy Fawkes, from the TV?" she asked, polite and innocent. Sandy swelled and preened. She did the Gracious Lady routine, asking just which program had you seen me on, was it such or so? What did you like best, dear? Then she saw me grinning in the background. The fluent flow of invective would have blistered a warship's paint, and it certainly stopped the bar dead. For Sandy, whom I'd seen dispatch at full volume some podgy punter in a gold necklace with: "I never did like you, you fat queen, just because you've got money," it was business as usual.

She enjoyed the joke, and we chatted. She said she'd given up on the tryout and was going to take her time going back to Florida. We said we'd see her back there, and parted amicably. Two weeks or so later, she took a call at the office from West Palm Beach police. The girlfriend she'd been staying with had just been attacked by the man to whom Sandy had introduced her a day or two previously. The story came out: Sandy had met 'Daryl Golden' a smartly-dressed and personable late-20s 'investor' in an Atlanta bar and had spent a week with him, driving back to Florida. He confided that he was going to be killed soon, and had recorded some tapes which would 'make a world news story.'

The police who arrested him for the attempted rape in Palm Beach filled in the facts. 'Daryl' was John Paul Knowles, a serial killer who had murdered at least 18 people in the past six months. He had killed two the day before he met Sandy, one of them a 15 years old girl he'd raped and strangled. The car he drove was taken from a man he'd killed four months before. Even his clothes came from one of his victims. Sandy never knew why he didn't kill her, and he couldn't explain, as the Georgia police shot him dead during an escape attempt. Those cops treated Sandy with suspicion. Why had she not been killed? Was she involved in murders? Later, Sandy delivered her assessment: "Police in Macon make Rod Steiger look like a fairy." She never went back to Georgia.

INSIDE THE TABLOID BEAST

———————

Fear of Firing

L ife at the Enquirer had a flavor all its own, and, I was finding out, it often tasted like fear. A transplanted Brit, I'd taken a job as a reporter far from my native industrial landscapes. I found myself one of a small band of journo expatriates plonked down in south Florida, a mid-1970s land of orange groves, air conditioning and retirees in gaudy golfing pants with matching white shoes and belts. Like the cuisine, which included conch chowder, unusual adjuncts like jelly served alongside bacon and eggs, or all-you-can-eat crab feasts, it was a place of novel experiences. We'd never heard of peanut butter and jelly sandwiches, for instance, and although I'd come across pizza once, in Holland, it hadn't made its way onto UK menus in the mid 1970s. Friends of ours, an expat couple fresh in from Zimbabwe, ventured out of their Holiday Inn for an American dinner and found themselves at a pizza parlor. They seated their two small children and looked at the menu. The prices seemed in line with their Holiday Inn dinners, so they ordered a large pizza for papa, a medium for mama and two small pizzas for the children. The waitress never blinked. Piles of pizza appeared, and the Treadgolds did their best, but were still left with several days' worth of meals. That was when another cultural difference surfaced. Brits didn't know of the concept of the doggie bag. Jan Treadgold's Leicestershire upbringing surfaced. She wasn't going to abandon good food, so she collared a handful of paper napkins and started folding pizza into her handbag, her husband's pockets and the toddlers' toy basket. When the phlegmatic waitress returned, all the pizza had vanished. Once again, she never blinked, though she must have marveled at the appetites of these Brits...

The differences sneaked up on you, too. When Lee Harrison and I wanted to mail postcards back to the UK, we had a problem. We found a US Postal Service mailbox ('post box' in English) but there was no familiar slot to accept letters. We circled the blue metal construction a couple of times, but no orifice was obvious. Two highly-trained investigative journos, we nodded sagely, and waited for a few minutes until someone came along and used the thing by pulling down the hinged lid. Oh. Vocabulary was another minefield. We all know about bonnets, boots and wings on UK cars, but my wife was bewildered to find that a handbag was a purse, a purse was a wallet, critters were unidentified small animals and a breakfront was, well, what WAS a breakfront?

There were other small but significant differences, too. Traffic signals were on the other side of the junction, so it was perilous to pull up to them before stopping. Traffic cops didn't pull in front of you to make a stop, British style, they stopped behind you. This led to an interesting experience for one Englishwoman, who drove about a mile along the shoulder of I-95 at slow speed, waiting for the uniformed idiot with the blue flashing lights to come by and stop her. But the sunshine, the beautiful ocean and the all-in-it-togetherness of the expat journo community compensated for a lot. There was golf, tennis and soccer, ocean fishing and snorkeling, picnics and even Christmas dinner on the beach. It was all new and different.

The working experience in Lantana, a small Intracoastal town astride Florida's Highway One, was certainly different, too. Being employed by the Enquirer was an edgy adventure, if sometimes a dangerous one for your career, because publisher and owner Gene Pope ran a very tight ship. His instructions to his hatchet men: fire at will. Or, if not at will, at least when he said to fire.

And they did. It was normal on Friday afternoons to see small knots of red-eyed young women sobbing farewell to one of their friends, who'd lost her job at short notice. Yet dismissal wasn't really that bad. Many editorial staff who were fired, hung around the area freelancing. They got handsome fees, seemed to work only a fraction as hard as the staffers and were not obliged to take the last-minute assignments that shunted us out of town at ultra-short notice, usually, it seemed, on a weekend. As the months went by, we more and more envied the freelancers, their days at the Banana Boat bar, their freedom. It seemed they'd been playing the tuba the day it rained gold coins. Then Pope took the legs out from under his former employees. He issued an edict, ex cathedra: no Florida-based freelancers would be employed. The expected exodus happened, and in one easy move, Pope put fear of firing back into staffers' lives and increased the flow of ideas from other parts of the US.

Despot Publisher

It was only one of the ways Pope kept control. GP was the godson of Mafia mobster Frank Costello, and he knew much about power and influence. His father, Generoso Sr was said to 'run New York,' and GP's boast was that he was there at the restaurant the day Costello was gunned down. I took that to mean he was a witness, not a hit man. The Popes were connected, but when three of the New York mob families went to war, Costello got sent down, and his grip on power began slipping away. Pope later said Frank made some bad decisions, and Pope's New York Enquirer became a victim. GP had to ship the paper from its New Jersey printing works, and there was a dispute with the Teamsters union. The story went round that one of GP's delivery drivers had been found dead in the back of his truck, a note pinned to the body with a knife stuck through the man's heart. The note said simply "Don't fuck with us." Pope got the message. His papers, his guy, he'd be next. He announced that the Enquirer was headed south, to union-free Florida.

The Enquirer employees were told to show up at Pennsylvania Station with their families for the train ride south—GP didn't fly —and there, his minions started handing out train tickets. That was when stunned employees found out if they had a job or not. Most of the 80 or so families had sold or rented out their homes, packed their goods for shipment. They were going to a new life. They showed up to the station expecting to embark on a new adventure, but one family in three found they had no tickets. They were not along for the ride. They were fired. Tough about your home, tough about packing your goods. It was Pope's way. A man who'd let his dog eat right off his dinner plate, he had a mental disconnect when it came to indifference to others' feelings or futures.

Yet he saw some things extremely clearly. A dictator, GP was also a marketing genius. He'd bought the paper for $75,000—some said $18,000—in 1952 and boosted circulation with headlines like: "I Used My Dead Baby's Face as an Ashtray," and "I'm Sorry I Killed My Mother, But I'm Glad I Killed My Father!" "I didn't know a damn thing about the business, I was groping. I had nothing to lose and it didn't matter what I put in the paper," he said, years later, noting that the paper had grown by then to around a million copies a week. But in the late 1960s, he was forced to change the tone of the Enquirer. Supermarkets were his new storefront and they weren't ready for raunchiness.

Pope repackaged the magazine with upbeat material: psychics and celebrities, government waste and medical insights, self-analysis and human interest pieces. They were brightly-written, positive, simple stories. No scientific discourse, either. The Enquirer didn't present 'confusing' debate between experts, they presented simple, black and white tales that were often only half-truth stories. The editor of the Enquirer's sister paper, National Examiner, once explained the lack of bustle and library-like silence in his newsroom to a friend who queried why the place was so unnaturally peaceful. "There were no phones ringing, no anxious voices trying to coax info out of reluctant witnesses, hardly any typewriters clacking. "Why is this, Bill?" he asked. "Why," the editor responded, "should we call up people and bother them when we have our own experts sitting right here?"

Invented or not, at the tabloids, everything was aimed at the hypothetical 'Missy Smith from Kansas City,' a middle-class housewife who'd be intrigued by the tempting headlines at the checkout line. It worked. Circulation quadrupled, but by the late 1970s, the paper's reputation for lack of accuracy was proving a dead weight. Medical experts, researchers, reputable sources who'd been burned by inaccurate stories that distorted or sensationalized their work refused to be interviewed again. Only the spurious experts stayed on. Celebrities mindful that their garbage could be collected and analyzed, or that their private misbehaviors might be documented by paid informers, hated the magazine. Publicists and agents avoided us, and actively banned tabloid reporters from their junkets and media events. Part of the problem was the tyranny Pope established. A story idea, condensed onto a 'lead sheet' would be evaluated and OK'ed. The problem was that too often a reporter would find that the original, one-line idea wasn't exactly what was out there. A similar story, maybe even better than the original, was the truth, but what was on the lead sheet was what GP wanted. Nervous editors were not going to budge from the original premise and incur the wrath of the Boss. Reporters had to find sources to support the original pitch, not to report what was actually there. We'd find several sources who agreed with the original line, and simply ignore others who didn't. It was a good way to keep your well-paid job, and besides, the editor told the Miami Herald, "Debates only confuse the reader."

Fabricating Facts

As corporate policy, Pope pitted editorial teams against each other, with the threatened loss of their jobs the penalty for the losing team, or at least for its editor. On a bulletin board near the vending machine (where naughty reporters sometimes substituted raw eggs for the hardboiled ones) Pope had lists and a Gant chart posted to show how individual editors were performing. The color-coded graph showed who'd had the most front page stories, what they'd done for circulation, and who'd had the most stories approved. Every so often, two editors were sent out with their teams to a distant city to battle head to head for a week and see who did better. The implied threat to the losing gladiator was dismissal. As the stress levels rose, editors eager to preserve their expensive lifestyles lowered the bar of their standards even further. Celebrities who'd once regarded the magazines cordially began to retreat behind a wall of flunkeys and mouthpieces who simply refused to truck with the tabloids. One editor made a specialty of writing stories which showed celebs in a favorable light, reasoning they wouldn't or couldn't sue to prove him wrong. Others simply retreated into fabrication.

Their philosophy was simple enough. If you lampooned or ridiculed a politician, say, you could exaggerate and embellish at will —so long as you had a grain or two of truth in the story. In an odd way, it made for more accurate coverage than you'd guess. Insiders were usually eager to provide a few juicy details, and the tab editors would invent the rest. Better a slightly-inaccurate story than no story at all, the editors reasoned. It was an unusual but effective way of covering the nation's political leaders, many of whom didn't care what we wrote, anyway. And, it sold papers. In time, as electronics improved, the papers distanced themselves a little from the dirty work, and got even better stories. They used private investigators to illegally obtain surveillance data that let them peer over the celebs' walls of privacy. Ex-cops would hack credit, email and other records, bug a room, tap telephones, even set a honey trap to video their target in a sexual situation. Editors did it to stand up their tipsters' stories, gathering information inadmissible in court, but still valuable. A celeb faced with undeniable dirt can be blackmailed into admitting old scandals in return for having the current one dropped. So, you'd read how a celeb bravely admitted to a lifelong struggle with addiction, while the current sex scandal was quietly buried. The celeb looks heroic, the magazine gets its exclusive. And, underscoring everything, was the fact of life for tabloid editors that if they didn't perform, they'd be dismissed. Although he rarely delivered the coup de grace himself, Pope liked to fire employees. Once, he pink-slipped the whole public relations department of about 20 people at two hours' notice. Another time, when he came across a memo with a word misspelled by a photo assistant, he didn't even ask whose error it was. He just growled "Fire the dummy." GP's dictatorial ways continued at home, where he ordered his wife Lois to keep out of his business. His usual question to her, she later told an interviewer, was "What do you want from me?"

The Pulitzer That Got Away

The tyrant brooked no resistance. When a bold new editor spoke up in a 1978 meeting and said he had a story that could win a Pulitzer, Pope sneered and stage-whispered to editor Iain Calder: "Tell Mr Dougherty what I think of the Pulitzer Prize." As expected, that triggered a roomful of sycophantic laughter. (Years later, in 2010, when the Enquirer lobbied for, but failed to earn a Pulitzer, this story would be recalled as the One That Got Away.) Paul Dougherty plowed on. His stringer had uncovered a cult of brainwashed Americans in Guyana whose abusive leader had them practicing suicide drills. The place was called Jonestown, the cult leader was Jim Jones. Pope disparaged the idea, was obviously irritated that Dougherty dared revive it the following week and his impatient foot-tapping signaled to his lackeys to mock the upstart. When the Jonestown tragedy came down a week or so later, leaving a US congressman murdered and 919 dead, nobody opened a dialogue about it with Pope, whose paper's intervention might have averted the whole thing. Instead, Paul Dougherty was soon fired. You couldn't have someone walking around the office who was a living reminder that Gene Pope had blundered.

Pope even canned the guy who likely saved his life. While the paper was still in New York, GP was travelling to a lunch appointment, taking along editor Ted Mutch, who told me the story years later, still bemused. An oncoming truck swerved into their lane. Faced with a head-on, Pope's chauffeur pulled off a miracle of evasion, swerving up the sidewalk and around a telegraph pole before bouncing back into the roadway. Ted was shaken, GP never said a word. After lunch, at which Pope had his favorite meal of chicken soup, which he believed kept him healthy, followed by pasta, Ted was surprised to find the limo outside the restaurant, with no chauffeur in sight. "You drive, Ted," said Pope. "Yes, sir," said Ted. "Where'd the chauffeur get to?" "Hadda fire the stiff. He nearly got us killed," said Pope. At the other end of the scale, Pope could be protective of his crew. Ted told me once of taking a glamorous woman to dinner. As they entered the restaurant, a couple of drunks made a crude remark to her. Ted, a mild-mannered man, left it alone and checked in with the maitre d', who recognized him as the new editor of the Enquirer. They got a good table, and a complimentary bottle of wine. Ten minutes into dinner, Ted saw four large men enter and efficiently remove the two drunks. "I excused myself for a moment and slipped outside," Mutch said. "In the alleyway alongside the restaurant, the large men were using baseball bats to give the drunks a bad beating. One of them stopped to nod to me. "Mr Pope's compliments," he said. "The maitre d' had called someone, who'd called the Boss, and told him about the insult. Who gave what orders I never knew." It was Pope's way. He could gift you with protection, or he could fire you. That message was plainly on the wall for all of us, and emphasized in my second month at the paper, when a Scots editor held a 'bank balance party.'

Over beers and pizza, Bruce Camlin wanted to celebrate the fact that he now had enough in his bank account to move back to Scotland if he got fired in Florida. It was an eerie feeling: celebrating ahead of the axeman. In fact, Bruce hung on for years, but a metaphorical sword was dangling over his and all of our heads the whole time. Nobody was exempt. When one of Pope's closest henchmen, Guy Galiardo, who was company secretary as well as a lifelong friend, was looking over the Christmas-ready office gardens with GP's wife Lois, she ordered some changes to the decorations. Pope noticed the differences and brought up the matter with Galiardo. "Why'd you move that?" he growled. "Because Lois told me to." "See if you can get her to sign your pay check next week," Pope glowered. "Meantime, move it back the way it was." An even-handed despot, Pope would not be denied, and equally hated to be beholden to anyone. When an editor presented him with an extremely expensive bottle of Scotch at a meeting, the others present recognized it as a bad error., GP had just been publicly put in a position of having to return a favor. At the next meeting of the same group, Pope handled the matter in his own inimitable way. "I took a sip of that cheap booze you gave me," he said, showing his large teeth. "I must not be paying you enough, Stuff tasted like kerosene. I used it to clean the carb on my Chevy." The gift giver blanched, the other editors took mental note, and GP didn't get any suck-up gifts after that. Once, I did present him with a copy of a book I'd authored, appropriately inscribed, as a thanks for his permission to use some of the magazine's material. I have to admit, I was highly nervous about the offering but decided it might be worse not to pay tribute. I chose my time carefully, going the day after the paper locked up, when he was least stressed, and right after lunch, when he'd cooked his own hamburger as usual. I also insured my safety with a discreet phone call to one of his secretaries to see how mellow he was at the moment. The planets were in conjunction and he took my Danegeld affably, but it was always a challenge to the heart monitor to enter his office...

Papal Habits

Sometimes, the mountain came to Mahomet, and the boss would patrol the buildings with a sergeant major's inspecting eye. Once, when he used the staff men's room instead of his private one, Pope noticed a couple of cigarette butts in a urinal. Within minutes, a sign went up in the toilet, over his initials in the red ink only he was allowed to use in the office. "Anyone caught throwing cigarette butts in the urinals will have to remove them with his teeth." The urinals remained clean after that. But you never knew it all, with GP. When his wife Lois and her mother walked past a line of people waiting to view the Enquirer's Christmas decorations, Pope called them back. "Where do you guys think you're going?" he demanded. "No cheating. Everyone waits in line here." His wife and mother in law turned, humiliated, and joined the end of the line. "This place is a democracy," Pope told his attendant editor, who was so afraid of the democratic despot he didn't repeat the story for a couple of years.

Of itself, the decoration of the Enquirer grounds is worth reporting. When Pope moved to Florida in 1971, he brought with him memories of large public Christmas trees in snowy New York. At Christmas '72, he had his first big tree, a 45 footer, decorating the office's extensive gardens. Traffic backed up on adjacent Highway One, as people gawked. GP was gratified. He wasn't a man to seek attention, and in his grey button-down short-sleeved Sears shirt and grey pants, with his comfortable re-soled Florsheim moccasins, strangers didn't pay him heed. He might speak like his favorite movie actor, Humphrey Bogart, but he looked more like a janitor or gardener than a mob-connected, big-time publisher.

There was no budget for decorating the gardens and acquiring the tree. It cost whatever it cost, "How many hamburgers do I need to eat?" Pope would growl if the question of profits came up. The tab for the giant spruce, and the gardens display was around a million dollars a year almost immediately. "Mr Pope loved the three or four weeks before Christmas, when he opened up the gardens, with the tree and Christmas display," said a former articles editor. "He disliked Christmas itself, it upset his beloved routine. He'd be morose around the house and play Mario Lanza songs, one after another, but getting ready to make the visitors happy gave him a deep satisfaction, and he got to show off his prized gardens." The manicured, lush gardens really were his pride and joy. He had a few plants in that reminded him of New Jersey, and although it wasn't a showpiece of rare and exotic plants, it was lush and green. The hedges were trimmed to an exact 9ft 6ins height, the lawns of Bermuda grass were cut exactly three inches high—he used a ruler to check on the gardeners' accuracy—and it was, well, an engineer's idea of nature as it should be.

"He had aerial photographs taken and studied them. He at once saw that the gardeners had followed the same tracks when they mowed the grass, both at his home or at the office," said the former editor. "GP was not pleased. He said it left ridges. You might not be able to see the marks from ground level, but they were clear from the air. The gardeners had to vary their routine. The lawns had to be perfect." Yet The Boss never minded that the grass got trampled by the Christmas crowds who jostled through the displays and peeked in the windows in hopes of seeing a space alien, or maybe, the Tortoise That Could Do Trigonometry. GP would actually beam at some of them while he supervised every detail of where the model railroad went, how the lights were hung. It was like a kid playing with his best toys.

O Christmas Tree

All across the Enquirer's manicured grounds and lawns of Bermuda grass at Christmas stood an array of individual displays. They were Toytown landscapes, complex model railroad layouts, animated Santas and elves, reindeer and chimneys. Gawking busloads of tourists nightly strolled the displays to canned music of Bing

Crosby, Mario Lanza or Frank Sinatra, all under the illumination of almost half a million lights strung through the trees and shrubs. The displays were something, but the prime attraction, the mind-boggler to end them all, was The Tree. GP wasn't playing. Being the man he was, he decided his paper was going to have the world's largest Christmas tree, and he'd display it in a decorated landscape suitable to its status. He knew the value of a headline, and juxtaposing 'World's Biggest' and 'Enquirer' appealed to him. If the Rockefeller Center had a 70 ft tree, he'd have a 140ft one. Pope's forest giant wasn't just any tree. His colossus of conifers would be the world's biggest, an Enquirer exclusive, enormous evergreen. A serious, million-dollar contender for the title of the World's Biggest Christmas Tree, it would belittle the efforts of pretenders like the White House, Rockefeller Center, and the Norwegian parliament. Pope's pine was to be the spruce de resistance, centerpiece of his highly-decorated gardens and a world champion, he decided.

Over the 17 years the mega-trees were erected, maybe four million pilgrims from across North America came to view it. A December day in frozen Michigan or New Jersey can be a powerful argument to take a trip to see the world's biggest Christmas tree in balmy Florida. The pine pilgrims came in busloads, carloads and, for the last few yards, often on walkers. The first year the tree was lit, an old dear was driving the curve of Highway One into which the tree was tucked and happened by just at the moment some tired comedian from Pope's youth was throwing the switch to turn on the lights. To the old lady's startled eyes, a giant lighted Christmas tree seemed to leap out into the road in front of her, causing her to swerve onto the railroad tracks alongside and get a nose bleed. That made a paragraph or two in the next day's local paper, and in following years, the Highway Patrol halted US1 traffic for the vital minutes, but the locals never did have the untold story of how the traffic-threatening giant got there.

When GP wanted to find Utopia, he sent a reporter. When he wanted to locate the biggest Big Tree, he delegated the task of finding and fetching it home to one of my friends, wily Aussie Hayden Cameron. Hayden was a former Daily Mail man, who'd nabbed the title of Britain's junior journo of the year, and was the sole survivor of the Enquirer's PR department purge. That escape probably owed much to Cameron's Dale Carnegie training, finely-honed instincts and seeming ability to teleport himself away from any threats that entered his personal zip code. For the last few years of the hunt for The Tree, Cameron flew to the Pacific Northwest in the fall and spent weeks with check-shirted, big-booted loggers, searching Oregon and Washington for the perfect spruce, that is, one shapely, full and tall enough to please the boss. Most years, the job was reasonably routine, but when GP heard of a 120 footer put up for the opening of an Oregon mall, every competitive instinct surfaced. "That," he growled around his Marlboro, "won't be enough." After three weeks of soggy tramping through Bureau of Land Management wilderness, Cameron's Tree Team joyfully located a 135 ft beauty, sank a reviving cordial or two and called the office. Enquirer business manager Dino Gallo flew west. The spruce earned his nod. He called in a team of loggers and had Southern Pacific roll up a rail flatcar to carry the forest giant 3,000 miles to its illustrious future in Florida. All was ready, chainsaws primed, when a uniformed ranger stopped the show. "No trees can be cut this year," he said. "Conditions are too dry. There's too high a fire danger. Dragging that through the forest could cause a friction fire." Thwarted momentarily, the team remembered another tree, 126 feet tall, they'd surveyed on a nearby Indian reservation. Native Americans, Dino reasoned, lived outside federal laws and the white man's fire precautions would be less strictly enforced. After considerable negotiation with the tribe, a deal was struck. The Indians would do a rain dance, soaking the ground and safely prepping the area against fire hazards, and the tree could be cut. Bundles of cash changed hands. The rain dance, however, was a bust. "The old guys can't remember it properly," explained one brave, folding a wad of readies into the back pocket of his Wranglers. That was when the Indians' memories improved about how much trouble they'd be in if they started a forest fire. The deal was off and they faded into the undergrowth, the white man scalped again.

Dino went upstairs. He made for the state capitol in Olympia and talked to the lawmakers. Which lobbyists got what we'll never know, but a special tree-cutting permit was arranged, with conditions. Platoons of firefighters on five engines joined the Enquirer payroll for the day, an air tanker carrying tons of fire retardant circled overhead and a US Army Chinook helicopter was employed to hook the tree into the sky and deliver it undragged to the waiting rail car, obviating any danger of fire-producing friction. The operation was a success, and a week later, the rail car halted on the line alongside the Enquirer office. The million-dollar tree was delivered. All was ready. GP had ordered a six foot deep concrete sleeve set into the ground, with a Stonehenge of concrete piers and an array of stout guy wires around it. This footing and support would hold a tree that was usually around 120 feet tall, and withstand 80 mph winds, or 'strong gale' Force Nine on Sir Francis Beaufort's Scale. The sump was filled with water, to reduce the chance of the tree becoming a burning bush, and to keep it hydrated for its two weeks of gawker fame.

Once erected, the giant spruce was given some artificial aid. Because very large trees usually don't have branches for the first 25 feet or so of their trunks, they don't look much like the traditional six-foot Douglas fir with its branches low to the ground that we see in our living rooms at Christmas. Pope looked at his untraditional Christkindlein's Baum with enough room to park a double-deck bus where the presents should go and decreed: "Give it more branches!" A crew of leather-clad, tattooed bikers, employed to hang the decorations on the tree, found themselves affixing giant fir boughs to the trunk, boughs so long they were too heavy just to be nailed on, but also needed to be suspended from above with hidden cables. Only then, with massive creaking boughs sweeping low over the onlookers' heads, was the tree decorated with its 15,000 light bulbs, mile of garland and 1,000 oversized ornaments. Several hundred red bows added the finishing touch. But there was a snag. Despite all the time, effort, and money, the quarter million annual visitors were not viewing the world's biggest Christmas tree.

Some quivering wretch notified an incredulous Pope that the Oregon mall's tree, a contender grown more or less on the mall's own doorstep, was 14 feet taller, at a certified 150 feet, and had been awarded the title of World's Biggest in the Guinness Book of World Records. The Enquirer tree might have qualified as the world's most expensive evergreen, but it was in second place in the height department. Cameron went into teleport mode. Pope promoted the spruce anyway as the world's tallest, using qualifying phrases to eliminate the competition. He even set a series of editors to cajole, admonish or negotiate with the McWhirter twins who compiled the record book. Ross and Norris were adamant. Uncompromisingly, they had already disqualified a towering smokestack decorated as an artificial tree. They'd turned down a giant Tasmanian tree because it was a eucalyptus, not a spruce. They certainly would not concede the Enquirer's tall Tannenbaum the official nod when it was topped by its Oregon rival. GP for once had to be content on the lower step of the podium. He probably never knew which was worse: losing the tree title, or being unable to fire the McWhirters.

Money Matters

There was a feature of Enquirer life I personally viewed with very mixed feelings. Meet the Friday night office party. It started innocently enough as an annual event, a Christmas bash, when the janitors would hand out a turkey or a canned ham to each staffer, largesse to take home. Then the place would shut up shop early, a buffet would be laid out between the desks, and we'd eat, drink and applaud as a silver-throated tenor of a Yorkshireman sang 'Danny Boy' because it made GP get sentimental. All the while, we'd be sneaking peeks at the clock or wondering which of the pretty assistants would end up in a closet with one of the office Lotharios, again. In time, the annual party became a more modest weekly one, to promote office morale, they said, but probably because Pope liked to hold court. It was a dangerous thing, because the bar was open and free and incautious people who drank too much were liable to indiscretions that could be fatal to their careers. GP would emerge from his office, cigarette between his set teeth, and sit in the middle of the newsroom, where he was a sun surrounded by a planetary system of constantly-smiling, jolly editors. Their relaxed demeanors, we reporters knew, owed much to the small pharmacies they kept in their desk drawers.

The chief editor and hatchet man rejoiced in the nickname Icepick and was noted for his whinnying bray of 'But how do we knooooow that?' His mumbling deputy and fellow Scot, popularly known as Captain Cruel, was rated as a 'fair' lay by one of our female journos, who said his post-coital activity was to roll over, burp, fart, and go straight to sleep. The others included a large, clever American editor who claimed his job was safe for ever because he fostered the Enquirer dog, Lucky. This was a mutt rescued from doggy Death Row for a career of being photographed with a series of celebrities and their pets. In the future, the editor/dogsitter would come unstuck over the small matter of a suspicious expense account. Then there was the nervous little guy from Tennessee who flew in a pretty Alaskan psychic to live with him on the strength of a saucy photo she'd sent. One of the reporters found her poolside at the editor's condo and took down her particulars, which she'd probably predicted. The editor later ditched his news career to open a toyshop before going back to the Blue Ridge Mountains and a local paper.

Jostling for the boss' goodwill also were the hugely-overweight diabetic from Philly who had several heart operations at Pope's expense; the sardonic socialite who stayed on the payroll for years after he moved to Spain because he was key to a big libel action; the aggressive Aussie with a brood of kids and the smooth young Aussie who told me his key to success was to nod and smile a lot and say "Yes, Mister Pope." As cautious as naked swimmers in a shark tank, they watched the predator's every move, laughed uproariously at his witticisms and competed to outdo each other before Caligula turned his thumbs down on someone. Of course, the imperial thumb could turn down at any time, but the Red Zone was inside GP's office. You entered the sanctum sanctorum through his secretaries' office. One was a wispy blonde, a transplanted Brit, the other a bustling, self-important woman with an aggressive-looking arse and a screw-you manner. Enter, and keep on the left Pope's private bathroom and the galley-like kitchen where he cooked his daily hamburger, or unwrapped the cheese, lettuce and tomato sandwich Lois had made for him that morning. Look right across the swathe of green carpet and GP, at his large desk had his back to the light, so his face was somewhat shadowed. The windows overlooked the lush subtropical gardens and were rumored to be bulletproof, which seemed sensible considering the family's affiliations and employment. Typically, six or eight people would attend a GP call to arms, dropping everything at the summons. The secretaries would trot out into the bustling newsroom to call in the troops, who'd drag their way in, all carrying important-looking papers to the latest Page One meeting.

If Pope himself called you, his grating "Gorra minute?" was a guarantee you'd be there, and fast. You wanted to keep that well-paid job, and it was well-paid. In the mid-1970s, a seasoned reporter at a well-respected daily newspaper would be receiving a salary around $15,000. At the Enquirer, reporters fresh from college started at $22,000, and my senior reporter's pay was around $40,000, and kept nudging upwards at regular, short intervals. Editors took in around $60k, and even the rewrite people were paid around that figure. Freelancers were paid by the story, of course, at $450 for a lesser, downpage ('D') tale, or $720 for a page top ('T') story. In addition, whoever came up with the story idea—so long as it wasn't an editor's—got a bonus of $180 for the downpage piece or $360 for a 'T'. An idea that made the page one headline earned a bonus of $2,000, with smaller bonuses for page one mentions in the 'ears' at the top of page one.. Story tipsters and those sources who were quoted, typically received a few hundred dollars for routine story assistance, or payments up to the tens of thousands for a major celebrity article. As I said, it was like being a tuba player on the day it rained gold coins, and the rain continued, as salaries climbed. By the early 1980s, before Pope's death, senior reporters were enjoying six-figure salaries, and that didn't take into account the unlimited expense account, which wasn't a source of income, as everything had to be receipted, but was a very pleasant perquisite and provided some fine dinners for travelling reporters..

Post-GP, matters were much more restrained. The story fees for freelancers actually declined so that by 2010, a celeb-oriented story that 30 years before was worth $1,500 might garner just $700. No cost of living increase there. It was the result of seeing circulation sink from four million a week to about a half-mill, although today's management, who applied for bankruptcy protection in 2011, quietly boosts the newsstand price every so often. What once cost 40 cents is now in the four-dollar range, so the papers still make money although the once-vast freelancer network doesn't, and has ebbed away.

The Enquirer had a cumbersome system of editorial management. There were a couple of bureaux—Hollywood and New York, and at one time six or seven staffers who were based singly in places like Boston, Houston and Atlanta, while the Florida staff was divided into teams of six or so reporters—about 80 in total at the height of things—each working for one editor. There were sub-sets of specialists: one articles editor handled medical stories, for example, but nobody had an exclusive grip on a subject, all were generalists and two or three teams might be combined for a major assignment, like a royal wedding, or the story of the first test tube baby. Photo operated separately, and then there were evaluators whose sole job was to decide the importance of each story and precis it so someone somewhere could comprehend it at a glance. Story control assigned each approved story idea a number and rank (T for top of the page, D for down page, or less-important stories) and kept an inventory of a year or two's supply of category stories like how-to's, human interest, Why I Love My Pet, horoscopes, Honest Person tales, diets, and money-saving tips. They also kept a current display of the upcoming week's stories (with a few, secret exceptions) on display for all to see, correct, and critique.

The most relaxed people in the office seemed to be the book editor, who'd dole out review copies for us to scour for ideas at $35 a book, and the writers whose job it was to take the vast file a reporter (or several) had prepared and turn it into final copy of a few hundred words at best. The writers would wander into the story control room and paw through the files to find, say, an occult story for the upcoming issue, which was created to a formula of X number of this category of story, Y of that. File chosen, the writers would condense the reporter's 2,500 or more words, which didn't say just that the subject was a doctor, but which hospital he'd interned at, what other qualifications he had and just about everything down to his shoe size. It was a totally unnecessary step, as most of the staff reporters had worked on daily newspapers and were perfectly capable of writing a 500-word piece ready for the printer, but GP didn't trust anyone, and he wanted to know that the Facts Were Right. Making the reporter back up every assertion, he thought, would ensure that. In practice, wily reporters learned to subvert the system, knowing that if they could get an expert to admit something was at least possible, they had the headline. We also reasoned that if we weren't trusted, at least we could test the efficiency of the God Squad known as Research.

That department began life as reporters' aides, digging out

contact numbers, statistics or other useful info for us, but rapidly became an adversarial inquisition, checking their version of the facts against the reporters' copy. Headed by a former Time-Life veteran, the department had a staff of 30 and a $2 million annual budget, and that didn't include legal fees of $30,000 a month to review final copy before it went into the magazine. Research even required that every direct quote in the paper had to be recorded on tape, and reporters were instructed that we had to advise interview subjects that we were taping them, an act which often inspired unease in the tipster's heart. So, you'd hear some canny reporter mutter unclearly: "Excuse me, I'll just tape some notes," at the beginning of a phone interview, and that hurdle was crossed. Research of course hated this, and as an almost all-woman department led by a toughie we felt was out to wreck our stories, the chauvinist reporters did what they could to undermine the research females, making disparaging remarks on interview tapes we knew they'd have to monitor. They fought back. It wasn't long before they got me. I'd hurried out a story that needed a shrink's comments, and I'd called one of the Enquirer's good friends, New York psychologist Elayne Kahn, whose book : '1001 Ways to Tell Your Personality' seemed to have been run in the Enquirer, at one Tell per week, for 1001 weeks.

In my hurry, I'd described Elayne as a psychiatrist, not psychologist. It was an honest and rare error, and I say that humbly. Research caught it. My editor called me over to the center of the newsroom, where he was in anxious consultation with a triumphant chief researcher. She was demanding I be fired for trying to slip a mere psychologist past them disguised as a full-blown psychiatrist. The Errand Boy, as Lois Pope called her husband's chief editor, was clucking feebly and pulling at his jaw. I was incensed. I pointed out that I was a senior reporter, I'd never had so much as a threat of legal action and if they really thought I'd pass Elayne off as a psychiatrist, and expect to slip it through, they were even better qualified than I'd guessed to be the poster children for stupidity. It blew over, but you can bet I was a target in that department for a while, and I made sure my interview tapes were dead-on. The system called for reporter's tapes to go to research. where some poor soul spent the day listening to other people's interviews, and she'd check off the quotes in the finished stories, putting a dot over every single, checked word in the story. Of course, the journalists found short cuts. One enterprising California couple was noted as a story factory, sending over scores of celeb tales all immaculately documented with sources and audio-taped readbacks.

Research spent much time listening to those tapes before they discovered that the writers were reading back their invented stories to friends who pretended to be interviewees, in return for 'tipster' payments from the paper. The couple had cleared a rumored $300,000 over a couple of years before their house of tapes collapsed. They'd had an A-List actor romancing an A-List actress at a time when he was in Hawaii and she was in Germany. The 'oops!' was heard widely, investigations began and the makeup artists retired from the celeb gossip biz. In the aftermath of that case, Pope randomly chose 20 or so celebrity interviews and had the tapes sent to the celebs' agents, to confirm that the voices on the tapes really were who they were supposed to be. Some stories were definitely not invented, however, and one moustachio'ed leading man was furious at the flow of embarrassing info about him, and wanted to know who kept ratting him out. The actor hired a dashing private eye who began dating one of the matronly ladies in the Enquirer's accounts department. She allowed him access to more than her charms, and he found out which of the actor's close associates was being paid for info about his client, which led to much squawking in the chicken house and a hasty revamping of the way tipsters and others were paid. From then on, the advice note with the cheque carried not much more than a story number, to foil minds that were inquiring too much.

For a paper with competitors, the Enquirer was remarkably open. Except for a few major stories, page proofs of the upcoming issue were pinned up for all to read, presumably for inaccuracies. Story discussions weren't held in confidential closeness, either. When GP called a meeting, articles editors, photo editors, evaluators, writers, researchers, story control and layout people would all hurry to his office, leaving the editorial assistants and the reporters behind to yawn and scratch in the suddenly-peaceful newsroom. It made little sense to me that everyone and his dog was in on the discussion, everyone that is, except the reporter who'd dug out the story, had actually visited and interviewed the story subjects, and had written the piece. Some evaluator whose only job was to decide if it rated 250 or 500 words in the paper would be in there answering questions about it and deciding its fate with the rewrite guy. It made little sense, and, like a horse designed by a committee, it often emerged as a camel.

One lockup evening, I was waiting around impatiently in the newsroom. GP had called in a squad of editors and the usual assortment of auxiliaries to work on a story I'd done on life after death. The details are a bit blurry, but I remember they involved my interview with a scientist in snowy Madison, Wisconsin, a man cautious about dealing with the Enquirer, but who'd given me a decent interview. He had not, however, come up with what the half-baked editor on our team called 'the money quote,' but had intelligently been cautious about his interpretation of the results of some evidence of a psychic wonder. The editor rushed out of Pope's office to get me. "Mr Pope wants to ask you a question," he announced. I was surprised. They rarely consulted the person who actually knew most about the story. I went in and the atmosphere in GP's office was about what you'd expect at a public execution. Pope had my story file open on his desk. "This quote here, Paul," he said, surprising me by remembering my name. "What's this?" My typed copy had been scribbled out and my editor's handwriting above it showed the 'money quote' he wanted, but which the scientist had certainly not said. I had taken the precaution of carrying in my original story, and I put that on GP's desk. "This is my piece, Mr Pope," I said, primly virtuous. "This is what I wrote. It's a clumsy quote, but it's what the man said. Exactly." I was looking at the clown who'd changed my copy without consultation. Pope looked at the altered story and glared around the room. I noticed that everyone had turned wallpaper-color and invisible, and that my editor was ashen-faced. I moved away from Pope's desk. "Who wrote this?" GP snarled. "Whose is this handwriting?" The culprit wriggled across the carpet like a penitent dog. "Er, that looks like mine," he whispered. Pope looked ferocious. "Ya changed the copy, Lon! "That's a no-no, Lon! And what's another no-no, Lon, is ya made it worse!" He slammed his hand on the desk, and I honestly thought the poor little editor was going to faint. He didn't unilaterally tinker with my copy ever again, though.

Routine Matters

On Fridays, you were expected to work or party until around 8pm, but not to mix the two. Leaving the party early was injudicious, your loyalty could be questioned. It was wise to sit in the background hammering away at your typewriter - computers didn't arrive until the early 1980s. The editors schmoozed with the boss, but what they talked about as he didn't travel, had no interest in sport and cared only for the magazine was a small mystery. He did have one favored topic of conversation, though. A Massachusetts Institute of Technology graduate in chemical engineering who'd had a short time with the CIA, he claimed a mysterious and comprehensive automotive knowledge. The boss bought himself a new white or pale blue Chevrolet Caprice four-door every year, just for the two-mile drive from his beachfront home to the office, and he claimed he never changed the oil. "You only need to change the filter," he explained, loftily, as MIT taught him. Everyone agreed. Most of us knew that his garage guy just didn't bother to charge him for new oil, but changed it anyway, and GP would sometimes 'prove' his theory by displaying the clean oil on the dipstick. The unostentatious Chevy, by the way, was one of Pope's concessions to security. Driving an inconspicuous car made him more invisible, he felt— although we noted he had a personalized plate with a papal 'P' on it. His wife Lois, a onetime club singer with a pleasing voice, drove a modest Porsche 924 and urged her husband to get something a little classier than a Chevy, so he bought a limo which he used once or twice a week, when their driver would take them to dinner. Pope was a creature of set routine. He'd rise at 7.15am, shower while listening to the same news radio station, and dress in those drab Sears clothes. He'd collect his belt, keys, wallet and coins from the neat piles on his dresser—doom for the maid who moved them—and take his morning coffee, prune juice and eggs in the kitchen while he read the Palm Beach Post and ignored conversational sallies. He'd fold up the New York Times to read at the office and stroll outside where his Chevy was parked on the macadam. Its windows were always sparkling because he ordered them washed every morning and God forbid there should be water spots. GP believed that seeing out clearly was a vital driving aid. The car had to be parked just so on the circular driveway, no obstructions. Lois once left her car in the way, after collecting the kids. She'd pulled over so GP could drive by, but one tire was on the lawn (cut three inches high and measured with a ruler). Pope was incensed. "Get that off the grass," Pope told his wife, who fired back something about what was more important, the kids or a blade of grass? "A blade of grass. Now move the fucking car!" Pope told his Best Beloved. Lois moved it. She knew her man. He issued orders, and they had to be obeyed.

Pope did allow his Great Dane, Batman, to eat from his plate but that was about the sum total of his warmth and geniality that we ever discovered. We mused that the security guards who checked under his car with a mirror before he left for work, and again before he took it from the parking lot at the office could easily be foiled. It would take, we plotted, a team in a speedboat on the Intracoastal Waterway, a rocket launcher and a bead on Lantana bridge as GP drove to or from his oceanfront home on Hypoluxo Island. One squeeze, and the hitmen could be done with the whack and on their watery way unchased, even by the two security guys who followed him to and from the office. Best to do the job in the mornings, he was more punctual then, we reasoned in the safety of the Oyster Bar. Some nights, he'd leave the office later, and you wouldn't want to hang around waiting...

Pope didn't travel. He built a routine, and he stayed with it. He'd lived in Boston, New York and New Jersey before moving to Florida, and he said he'd done everything he wanted to do. He wouldn't fly because he said he'd once had to deliver the news of a friend's death in a plane crash. He wouldn't have his own railroad carriage, an idea Lois suggested because she knew he liked to be near his own doctors and hospital, and she reasoned he could get doctors to travel with him on a train. I did spot him at the rail of a large motor yacht on the Intracoastal Waterway once, when I was in a (much smaller) boat with friends. I had a hard time convincing my pals back at the office the next day that he'd ventured out of his home on a Sunday, but then again, the sighting was made within two miles of his house. When Lois wanted to visit Europe with her children, GP had everything planned for her, right down to an audience with the Pope, and he told her where she wasn't to go, too. He stayed home, and when she returned he told her he didn't want her to go again. It had upset the routine too much. On Saturdays, when he didn't have the Enquirer to run, he went into the office anyway, listened to opera or watched an old movie (Casablanca was his favorite film, Hogan's Heroes his most-favored TV show) on his office TV. On Sundays, he read every word of the New York Times and its supplements, perused a stack of story ideas he'd brought home from the office and sat poolside in a sun lounger, separated from his wife by a small glass table, while they both read.

Desktop Dancer

Pope also liked Friday office party nights, when he'd hang out at the office until 8pm or so. Those of us excluded from the inner coterie would pretend to work. We'd be there, without being there, so to speak. We'd sneak a coffee cup full of Scotch back to our desks, where we'd type ostentatiously. Such was the situation one Friday when a curly-haired whirlwind called Richard Simmons burst in. A fey little exercise guru, Simmons was a popular TV personality and wanted to impress the tabloid whose readers were his best fans. He was wearing star-spangled hot pants and a wife-beater tank top and he started doing his dance exercises on desktops, including mine. It had to happen and it did. He kicked over my cup of Scotch and Pope noticed."What ya got there, Paul?" he asked as the amber liquid dripped from my desk. "Oh, it's OK, Mr Pope," I said, praying he wouldn't come over and smell the booze. "It's English tea. Cold tea." "Limeys!" he said to one of his editors, turning away. A few weeks later, GP would demonstrate his powerful memory, and leave me feeling uncomfortably that he knew well what kind of cold tea I'd been drinking, but more on that later. He probably knew a lot more about almost everything than we employees suspected at the time. Years later, his son Paul admitted freely that he'd been employed at the paper to check up on various departments to make sure 'nobody was stealing from us.' Just like his editors had their celeb informants, GP had his spies, too. He employed a handful of general-purpose security guys who worked at his home and in the office, where their windows overlooked the main entrance to the sprawling, single-storey complex so they could monitor who was coming in late or leaving early. They were rumored to be sent out of state to follow employees to ensure they were doing what they were supposed to, trailing the unsuspecting reporter or circulation guy for a week at a time. When Pope paid for television advertising, he had employees around the nation sit up until 3am or so, making sure the ads really were aired on the stations, just as he was paying for them to be. His family later said it was his CIA training, but other factors may have been at work. He certainly wanted to keep a close eye on things and I personally was called on once to visit a restaurant in San Francisco, under cloak of great secrecy, to collect an original meal receipt. Somehow, Pope had found out that one of his editors had milked an extra $100 or so on his expense account. The original receipt had been altered, the man was fired, and he lost a $150,000 job for a petty theft. GP even admitted to his wife that he'd had her phones tapped and conversations recorded when she was his fiancee, and that he'd had her followed for considerable lengths of time. "You were nice to that lady in the elevator," he once said casually. Lois had helped a woman who was taken ill, and one of Pope's goons had been in the elevator with them, observing and reporting back. "Sure, I had you watched. I hadda make sure you were a nice person," Gene explained to his wife. No wonder she admitted she was considering divorce shortly before he died. With that background, imagine my feelings one night several weeks later. My wife and I were eating at a small Italian restaurant in Boynton Beach when GP and Lois came in. They were seated without noticing us, then Pope spotted me and stared without smiling. I made some obeisance. A minute later the waiter was at my elbow with a bottle of wine. Mr Pope, he said, hoped I'd enjoy this more than cold English tea. My wife looked puzzled, but I knew. That bloody Richard Simmons. My sickly smile and nod of grateful thanks must have warmed Pope's stony heart.

Smoochy Pooch

British newspapermen of a certain vintage have a culture of their own, a blend of overblown theater, piracy and self-conscious delight in mild naughtiness. We're in a club, is their unspoken attitude, we're in this together, let's enjoy it. I've encountered similar attitudes among my fellow rugby players—we're in this nonsense together, we're all brothers under the skin, we're the 'we' in 'we and they.' Newspaper people of my era rarely attended university but learned their trade empirically. We're generally an unpapered, degree-free generation although, we're usually quick to point out, we had a superior education from the old grammar schools. Schoolboy Latin, maths, languages, chemistry and physics and a decent grounding in the arts were rounded off by the National Union of Journalists' own training courses and many of us were mentored by older, wiser journalists, too. They were the ones whose phenomenal memories let them catch the mistakes of others, who knew it was Telstar, not Telestar or that Walter Cronkite covered the D-Day landings from a warplane, not from a beach head. They could explain the origins of a wayzgoose, could list the rankings of the English aristocracy and knew the correct way to address a bishop, but only a very few were noted as cerebral. There were exceptions. Before the broadsheet Manchester Guardian moved its major editorial staff and printing operations disastrously to London, where it became known as the Grauniad for the quality and quantity of its literal errors, its newsroom was a temple of quiet. It was peopled by those who wrote for the literati, and the news editor refused to allow a telephone to be installed where the reporters worked "because it might interrupt the flow of their prose." One of my friends, a sub editor, swore he heard a reporter answer the editorial telephone, which was in the subs' room, in "shocked tones." "He said: "Madam, the Manchester Guardian does not take murders down the telephone." It wasn't so on the Brit tabloids. In those pre-Enquirer/Globe/Star days, I was a staff reporter for a daily newspaper. At weekends, I worked as a freelance, on lucrative day hire 'shifts' for the northern England office of The People, a Sunday newspaper most interested in the seamier sides of life. It was the best job I ever had, as my duty was to cover the 9pm – 4am Dog Watch and was basically on standby in case a major story broke. At 9.20pm, someone came around with our cash-heavy pay packets. By 9.30pm a poker game had broken out and a wonderful fellow called Mike Arnold had produced a vat of steaming curry. We ate at the news desk, played cards and called the local police from time to time to see that nobody had stolen the town hall clock. Occasionally, the paper called me during the week to carry out an assignment, and once sent me to investigate a report that a local clergyman, the Vicar of Worsley, was tampering with the choir mistress when he was supposed to be walking her to the bus stop after evening choir practice. A photographer and I did some lurking in the rhododendrons between the vestry and the bus stop, and found that the innocent vicar was a perfect gentleman. He walked the girl courteously and with the utmost propriety to the bus stop, waited until her transport arrived, raised his hat and walked back through the dark woods. I called it in as a non-starter. "Not true," I said. "File a memo," said the news editor. When I next saw the paper, I was startled to see a story about the vicar and the choir mistress. "Hands Off The Vicar, You Peeping Toms!" said the headline, after which it diligently repeated all the rumors. Former Mirror executive Revel Barker, whose towering 6ft 7inches are not the only reason he is regarded as a colossus of news rooms, heard the story and told me a similar one. One of his Yorkshire friends was sent to follow up a reader's letter from an elderly couple who were complaining about the antics in the Lovers' Lane below their bedroom window. Revel's friend wrote the piece, which appeared in the paper totally rejigged as "Leave these kids alone, you interfering old Peeping Toms!" He questioned this and was told there had been a change of policy during the week. The editor was now going for the Youth Market. "That's a funny old way to do things," said the reporter. The news editor brooked no nonsense. "Look," he told the journo. "You just shovel the shit. We will turn it into gold."

Veteran journo Joe Mullins, whose battle honors include stints at the Daily Herald, Sun and Daily Mail, where he claimed he was kept 'busier than a bishop's hat', said that's the way tabloids work. He told of turning in a carefully-crafted crime story to the Mail news-desk. The night newseditor read it, then boomed across the office at foghorn intensity: "Total piece of f---ing shit, Joe." (pause) "Just what we wanted!" As an Enquirer staffer, Joe interviewed the acid funnyman Rodney Dangerfield. The comedian shared a New York brownstone with his snappy, mean-tempered little Chihuahua and an older couple who tended the dog when he was away. Rodney got a new gig in Las Vegas and wrote to the couple asking them to tend to the dog for a few months, which grew into half a year. Finally, they wrote to Dangerfield and asked him to either collect the nasty little canine or send some money towards its upkeep. Dangerfield fired back with a "Throw the little ****** in the East River." "For some reason," said Mullins, "they sent the letter to me. Maybe I'd just done something nice about him." Mullins and photographer Scott McKiernan, with whom I worked in Colorado and watched him ace the JonBenet Ramsey murder story with some world exclusives, went to meet the old couple. On their dresser they displayed a framed photo of Dangerfield. Mullins and McKiernan exchanged glances. Within moments, they'd smeared the photograph with bacon grease, had the Nikon focused and the dog at the ready. "The little dog just about had an orgasm," said Mullins. "He was slobbering all over the picture. It looked exactly like he was missing and kissing Rodney. The pic made the top of the cover with a rag out of a letter, too." A few years later, Mullins met Dangerfield in Jimmy's, in Beverly Hills and told him about the picture. "He laughed like a drain and said he knew it had been faked because although it was his dog, it hated him and would bite him when he was asleep."

Getting the Picture

The food-as-reward photographer's technique isn't unknown. Super-snapper Jeffrey Joffe and I used a version of it when we were sent in a hurry to Honduras, where Hurricane Fifi was rampaging ashore. The storm is rated as the fourth-worst hurricane ever. It was big enough to smash across the mountains from Atlantic to Pacific, and it caused the death of about 12,000 people. We were dispatched from Florida even before the monster storm had reached the Pacific, and after a nightmare flight landed in Guatemala City on the last inbound flight. We rented a 4WD Toyota Land Cruiser, bought a supply of canned goods, bottled water and a jerrycan of extra fuel and set off. We slogged through the skirts of the storm on a 28-hour journey around the mountains that form the spine of the isthmus. Crossing the borders was educational. We had to leave Guatemala and enter Salvador, then exit that country for Honduras. At each exit and entry point were three sets of controls on each side of the border. Vehicle control, immigration and customs had to be cleared, separately. The technique was pure South American and called for la mordida, the 'little bite.' I had a two-inch stack of paperwork for the rental vehicle. I put most of it aside, pocketed two pieces and presented four or five forms to the waiting official. Because we'd arrived in the early evening, our first encounter with a border official was late at night, an unusual time for gringos to be showing up at a crossing. This was a factor in the transaction—we were obviously in a hurry to get somewhere. The vehicle control official was seated when he took the forms I offered him. He stamped the first and moved it aside, then processed the next. From the third, with a hand speed that would have won him first prize at any conjurers' convention, he extracted the two dollar bills I'd inserted between the document's pages and jammed them between his knees under the desk. At the same time, he was rubber-stamping the log with his other hand. Two bucks was OK. He slammed his stamp on the last document and handed everything back with a gracious 'Gracias, senor.' Then we walked into immigration and customs to do the same thing.

The only snag came as we exited El Salvador. Until then, every official had been happy with two or three dollars, and the small knots of peasants patiently waiting—some had been there for hours, to judge by the remains of food and the sleeping children around them—showed us what would happen if we didn't submit to a little bite. But the Salvadorean vehicle control official at the Honduras frontier wasn't content with $2. "Mas?" he asked. I produced another dollar-salted document. He stamped it and spirited away the banknote. "Mas?" Another buck. "Mas?" We feigned ignorance. He managed to convey to us that we had no receipt to show we'd brought the vehicle into Salvador. We showed our passports, time-stamped that day, demonstrating our arrival in his charming country. He shrugged. Standoff. I looked at the eight or nine dozing peasants littered around the border post. They weren't going to pay the $2 to go through the express lane, they'd just wait six or eight hours until the smell or his shift change persuaded the official to wave them through. "Time for the big one, Jeff." I slid a five dollar bill from my wallet, taking care not to let the official see the other contents. I folded the bill in four, palmed it and shook hands while telling him Salvador was an untapped tourist destination and he should be proud. He squinted at the denomination and the side of his mouth moved. He got up, put on his dark green uniform jacket, twitched it straight and sat down at a battered upright Underwood typewriter. It took probably 10 minutes, but he painstakingly filled in the missing form, handed it to himself, stamped it, and shook our hands.We were now free to visit his colleagues in immigration and customs. Buenas dias, senores. As we walked by the unglazed hole that was his window, I glanced in. He was throwing the form into the waste bin.

We arrived in Choloma, north of San Pedro Sula, to a scene from hell. In the mountains, Fifi had levelled huge swathes of Honduran hardwood, which had been swept down the rivers towards the Atlantic. Just a few years before, the Hondurans had built a chain of bridges along the coast. As the hardwood wreckage hit them, it dammed the rivers, and the backed-up water pressure blew the bridges one by one. Those burst dams released towering walls of water and felled timber. Any settlement on the ocean side of the highway was doomed. Such was Choloma. The place was nine feet deep in grey silt, a few homes still standing, many shanties simply vanished. Tiredly, I parked our vehicle on a bank of drying sand. We shot away to record the chaos and talk to survivors. Two hours later, we found our vehicle, sunk three feet deep in the silt. We had to call away people who were digging out their homes and searching for loved ones to rescue our vehicle. Happily, I'd bought a couple of boxes of emergency food in Gua City, and shared them and some of the precious gallons of clean water we'd brought. We handed over our supplies happily. It was just about all those poor survivors had. Over the next week, we gathered a dozen stories, from the nuns who saved the orphans to the youth who'd been swept far out to sea on a log and had survived three days before being washed back to rescue. We met reporter Bill Cole and photogger Vince Eckersley, another team from the paper, and briefed them as they went off elsewhere. During our rendezvous at the military base which was the center for rescue efforts, smitten photographer Vince had met the next Mrs Eckersley, he said. We gave her a ride to town while Vince flew out, vowing to see her in a week's time. She certainly was a stunning girl and Jeff and I arranged to meet her in the bar of our San Pedro hotel that evening. We'd tell her about her next husband, we said, although she didn't have a word of English and our Spanish was only basic. We got back late. Jeff had something urgent to send from the hotel. I let him out and as I drove off to return our interpreter home, spotted the Next Mrs Eckersley waiting in the lobby, a vision of Latina beauty in a tight white dress. Half an hour later, I was back at the lobby. No sign of the NME. Jeff hadn't seen her either. In the bar I chatted to some British squaddies down from Belize, one of the last pink bits on the map of the British Empire. "What goes on up there?" I asked. "Not much," said a friendly sergeant of the Durham Light Infantry. "No trade, nothing really. About all they export is hookers, but don't go near them, they're all poxed with something terrible. "But they do get around. There was one in here just now, in a tight white dress...." The next day, we continued our search for The Picture. Every disaster generates an iconic image. The bombing in Oklahoma City had a firefighter carrying a toddler from the ruined building. London's Blitz had the photograph of St Paul's lit by flames, and the World Trade Center attacks had the smoke-billowed towers dominating New York. We wanted one heart-rending picture to capture the disaster that was Fifi. Jeff had an idea, based on the relief of Mafeking, I suspected. We'd take supplies to a starving village, one of the many cut off by floods. We'd rent a packhorse because the roads were impassable and I would play Lady Bountiful. Jeff thought he'd get pictures of a crowd of grateful villagers thanking generous Enquirer readers for their donations.

It didn't work out quite that way. We couldn't get much more than a supply of oranges, some musty Scots Porage Oats and some canned green beans, as there had been a run on the grocery stores. I bought a machete but they're sold unsharpened and I had no way to change that, so it served merely as a colorful prop for Jeff's pictures as I marched along with it over my shoulder like a Ruritanian sentry, dragging the horse. After a half day's hike through intense heat and humidity, we wearily delivered the oats to several puzzled villagers, took a few photographs and left. I gave the useless machete to a baffled greybeard. It was the end of the cavalry action. From then on, we used the Landcruiser. Each day, we'd drive out to a different area and seek out stories. Soon, I came across one we couldn't publish. I was talking to an educated Honduran, a senior manager who oversaw road building crews and I idly commented on the fact that he was wearing a holstered semi-automatic pistol at his hip. "Snakes?" I asked, knowing that a number of people who'd climbed trees to escape the floods had been found dead in the branches, victims of snakebites from reptiles that had also taken refuge there. "My workers," he said, grimly. He said he'd shot and killed three men, members of his work crews, over the past few years. The story was similar each time, he said. At week's end, working in some remote area, the crew would be paid off and seek the hospitality of a local bar. At some stage of the alcohol-fuelled evening, a ditch digger with a grudge would go after the boss with a knife or machete. Remembering the adage about taking a knife to a gun fight, the boss wore a pistol and was still around to tell the story, but three men had been quietly buried in the Honduran jungles and some tale of snakebite or road accident plus a compensatory payment had gone back to their relatives....

Our work as a pair of unarmed journalists also involved keeping an eye out for snakes, as well as driving through several rivers each day, as the bridges had been destroyed by the lumber-loaded floodwaters. With yellow sticky tape, we lettered up the windshield with 'Prensa' to declare our press affiliation and we'd drive down the line of refugees with their handcarts and the occasional car that waited on each side of each river. We'd blast our horn, and whoever wasn't driving would wave a piece of paper out of the window as if we were bringing the good news from Ghent. We became such a regular sight we actually got cheers and waves from the locals from time to time. At the head of the line we'd bypassed, we'd skid the truck to a halt in a cloud of dust and shout for the soldier controlling the river crossing, which typically would be several feet deep and about a quarter mile wide. The soldiers knew our act, too, and they'd trot over to receive a discreet dollar or two, then blow their whistles to halt the few vehicles and pedestrians they allowed to cross at one time, and we'd plow through the snake-infested floodwaters, to drive on to the next crossing and repeat the process. It went well enough until one night we were wearily coming back from a day in the field. On cue, we skidded to a stop as a young soldier approached for his mordida. I fished around in my pockets and found nothing less than a $20 bill. Jeff had no small bills, either. I knew it would ruin the economy for us if once we handed over such a small fortune. The word would be out, we'd be bankrupt in a week. The soldier was almost at my elbow. I snatched up a knife we had jammed in the air vent and slashed in half a loaf of week-old fruitbread that had been baked by the sun into the consistency of a house brick. "Por Usted, officier!" I beamed, handing over the tooth-shattering baked goods. His eyes widened, he shiftily snatched the half loaf from me and jammed it inside his uniform jacket, simultaneously and enthusiastically blasting on his whistle to clear our way. The reaction startled us both and we talked it through: the soldier liked the food, it was a luxury and much, much more acceptable than a dollar or two you couldn't easily change. Life became sweet. We still had a box of emergency rations: canned goods like beans and sardines. "Here, my good man," I'd say grandly, "have this tin of pilchards for your trouble. Keep the change." I've never handed out gratuities with a greater sense of satisfaction.

Back in San Pedro, we met an affable USAF pilot and his helicopter crew, and they offered to let us ride along on their next mercy mission, delivering 120 lbs sacks of rice or beans to villages cut off by floods. We understood we'd have to help unload the sacks, though I noticed Jeff muttered about taking pictures while I did it, but agreed to the plan. At the temporary air base, I eyed the Huey, a huge machine with a cargo bay as big as a small warehouse. It was stacked with hessian sacks full of the precious food. The crew clambered into their cockpit, high above the loading platform and an affable sergeant instructed us on where to sit: on a narrow edge of the platform, with our feet outside, resting on the landing skids. He grinned as he handed us a seatbelt each, with a sort of dog leash clip on each end. We snapped the clips into D-rings that were part of the steel floor, tightened the belts across our laps and found ourselves sitting on a 10-inch metal ledge, facing out sideways from the chopper, feet on the skids outside. Our backs were supported against the wall of sacks, whose contents shifted slightly as we wriggled back against them. I fastened my clothes tightly around me, against the 120 mph slipstream we'd get once we clattered into the sky, and anticipated the thrill.

The co-pilot looked down and back at us, inscrutable behind his face mask, and gave us a thumbs-up query. Jeff and I waved back and the big Huey lifted off. I was enjoying this. We were at about 500 feet when the pilot began circling to port in a steepening curve. I looked up and could see that his and the co-pilot's eyes were crinkled, in laughter. I worked it out: they were throwing a scare into the Limeys as we began facing increasingly towards the ground. For the moment, I was enjoying matters, though I heard Jeff shout a rude phrase of alarm. After all, I'd been a rock climber for six years. Heights didn't bother me. Then a new factor entered the equation. The rice and beans began to shift, pressing Jeff and I against our lap straps. I glanced down at the dog-leash clip and wondered in growing panic how strong it was. If the tons of beans that were pushing harder by the moment against my back popped one of those clips, I'd have no choice but to learn to fly before I hit the ground. I had nothing to hang onto. I couldn't even get my fingers inside the lap strap, because it was strained so tight. I glanced up to the pilot frantically, he recognized the urgency and, satisfied that they'd scared the media hacks, levelled out and clattered across the sky to our first drop. When he heard our side of the prank, he had the decency to go pale and stammer apologies. I don't suppose it would have done his career a lot of good to kill a couple of news men, but then, it would probably have hindered ours, too.

And, we still needed a picture. We got it a day or so later, just across from the parking lot of our hotel. A couple of shanties stood in a thicket of palmetto and two toddlers were playing. One of them was a very light-skinned mestizo girl, very pretty, about three years old. Her granny smiled at me, I walked over. The place looked ruined. Jeff wandered up. "Could we photograph your little girl?" he asked. Smiles all around. She sat, a dirty-faced, barefoot angel in a ragged dress, among the jungly background. I gave her a Coca Cola and she started to drink it. Then I took it away. Jeff's picture of the broken-hearted, orphan in the jungle, crying over the disaster that Fifi had brought, had the best success of all our efforts. Publisher Gene Pope loved the picture, but was grumpy about some of the stories. He spiked my piece about the teen washed from his home and out into the Atlantic, where he clung to debris for three days before fishermen rescued him. "That ain't a hurricane story, that's a lost at sea story!" he snapped.

The same went for much of the copy we'd wired back so urgently. It took five months before the rewrite guys could find an intro to the one story that Pope found acceptable, by which time we asking plaintively: "Does anyone remember that hurricane?" Finally, the elephant strained and brought forth a gnat. The final version of the

Enquirer's recounting of one of the world's worst hurricanes read like a ski report. It began: "Death rode the slopes to Choloma ..." and didn't inspire even one reader to send a donation to the victims. Not every story could be a Baffling Chair of Death, the story at the hinge of my personal history, it seemed. I moaned my disappointment aloud at the Nostalgia pub, known by us as The Neuralgia. "Editors," said a fellow sufferer. "always disappoint. You wind them up, put them on the table and they clank off importantly. But they always fall off the other end of the furniture."

Sally, Enge and Operation Elvis

Celebrities were a big slice of the Enquirer pie, but were not my favorite area of work. Frankly, I've never considered the intimate details of the lives of trivial play actors to be of global importance, but many people regard those they see on screen as members of their extended family, and thirst for news of their doings. Translation: celebs sell papers. Almost as a public service, not to mention keeping my job, I did some celebrity stories. Back in the late 70s, when Sally Field was breaking up again with Burt Reynolds, I was sent on a nonsense mission to interview her. Yet another editor who'd never been on the road as a working reporter had fanciful ideas that someone else could get the impossible. Although dealing with celebs has left me in more tight places than a shepherd's arm, I heard and obeyed, just like Christ's centurion. Reluctantly, I went to California. I got Sally's address in Los Angeles and showed up to find the house, gated and at the end of a cul de sac, with a real estate agent's For Sale sign on prominent display. As I sat in my car, the gates opened, Sally drove past me and unloaded her small sons Peter and Elijah, whom she'd seemingly just brought home from school. I walked through the now-open gates and rang the doorbell. A housekeeper answered. The first thing to come to my mind was to ask if the house was still for sale. Seconds later, ushered in, I was standing in the hall as a beaming, totally-friendly Ms Field was approaching. I apologized for intruding, she assured me I was welcome, and I asked if she'd care to comment on her relationship with Mr Reynolds. The roof fell in. I still have a vivid memory of the 5ft 2ins Gidget bouncing up and down alongside me as I made for the door. She was livid with fury, screaming like a howler monkey in outrage and frustration. "You're from the Enquirer, aren't you? The Enquirer!" I've deleted the unladylike expletives, by the way. How could she have known? Later, when I saw her simulate anger at Robin Williams in "Mrs Doubtfire," I grinned. I'd seen the real thing, a Field in a frenzy. Robin, I thought, you never saw the half of it.

At the other end of the welcoming scale was Englebert Humperdinck, whom I went to see just a year or so later, at his Pink Palace home on Sunset Boulevard. He gave me a full tour, showed me where Jayne Mansfield and Mickey Hargitay used to feed the lions in their specially-built pit and told of seeing Jayne's ghost on the stairs. He also told me his trade secret, about his moustache. Years before, Enge had grown super-long sideburns and dyed his hair black, and he'd been voted into fourth place in a Most Sexy Man poll. Fourth place... Enge studied the three who beat him. All, he noted, had moustaches. He grew his own, and topped the poll the next year. He's kept the 'tache since. It's the details that count.

All in all, my time at the tabloids was marked by a series of Big Stories. OJ and the Bruno Magli shoes, the Test Tube Baby, Monkey Business and the philandering pol, lately the Edwards' mistress and child saga, but the granddaddy of them all was Elvis. It's a long time ago, 1977, but anyone who saw that Enquirer cover with a picture of Elvis in his casket still has a memory of it. Well, I do, anyway. The Day The King Died, the Enquirer newsroom looked like a kicked-over beehive. All was a military-style frenzy, as a troop of reporters and editors loaded up on cash and cameras. Within a couple of hours, associate editor Tom Kuncl, one of a handful of American newsmen among the Brits, was on his way to Palm Beach International with four reporters and a photo editor. There, a Cessna Citation private jet was already warming up, and a flight plan for Memphis had been filed. In Lantana, we were working the phones and putting 20 or more journos in Tennessee on the payroll to feed contact information and news tips. The advance team arrived to find the top floor of an apartment building already rented as a war room and dormitory. Southern Bell linemen were busy installing 22 extra telephones. Just in case the rapidly-swelling team—it capped out at 22 staffers—was evicted, we'd ordered ten Winnebago recreation vehicles to be held on standby.

Over the following few days, reporters in Memphis and Lantana worked the phones. We quizzed dozens of Presley contacts, locking up the more vital ones with exclusivity contracts, to keep them away from the opposition. Kuncl estimated that the Enquirer put together a 400,000 word file, including material from the ambulance crew, Elvis' girl friend, autopsy doctors, (the team got their names by posing as reps from a medical stationery company) bodyguards and Elvis' stepmother, who was happy to peddle her memoirs. The team also handed out 15 mini-cameras to a stampede of 'Memphis Mafia' —Elvis' relatives and friends—who were told to secretly snatch Last Photographs of the singer in his coffin. We got about 20 images, several of them not bad at all, and ran one, black and white, on page one. That issue, with its cover picture of Elvis in his casket and six pages of coverage, sold a reputed 7.2 million copies, at 35 cents per. Not a bad return for the estimated $75,000 the magazine paid out to get its Untold Story including the 18 grand the lucky relative pocketed for his undercover work. A year or so later, there was a curious footnote. Three enterprising Enquirer employees tried to lift that photo to create Elvis-in-a-box tee shirts, posters and the like. An accomplice scared by the thought of consequences ratted them out and the 'buyer' waiting with $20,000 in a room of the Sheraton in West Palm Beach was a police detective. Once reporter Jeff Samuels accepted the plastic bag full of marked $50 and $100 bills, he was nailed. Right in the middle of the sting operation was the Enquirer's stork-like editor, who unfolded out of the motel room's closet screeching "Aha! You rogue! Why? Why?" and scared Samuels and the 'tec half to death. Not much came of it, and Jeff continued his wily ways as a well-regarded freelance in New York. Elvis, well, he went on to greater things, too.

The Rites of Bing

Publisher Gene Pope was no great admirer of The King, but he liked the big sale, and wanted another profitable Elvis cover. He or one of his minions hit on the idea of having a pic of the grieving widow, Priscilla, kneeling in prayer by the grave in Graceland. My photogger pal Vince Eckersley, jovial, larger than life, and quick minded, was given the job of getting that unsanctioned shot, for which Priscilla was to be paid. He kitted himself out with a shiny black suit and dog collar, hollowed out a fat Missal and inserted a baby Rollei camera. Who'd question a priest in prayer? We roared laughing at his dress rehearsal, especially when he began camping it up as a gay priest making overtures to a worldly altar boy. Vince flew out, to hang around a Holiday Inn in Memphis for a week. Priscilla blew hot and cold on the idea of the shoot, until her feet chilled so much that she opted right out of it. Before Vince could return to Florida, word came from Madrid. Bing Crosby had died and his body was being shipped to California for burial. Eckers was told: Scramble. Get yourself to Los Angeles and get a picture of Bing in his box.

Observers at dusk a day later might have seen a portly priest busy with a pocket knife. He was removing a diamond-shaped pane of glass from the window of St Paul's, Westwood, just at a place where a long lens might be inserted to get a fine view of the nave. The service was held early the next morning, to deter crowds, and that portly priest could now be seen at the back of the church, kneeling and murmuring over his Missal. "I looked up, and a big black-bearded priest was striding towards me with the light of battle in his eyes," Eckersley recalled. "I lowered my head, then cautiously looked again. It was Enquirer reporter Frank Zahour." He was the only journalist inside the church, thanks to the 'funeral director.' That, in sober suit, was Gerry Hunt, another Enquirer reporter who was at the door, diligently keeping the media out, while graciously accepting Kathryn Crosby's thanks for his work. Any indignant metro daily writer who protested at being excluded soon realised from Gerry's demeanor that he'd best stay where he was. Gerry was noted for his short fuse and Pearl Harbor attacks at the office pub, and his air of menace wasn't faked. The service ended, and as Zahour exited, one of the excluded hoi polloi asked him for the name of the officiating priest. "Father Ellwood Kieser," said Zahour, who then spelled it, adding: "But, my son..." (pause while the obedient hack waited, pen poised) "Check it. Check it!" At Holy Cross Cemetery, the Enquirer team were at graveside and the reporter who'd asked the now dog collar-less Zahour for the priest's name did a mouth-breather's double take. "A miracle, my son, a miracle," said Zahour, waving his fingers in blessing.

A couple of years later, an English journalist who was working at the Enq told me a sort of sequel to Bing's death. By then an articles editor at the paper, Terry Willows had been co-owner of a nine-hole golf course in Kent, and between running a news service for daily papers had labored for years to turn the course from a bramble patch into a manicured, green gem. It was a family business, and one day while Terry was slaving over a hot typewriter in Fleet Street, his son called to say that Bing Crosby had shown up at the course with a couple of other fellows. They wanted, said the boy, to see about playing 18 holes. Terry naturally enough urged his son to welcome them, abandoned journalism for the day and shot off to the course to see what the singer was up to. When Crosby came off the links, he was glowing. "This is one of the best small courses I've ever played," he told Terry. "Wanna sell?" Terry, aware that the singer collected golf courses the way some people collect postage stamps, gulped some answer and called his partner. They agreed on an outrageous price, four or five times their expected return, and Terry managed to stammer out their requirement without choking. Bing nodded casually, and said "OK. Done. This is my business manager. He'll get the details to you. I'll take it." Visions of sugar plums danced in Terry's head for 24 hours, drink was taken, plans made to buy an island in the South Pacific—each—and a rosy future beckoned. The next morning Terry opened up a newspaper. Bing had just died in Spain. His once-in-a-lifetime deal had evaporated. Back to the sweat-stained harness of journalism.

After a handful of years at the tabloid, I'd become accustomed to thinking big, on other people's money. The daily grind was often an exercise in big spending and big ideas, as the Enquirer's publisher and sole owner never minded sending a squad of reporters on important stories, and he spared no expense. I was working on a series of stories about the CIA attempting to develop psychic spies, and turned up a psychic's sketch of a Colombian airfield, seen from the sky. This said the 'remote viewer' was what he'd seen in his mind's eye during the experiment. Most publications would have gratefully used the sketch, with an explanation. I felt I knew our publisher better than that, and suggested we replicate the exact aerial viewpoint to show what was really there. The reader, I argued, would be more convinced of the psychic's accuracy if he could compare the sketch with the real thing. Pope nodded. A minor expense. Photographer Jimmy

Sutherland flew to San Andres, Colombia, rented a small plane and took a picture from that exact aerial viewpoint. It all matched—the airstrip with the ocean at one end, the terminal building with its large overhang, the beach. It was just one photo of a handful that illustrated the story, but it was typical GP style—only the exact thing would do.

The paper spent tens of millions annually on the editorial budget, but publisher Pope took only a few millions a year for himself. A graduate of the Massachusetts Institute of Technology, GP was reputedly a former CIA psychological warfare agent who considered Sophia Loren the world's most beautiful actress and Bob Hope the funniest comedian. He loved the TV show 'Hogan's Heroes,' drove a Chevy Caprice, cooked himself a lunchtime hamburger in his office kitchen, disliked flying and rarely travelled more than 20 or 30 miles from home. He lived in an oceanfront mansion two miles from the office, his wife Lois drove a hausfrau Porsche less luxurious than many of the cars in the staff parking lot, and their idea of a big night out seemed to be a meal in a modest Italian restaurant. "Whadda I need a lot of money for? How many hamburgers can you eat?" Pope would ask. All that changed when Pope died, and Lois sold the business for $412 million, but that didn't come until the late 1980s.

Pope didn't stint when it came to his staff, though. He paid us extremely well, and Enquirer reporters could live like lords while travelling. We could spend on anything, so long as we had a receipt. One rogue elephant of a reporter notoriously dined from the right side of the menu, selecting dishes solely by price. A balding Londoner at the Enquirer specialized in finding adult entertainment places and massage parlors with names like The Sports Lounge, where he could charge his libidinous tastes to the magazine, under the guise of 'entertaining story contacts.' He told us of receiving a massage from some skimpily-dressed girl. "I knew that the 'Executive Special' was going to be good when she got hold of my bum," he told us. "She gave me a sexy massage, and at the vital moment, I felt obliged to do it, so I reached up and grabbed her breasts." It went on his expense account as a $100 lunch, including tip, at The Sportsman's Club.

Expenses, as I said, were our heart's blood. One Expressman, Brian 'Vino' Vine had a lavish ex'es account and was rumored to support a string of race horses on it, an untrue assertion, although he did have an interest in several indifferent equine performers. Vino, who was the Express and later Daily Mail's man in New York, had a splendid place on Shelter Island where he entertained Manhattan society, and he was a fixture in Tim Costello's bar, the New York spiritual twin of El Vino's wine bar in Fleet Street. His time in New York came to an abrupt end when the New Yorker magazine profiled the monocle-wearing Brit and mentioned his 'estate,' his yacht and his race horses. Express proprietor Lord Matthews read the piece and is supposed to have said: "Blimey, he's richer than I am. Bring him back instantly!" Vino did go back to London, and, a motoring enthusiast, took with him a Cadillac convertible. After a liquid day at the races at Ascot, he was stopped by a policeman who asked if he'd been drinking. "Yes officer," said the virtuous Vino. "I'm completely pissed." The cop asked him to get out of the car to be breathalyzed and only then noticed the Caddy was left hand drive, and Vino's wife Beverley was actually the one behind the wheel. Vino had done it again.

When it came to on-the-road accommodations, many of us reporters rebooked our hotels. If the travel desk booked us, we'd be in an inexpensive motel near an airport. We preferred places downtown, modest hostelries like the Georges V in Paris or the Cavalieri Hilton in Rome, places we'd justify months later on expense reports as closer to the story source or vital for communications. The same went for rental cars. The airport desk staffs were always happy to scribble 'No mid size available' as we upgraded from the office-booked subcompacts. I discussed our modus operandi once with a reporter from National Geographic, He shrugged. They had great expense accounts, too. They even had a pre-printed expense account form, he said. Down near the bottom was an entry that was much used. It was labeled: "Gratuities to natives." Top that. Of course, our sins tested the internal auditor, but we made sure to bring back from foreign trips the right kind of Cuban cigars for him, and sometimes we were forgiven. Once, coming back from Europe, I listed 'cigars' on the customs form. The officer at JFK in New York ignored everything else on the list. "What kind of cigars are those?" "I got them in Holland, Dutch cigars," I said. "The Dutch don't make cigars," he told me. I said I didn't know that, I didn't smoke, they weren't for me, I was just a Good Samaritan, what did I know? He looked at the box. Havana. "They're Cuban. They're contraband," he said. More protests from Innocent Me. The customs man took out a pocket knife. I had visions he was going to cut them up and started to squawk. "OK, OK," he said, delicately cutting the band off the cigar. "What's that?" as he held it up. "Cigar?" I said. "Yep. If there's no band on it ya can't tell." That customs officer loaned me his knife and stood patiently as I cut the bands off 25 Cuban cigars, standing in full view in the customs hall. I packed them neatly back in their box as he scribbled my clearance, then offered him one. He put his hand on his heart. "What?" he pretended to splutter. "Ya want me to commit a crime?"

Royal and Ancient

My travels went on. In June 1978, 600 invited guests including Gregory Peck and Frank Sinatra, travelled to Monaco for the short-lived marriage of Princess Caroline, Grace Kelly's daughter. Uninvited, but trailing along like hyenas, was an Enquirer team. We arrived a few days early, did our prep work and readied for the big day. Free of duties, I strolled out to take an hour or so off and explore Monte Carlo. Down the sidewalk towards me came the cheerful face of a Cockney friend, photographer Davy Jones. 'Hallo my son, whassup?' Davy was there, he told me for the Mirror, and what about a drink? We turned towards the pink and white confection called the Hotel de Paris and bumped into two short, bulky gents in checked suits who looked exactly what they were—two London bookmakers. Davy was delighted, he knew them, too, and yes they were ready for a snifter, eh, Davy boy? The hotel was a very grand place and I nudged Davy. I had walked out in shirt and pants, I had about $35 in my pocket, no wallet. "S'all right, mate, I got my ex'es." The Mirror had advanced Davy £400 which he hadn't bothered to convert. A glossy waiter approached. "Bottle of your finest champagne, gascon," said Davy. The bookies gurgled it down. Davy waved for another, and another. Cristal, expensive, I thought, then took another delicious bubbling mouthful. The worries evaporated. Time moved on, have to go, Davy. "Gascon, l'addition silver plate.' The waiter ignored the bad French and materialised a salver with the bill enfolded in polished, embossed leather. Davy dropped the stack of sterling onto the salver. "Take it outta that, my son," he said airily. The waiter didn't show a single flicker of emotion, nor did he even touch the banknotes, a foreign currency which he'd expertly evaluated just by the height of the pile. "That, m'sieu," he said, "will not be sufficient." IIe was right, and Davy spent a very difficult and dry week with empty pockets, dependent on his friends. The bookies fled, too. Nor did Davy even get the best pictures of the wedding. Some hang-gliding snapper from a German magazine swooped over the outdoor reception, got the pics, then dropped his film to a motorcyclist lurking by the beach. The biker evaded the chasing gendarmes, but the ones who caught the para-photogger determinedly exposed the film in his camera before releasing him. What they didn't know was it was useless blank film he'd cunningly loaded into the camera before landing.

I got back to Florida to find that the Baffling Chair of Death had raised its head again. The publishing house Grosset and Dunlap wanted a book on the occult, our obliging book editor pushed me forward and two weeks later, I'd regurgitated a couple of dozen stories from my files into book form. Strange Happenings didn't make my fortune, but it gave me a moment of near-fame when the publishing house wanted me to make a television commercial for it. They sent me a truly crappy script, which I rewrote, and flew me to Palm Springs. The fellow whose script I'd rewritten met me at the airport, a round little man in full tennis kit with matching sweatbands on head and both wrists. He drove me to his house in a vast limo, showed me his workroom, at the top of an octagonal tower. The entire north side of the walls was lined with bookshelves full of neatly-arranged three-ring binders. "Scripts," he explained. "I was a writer on 'My Favorite Martian.'" I was stunned. The guy had made a fortune writing for TV and I thought his stuff was rubbish. At the studio, I was shocked again. I almost couldn't believe my eyes. The Baffling Chair was standing, waiting. "I'm not sitting in that," I said. The director was soothing. "It's from a props house," he explained. Somehow, somewhere in Hollywood, someone who created movie magic had found the Baffling Chair's exact double and rented it for the shoot. I looked it over very carefully, to see it really was a replica, though, before I sat down. Even reporters of matters psychic can be cautious...

From my next assignment in France, it was an easy trip into Switzerland to meet the world's leading expert on ancient astronauts. Erich von Daniken, charming evangelist for the theory of long-ago visitors from space and author of 'Chariots of the Gods,' had invited me to his home in Zurich, where he terrified me and the local citizenry by race-driving the streets in a Chevrolet station wagon only slightly smaller than a nuclear submarine. He told me tales of tracking ancient astronauts, and focused on one area in particular. He'd followed the Hindu legends of astronauts 3,000 years ago to a ruined temple in Srinagar, Kashmir. There, he and his assistant Willie Dunenberger had detected faint traces of radiation that led in a 52-meter straight line from the temple door to the altar. This, Erich extrapolated, meant that the site was once a repair shop for starships—the radiation traces were left as they drove in and out, and the locals had later built the temple in hopes like those of New Guinea's Cargo Cults, of attracting their celestial visitors back again. It seemed very reasonable to me if I could get a trip to India out of it, but fellow reporter Harry Lewis, whose white suit and wintertime tan had lured me into this situation in the first place, was on his way home from Hong Kong or somewhere. Harry was instructed to stop off in India, take a hired academic along to the temple and independently verify matters. I knew what would happen, and it did. The Most Inventive Man in the Office didn't want to have to write anything, so he simply neglected to find the radiation with the geiger counter the academic brought along. As I watched my entertaining if unscientific story collapse, I pleaded with the editors. "Just let me add one word to the story. If I say it's an intermittent line of radiation, everything else stands up!" They weren't convinced, and the story ended on the spike. Back home in Lantana, sleek and glossy on expenses, Harry showed us pictures he'd taken in Macau on another story, and I sulked. "I suppose you got that one?" I snarked. "No, old boy, killed it, too," Harry smiled. He'd been half way around the world without writing a word.

But the ancient astronaut connection didn't fail me, and my next assignment was a keeper. Go to Mexico's Baja desert and find pictures of ancient flying saucers. The natives painted them on the walls of their caves, the editor said. They're everywhere. Take someone who knows about history with you. It would be a memorable assignment with my favorite snapper, Vince Eckersley, with whom I'd worked on a Honduran hurricane, on Elvis' death and other adventures. Vince was from the small market town of Leigh, Lancashire, and we'd both attended De La Salle College, Pendleton as schoolboys. The contingent at DLS who travelled daily from Leigh was noted for its lawlessness, cunning and skilful interpretation and avoidance of rules. All that made an admirable grounding for a photographer. Vince, a Leigh Boys ringleader, had a taste for safari clothes and SCUBA diving (not contemporaneously) that led him to Florida and the Enquirer. There, he was one of a handful of larcenous staff snappers who bought and sold their less-guileful American cousins week after week, smiling as they did it. I was delighted to have him along for what promised to be an adventure and probably a Forlorn Hope of a story. We didn't mind. Several weeks on muleback in the desert promised to be, well, interesting. The idea was that we'd examine the Cuevas Pintadas, the Painted Caves, on the mile-high mesas of the Sierra de San Francisco, above San Ignacio and see if the long-ago Cochimi indians had painted a few UFOs on the walls along with the deer, fish and turtle images.

I'd rounded up a couple from New Mexico as our academics. He was an archeologist, she was an anthropologist and they were supposed to be the truth squad who'd verify our findings. We equipped the expedition in San Diego in an hour. Camp Five sleeping bags, down-filled and toasty to five degrees below freezing ; a dozen blanket-wrapped, gallon-sized metal water bottles that kept the contents cool, Hillary backpacks, foil packets of freeze-dried food, tea, coffee, sugar, candy bars for any kids we'd meet, sheath knives, tools, desert boots, bandannas, sunscreen, flashlights and camping lights, all went to swell the bill. Shopping with Other People's Money is fun. We flew down in a twin-engined plane, the pilot buzzed the dusty main square of San Ignacio and we landed at the airstrip a few miles out of town, where a taxi alerted by the fly-by came to collect us. San Ignacio is an oasis town of date palms, nicely shaded in an arroyo called the Creek of Reeds that's watered by an underground stream. A sleepy, dusty, pretty place, it sits on the south side of the Viscaino Desert, cosily surrounded by high mesas, There's a central square in front of the old mission of St Ignatius of Loyola, a mortarless building constructed from local volcanic stone, which reportedly cost the Queen of Spain a million and a half pesos to build. The town boasted a collection of pastel-colored colonial houses, a modern motel, a couple of small cantinas and a sense that this quiet, friendly community won't ever really change. That night we ate squid cooked in its own ink and drank enough brandy to give us severe hangovers come daylight. It also led to an unfortunate accident involving inky vomit and a yellow carpet. Vince consoled me. "That," he intoned, "will be seen as the Face of Christ. This motel will become a place of pilgrimage!"

I paid for my sins with a badly hung-over head, battered in a 30 mile drive in the back of a pickup over bumpy jeep trails that led us to our guides. The first night, after our hungover jolting, we and our academics stayed at a rancheria, met the mules and their handlers, and sorted our gear for a dawn departure the next day. Vince and I had a few cold cervezas with the rancher and the muleteers, played with the rancher's dog and swapped yarns like the one about the Irish guy who broke his ankles trying to make coconut wine. Vince capped it with the story of taking his girlfriend to Bangkok. She went off shopping, he fell into conversation with a pretty girl in a doorway whose price was $200. "I was aghast, I thought it would be about $10 and told her so," he said. Vince met his lady for lunch and as they were walking back, passed the same girl. "See what you get for a tenner," she said.

Soon, it was dark and we climbed into our sleeping bags on the porch, but the muleteers' full-throttle snoring and gas emissions drove us off. We opted to sleep a hundred yards away, in the sand. I'd dozed off under the bright, familiar pattern of Orion when I woke, uneasily. Something heavy was lying across my shins. Rattlesnakes! The thought went through my mind at once. The thing shifted slightly. Alive. Warm. I thought it out: a snake had been attracted to my body heat and was curled up on top of my sleeping bag. Cautiously, I wriggled my arm free and grasped the flashlight by my head. I whispered urgently to Vince, who was several yards away. When the sawmill noises he'd been making eased, he heard me. "There's a giant snake on my legs!" Vince moved fast for a big man and was easily 25 yards away before he stopped to reassure me that they probably had snakebite antidote at the rancheria and he'd get some, eh? I extended my arm so if the snake did strike at the flashlight, which would probably be a world first, it wouldn't be close to my face. Click and squeeze eyes shut. In the beam, the ranch dog looked at me hopefully from where it was snoozing, head and paw across my legs in a friendly, possessive way. I scratched its ears and made my way back to the reverberatingly social porch, and the muleteers' choking emissions.

The eight major cave complexes we planned to visit on a 50 or 60 mile loop were not accessible by vehicle, so we now had a couple of weeks on the backs of horse/donkey hybrids, and very comfortable riding that is, too. It's conducted in a high-pommelled saddle on a sort of four-legged rocking chair that lets you doze while your mount plods along.The muleteers, a 60-something leathery old fellow called Tacho, short for Eustachio, and his two nephews, produced their food supply for the trip: a two-foot high stack of tortillas wrapped in what looked like a potato digger's retired undervest. We were to supply everything else edible, and somehow it worked out. We did get a night time symphony of gastric rumblings (they'd eaten freeze-dried beef bourguignon too enthusiastically) but Tacho and his nephews worked well. They took care of the seven mules and three burros who carried us and our equipment, they set up and tore down camp—not so difficult as we slept on the ground—and they did some truly awful cooking until Vince and I took over. Those good men, (hired at a day rate of $1.50 per man, $4 per mule) loved our supplies. They made their coffee so stiff with sugar we ran out after the first two days, and I don't think one child at any rancheria we visited got any candy. The guys ate it all first. Otherwise, the mishaps were minor. The vodka leaked and my mule inhaled the fumes, which was why he was stumbling and I was walking; and old Tacho was highly embarrassed. He'd contracted gringo tummy—the trots—from piling too much chicken a la king on his tortillas.

The routine was simple. We were up and about at 5am, fed, watered and on muleback by 6.30 and having a siesta by midday. We'd stop around 5pm, drop the stroganoff, goulash or garlic lamb with dumplings and petits pois into muddy boiling water for dinner and loll on our sleeping bags as we yarned in broken Spanglish around the evening campfire. Four times, we rode up to isolated rancherias where we found our man Tacho doubled as the local delivery guy. He took with him goods the ranchers ordered from mail order catalogs, or items they'd asked him to find in town. For one, he produced half a broken binocular he'd bought somewhere, as ordered. At two places, he delivered bits of hardware and some fabric for the new baby's layette. The ranchers were courteous and helpful and I bitterly regretted allowing the sugar-hungry muleteers into the candy, as the ranch children were delighted to see the gringos and would have enjoyed the treats. Vince himself was a treat, though. He was a great star at the rancherias, where, after ceremonial greetings, we'd sit on the porch. There, in sober ceremony we'd be served instant coffee of uncertain age with all the males and the oldest female resident while a couple of young wives brought us more hot water. I wore a folding Buck knife on my belt, but Mister Hollywood Photographer had not one but three sheath knives dangling from his ample waist, including a bone-handled cowboy weapon with an intriguing braided leather security cord. He also had a SCUBA diver's watch with impressively illuminated dial and mysterious features. At every stop, the men and boys would cluster around him to marvel at the watch and finger the sheath knives (Vince gave away two of them before the trip ended) which he airily assured them he'd used many times to kill sharks. "Tiburones!" they'd say in awe. I noticed that all the admiring glances were reserved for Eckers' knives. My eminently practical folding Buck was dismissed out of hand, however much I made encouraging noises and ostentatiously displayed it. Senor Vicente was The Man. I was just his acolyte. So much for monkeys with cameras. Every monkey has his day.

All the rancherias had groves of figs and citrus, grapevines and some grain crops, and our muleteers, who were quite the glamorous big-city boys out there, spruced up their wide leather chaps in the evenings by rubbing the hides with lemon halves. It brought up the color beautifully. The ranchers also kept a wonderful thing on their shaded porches—wineskins of water. The evaporation through the skin acted as a heat transfer device and the water was delightfully cool, a high point of the day when we'd been out in 100 degree heat. Our rented archeologist was dismayed to find what tabloid types he'd fallen amongst. We were a bit below his academic expectations, but he cooperated as he'd been unwise enough to show up without a camera. The scientific paper he'd hoped to write wasn't going to be much use without pictures, so he required our photo help, or would have to do the whole thing again by himself. His anthropologist wife, on the other hand, was pleasant and helpful as we trekked around the eight cave complexes and admired the colorful red, black and orange paintings of antlered deer, swimming fish and turtles and men with mysterious horned hats. She told us the works were executed with ground stone and the chewed end of a yucca plant and many were similar to Australian aboriginal art, or the motifs of the North African Tassili tribe. It suggested a possible telepathic link, as physical contact between those peoples seemed unlikely. Painting the images was a way of visualizing and creating success in the hunt, the anthropologist explained. The act of painting was a semi-religious experience and maybe the artists had 'dipped into a pool of cosmic consciousness' to share the images across thousands of miles, just by mindpower.

The caves had been occupied for centuries. In the middens, with the deer bones and bits of ancient rubbish, were abalone and clam shells, the remains of meals that the Cochimi had brought from the coast, though how they kept seafood fresh in that heat and over such distances was a mystery. Many of the paintings were indisputably older than 450 years, because descriptions of them were left by early explorers, so we looked eagerly and optimistically for evidence of pre-Industrial Revolution machinery, like flying saucers. Also intriguing and encouraging to our UFO search was that Jesuits who arrived in Baja in the 1500s had recorded a religious belief there of Men Who Came From the Sky. The legends told of winged serpents that carried these gods from beyond the stars and the moon, and were common to the Cochimi as well as the Aztecs and some Australian and African natives. Vince and I were focused on UFOs, though. There were plenty of 'horned hat men,' with helmeted and antenna'ed heads. Their arms were raised in a gesture of greeting similar to the one NASA sent out on the Mariner space probe. The story was tantalizingly almost there, but we just needed that one perfect bit of evidence, and a picture. We struck lucky. Fifteen feet up the wall of Soledad's La Pintada cave, we found a foot-long painting of an object that looked like a bowler hat with long flames shooting out of the underside. It was no animal we could think of, an image of nothing except the obvious. We'd found our UFO. It wasn't National Geographic quality, but it was good enough. For a tribe that had no boats, no fishing equipment, no technology when the Conquistadores arrived, it was an intriguing image. We just hoped it wasn't really a just a burning bowler hat.

DIRTY TRICKS

Presidents' Suite

Presidents, like showbiz people, are a favorite target of the tabloids, so White House occupants from the Carters to the Obamas were dialed into my reporter's sights and gave me plenty of page one headlines, thanks. Chronologically my first White House subject, Jimmy Carter wasn't too accessible to us, but his 'Bad Peanut' brother Billy was, and his he and his gas station drinking buddies from Plains knew me well enough to nod hello when colleague Rick Eyerdam and I gate-crashed the wedding of Billy and Sybil's daughter Jana. We watched as the wonderfully-named preacher Earl Duke performed a down-home ceremony by Billy's kidney-shaped swimming pool. There was a rowboat filled with ice, Billy Beer and pink champagne, Sybil Carter joined country singer Tom T. Hall to render 'It may be peanuts to you but it's love to us,' and President Jimmy, proud uncle, beamed right through the rain showers.

It was a time of peace between the Enquiring Minds and the celebs, a time I enjoyed so much more than the era of grubby muck-stirring that followed. Back in those innocent days of the mid-1970s, Jimmy's sister Gloria Spann openly introduced me to Miss Lillian as an Enquirer staffer when I showed up at her house. The ladies were playing cards, but treated me graciously. Life was good.

The nastiness between the tabs and the First Families came later, when the tabs decided that sordid secrets revealed were a circulation booster. It was a sort of 'see the bearded lady as she shaves' approach, and tab execs adopted gloves-off tactics. They didn't confine it to examining the garbage of the famous, either. In one instance, they sent reporters to Arkansas. Their mission was to follow then-governor Bill Clinton on his morning jog to see if he'd be tempted by the black hookers who mysteriously kept crossing his path. During the 1980s, there was some nastiness around the Reagans and their imperial management style, some mockery of Nancy's weakness for fortune tellers, but it wasn't until the Clinton era that full negativity was given free rein.

A look through my filing cabinets tells a lot. File tags with captions like 'Chelsea Wild Child,' 'Wedding Chaos,' 'Hillary's Butch Hair,' 'Hillary Divorce,' 'Clinton Divorce Pact,' 'Clinton Sex Addict,' 'Bill Clinton Depressed,' 'Hillary Exorcised,' and 'Bill and Belinda' show the trend. The tabs weren't exactly Clinton boosters, and nobody was exempt. First daughter Chelsea Clinton was regarded as fair game, and the tabs followed her college romances with glee. When I was sent to investigate her doings at Stanford University in the mid 1980s, I was intrigued to find that her dorm building had been secretly reinforced against possible rocket attack. The story didn't run. The tab editors weren't interested in tales of threats to her, they just wanted anecdotes about bad behavior, romance or conflict with her parents. Chelsea had never run for public office, and in my mind at least was not a legitimate target, but her indiscretions were meat and drink to the scandal sheets, where paparazzi pictures of her in what we used to call 'emotionally overtired' mode, exiting some Oxford pub with other students were run large.

It wasn't anything I was proud of, and I honestly attempted to sidestep celeb assignments, but the tabloids profited well from scandals, and soon even the so-called quality press happily joined the sensationalist hunts over Monica, and Whitewater and Chandra. The days of newspapers turning a blind eye to presidential flaws were over. The Oval Office wasn't a place the tabs or anyone else seemed to respect. After 1999, when all the tabloids were under one ownership, and the rivalry was lessened, the page one stories became an ongoing series of slurs and tattles about the presidents. There were Clinton's alleged dalliances, George W Bush's claimed drinking, reported domestic upheavals with Laura and coziness with Condi Rice. And then there were Obama's so-called relationships with Oprah, terrorists and gays. Most of these tales had doubtful provenance, many of them were shrieked in misleading headlines, and all seemed secured by the knowledge that no president would even acknowledge the slurs. There wasn't even a statute of limitations for some that should have been long-forgotten indiscretions.

In 2007, when Obama was running for president, he got the full bare-knuckle treatment, and I was part of it. I was sent to scratch around Hawaii and Los Angeles, to dig up stories of the teenage Obama's hormone storms with a onetime beach beauty who was now a fading escort-for-hire around Hollywood. Uneasy at publishing dirt on the next Leader of the Free World, I talked to a colleague who'd raised that very subject over a beer with one of the tabloid group's legal advisors. "He told me that presidents are a bit like cartoon characters, you can't really libel them," he explained, cheerfully. So the editors had reasonably free rein when they wanted a juicy headline.

Researched and Faked

Here's how it worked: an editor eager to run, say, a 'Bush Divorce Plans' headline would scour the dailies, web blogs, gossip columns or underside of a garbage can for some hint of domestic upheaval on Pennsylvania Avenue. That was the basis. Then, to add some credibility, a tabloid would have a rent-a-pundit declare that Laura looked strained, or a paid-off 'body language' expert would be called in to declare just how hostile the Bushes were to each other, on the evidence of this photograph of them staring in opposite directions. Even the thinnest speculation could work, because the tab editor would argue that this was already published, and he was simply reporting it, factually, with an 'expert' to help stand up the tale. It was the mixture as before: find the sources that supported your claim, ignore any opposing views and keep the story simple, so as 'not to confuse the readers.'

George Orwell warned against 'words used in a consciously dishonest way,' and some editors were masters of the consciously dishonest. Piously intoning that every claim must be supported by at least two sources, the editor would write the headline he wanted, sometimes even sketching out in a paragraph or two of instruction what logic might support his invented story. Then he'd let loose the dogs. The reporters could usually sniff out some political opponent who would claim to have inside knowledge, often at second or third hand, and that person would become a 'longtime family friend,' 'White House insider' or 'source close to the family.' His name wouldn't be used in print, but the tabloid's attorneys would be provided with it, and with contact details, as well as a brief thumbnail of who the source was. It might say: 'Trustworthy source we've used before, business acquaintance of Laura's best friend. Telephone: 555-455-5555.' After Enquirer publisher Gene Pope's death in 1988, the much-advertised but fallible fact-checking system collapsed. Post-Pope, I can remember only a few instances when source phone numbers were checked to see if anyone real or even alive was at the other end, much less whether they'd spoken the words they were supposed to have done.

The Enquirer's rep for accuracy had sunk so low by 2002 that a couple of Salt Lake Tribune reporters saw an opportunity. They provided, for $20,000, what they thought would be 'deep background' on a hoked-up story they thought would be lost in the welter of other tabloid sins. They'd been following the story of Elizabeth Smart, a young Utah girl who had been kidnapped from her bedroom by a crazed 'prophet' who kept her chained up for sex in a forest camp for eight months. The hunt for her, and subsequent rescue, captured attention worldwide. Coincidentally, I'd worked with her photographer uncle, Tom Smart, at an Antiques Roadshow TV taping some time before her abduction. I liked Tom a great deal. So, it was a shock during the time Elizabeth was missing to see an Enquirer story that Tom's brother and other men of the Smart family were involved in a 'gay sex ring.' There was no truth in it. Ironically, the fake Enquirer story, for which the paper apologized and paid up damages, wasn't the tabloid's creation. Even the Smarts' family attorney later admitted that the tabloid had 'acted very responsibly.' To the public, however, the sordid business was yet another Enquirer negative.

Here's the inside story of what really happened. Salt Lake Tribune crime reporters Michael Vigh and Kevin Cantera were gullible enough to believe their police sources when they heard some lurid nonsense about S&M, gay sex and other fairy tales. Then they were greedy enough to embellish the tall tales for a payoff. It began when the duo wrote in their newspaper that investigators were working on a theory that Elizabeth had been abducted by a family member. The fingers of their unnamed sources pointed right at Tom Smart, though he wasn't ID'ed until his own newspaper, the Trib's rival Deseret News, defended him. Enquirer freelancer Alan Butterfield heard of the 'family connection' to the abduction and rushed to talk to the journos. He conjured up sugarplum visions of a $100,000 payoff, and over a four-hour dinner heard their boastful stories. Later, the Trib's pair would say they were just sharing rumors, but they agreed that yes there was a journal, a sex diary and yes, they could flat-out confirm everything. Copper-bottomed sources, the real thing. Confirmed. Just pay us. Butterfield made sure his tape recorder was working when he called them back the next day to check the 'facts' they'd confided at dinner. The reporters said later that they told him what they felt he wanted to hear, though the offer he now made was only $10,000 each. They said they had a source or two for certain details, identified the FBI, Secret Service, Utah State Police and Salt Lake PD as giving them the information, and vouched for its truthfulness. All of it on tape.

One convincing detail was the sex diary, as the Smarts are Mormons, and the LDS church encourages its members to keep a journal of everyday events both good and bad. A record of misbehavior, attested to by cops. Great. Except, it wasn't real. The Enquirer's flawed fact-checking system failed. The magazine ran the story under the joint byline of five reporters: "Utah Cops: Secret Diary Exposes Family Sex Ring." It named Elizabeth's dad and two of her uncles as participants in the 'shocking gay sex scandal.' The Smarts suffered in silence, as their primary goal was to recover Elizabeth, and reacting to a slime attack could divert their efforts. For eight months they kept quiet, then Elizabeth was recovered and the family went about reclaiming their good name.

Attorney Randy Dryer considered the Smarts victims of the

investigators' leaks and wanted to find the no-name sources who had spread lies about them. Another consideration, now that Elizabeth was back, was that those leaky sources should be plugged, or prosecution of the abductor could be jeopardized. The Enquirer handed over source sheets that identified the two Tribune reporters as providing sex ring details. At the same time, the source sheets were edited to exclude informants who'd been promised confidentiality. The Trib reporters were first given probation for illicit freelancing, then were fired, and their editor, who seemed suited by his actions for a tabloid career, tried to keep the Enquirer connection under wraps. He, too, was forced out. And at the end of it all, the dunderheads who smirched a family under siege claimed they 'never dreamed' they were taking the Enquirer's cash for information. They thought that twenty grand was just for 'deep background' and that reporters from the Enquirer would do the work.

Chandra's Tragedy

The Smart case was a year old when another major legal crisis for the tabloids reared its head, and I was involved. California congressman Gary Condit was a person of great interest during the tragic story of Washington intern Chandra Levy. Chandra was taken in by the scuzzy politico, who had a fighter pilot haircut and some lowlife habits. It all came out when Chandra went missing and the police took a close interest in the relationship between the young woman and the married politician. It seemed not to be his only entanglement, and while East Coast correspondents were scouring Washington DC for stories, I was in Washington state, looking into his relationship with a United Airlines flight attendant. Congressman Condit, we heard, was in the habit of handing out his business cards on flights to any attractive woman, unselfishly offering to help in any way he could. This, claimed the flight attendant, led to her romantic entanglement with the Representative from Ceres, California.

That story and others about Chandra ran for months, culminating in headlines about an alleged telephone screamfest between his wife in California and Chandra in Washington. Soon after that claimed long-distance dispute, Chandra was murdered while jogging. Her body was not found for a year. The tabs were wrongly convinced that Condit had dark depths—a Salvadoran immigrant was convicted of the murder in late 2010—and were making hay while the scandal sun blazed down. One senior editor mysteriously acquired details of the angry phone call he said had been made between Condit's wife and his mistress. They ran the circulation-boosting tale, and to nobody's great surprise, the story backfired. It brought me some discomfort, because the piece included unrelated material I'd filed three weeks before. My copy was basically background color about Condit's behavior and it wasn't concerned with the claimed conversation. It came from three sources to whom I'd promised absolute confidentiality. Unfortunately, my name was among the multiple bylines on the 'telephone row' story, and Condit's attorneys scatter-gunned writs at everyone. My three sources unexpectedly faced being subpoenaed because the tab lawyers had no intention of honoring my 'must be confidential' memo. Although what my sources said had nothing to do with the contentious alleged phone call, the Condit suit was leveled at everyone even remotely concerned with the published piece and the attorneys were in rump-covering mode.

After Condit's lawyers came knocking, the tabloids' woodentops contacted my trio before offering them up to Condit's team. I was in a nutcracker, and made a few calls. Happily, my three played it deadpan to the defense legal eagles. They confirmed that they'd spoken to me, but claimed to know nothing, to have said nothing. I must have invented it. That sank my credibility, but kept my informants out of the case. No point handing over witnesses who couldn't support the defense, and as I was a freelance, the paper could hardly fire me. Anyway, I reasoned, if the tabs who stretched matters so far and demanded so much would so happily sell out my sources, breaking my promise, (and this, my only lawsuit in 30-plus years), they had small grounds for complaint. In the end, everyone seemed just to shrug and the boat sailed on, unrocked. I was interested, though, to see just how cavalier the papers' lawyers were about abandoning me, and made mental notes for the future. Condit won an undisclosed settlement over the alleged phone call, the editors continued their creative ways and the representative was dumped by voters at the next election. He began a new career selling ice cream.

Obama and the Birthers

A few years on, in 2007, when Globe called on me to investigate
Obama, I remembered those old stab wounds in my back and did
some derriere safety work of my own. "We want to look into Obama,
and we want New York Times-quality reporting," the senior editor
insisted, probably crossing his fingers behind his back. "This will be
looked at from the very top. Everything has to be accurate, backed
up and real." Then he did what the Times does not do. He outlined
what the still-unresearched story would contain. He emailed to me a
full, 700-word memo with subheads, of the story they wanted, headlines already written. Neatly capped-up over each section were the
teasers. First was: OBAMA'S LIES and CRIMINAL CONNECTION.
Next up: MUSLIM TIES. Finally: SCANDAL OF OBAMA DIARIES.
This last, the hoped-for diaries, was an especially low blow. The
Washington buzz, I was told, was that secret diaries contained
details of Obama's mother's 'rampant sexual exploits,' which I was
told 'would have a huge bearing on the issues of family values in
an election year.' It's almost needless to note that no such diaries
have been turned up, although the tabs did send someone to Jakarta
(and me to Hawaii and Los Angeles) in hopes of supporting those
preconceived headlines. I started with the LIES and CRIMINAL
CONNECTIONS, made a few calls, flew west, checked into an over-
priced, shabby hotel in Waikiki and began work.

Obama, I soon learned, had been packaged like a supermarket
brand. He'd shaped his career with precision, taking deliberate steps
to advance himself and to create political credibility. And he'd had
great help, as a rising star legislator. When he began his run for the
White House, Obama's highly-disciplined campaign's press strategy
was to control the media. They used web videos to focus the message,
and avoid having the candidate talk to reporters. When interviews
were needed, Obama gave them on live TV. That way, as communications director Anita Dunn later explained, "we determined what the
voters heard, as opposed to some editor in a TV station (wanted)."
The campaign was just as efficient when it came to Obama's back
story. A Cleanup Fairy seemed to have fluttered in to help with his
past. Someone had gone to Honolulu about ten months before I got
there in April 2007, swept up inconsistencies and buried, burnished

104 | TABLOID MAN

or mended any skeletons in the Obama closet, which was then hermetically sealed. Obama's island friends and enemies alike all seemed to have been approached, briefed, or cautioned. Nobody was openly willing to spill even a single Kona coffee bean about the young Obama's long-ago wild life. The candidate himself had addressed his teen years in his first autobio, frankly and disarmingly admitting to some indiscretions, including drug use and drinking. He wrote of being alienated from his peers by his skin color and of being salvaged from 'Junkie. Pothead... the final, fatal role of the young black man' by his mother. He wrote that Ann, on one of her visits to Hawaii, had challenged him about his druggie pals and the recent arrest of one of them. A starting point for grubbing around, I thought.

I scoured through Punahou School class lists, reunion planners, and locals, looking for leads, with only moderate success. Then I approached Keith Kakugawa, Obama's high school basketball team mate and mentor. Kakugawa, two years older than Obama, was once the laid-back leader of a group who called themselves the Choom Gang. 'Chooming' is Hawaiian slang for drug-taking, and Obama readily admitted he'd done cocaine and marijuana. The gang was important enough to him that in his senior yearbook, he thanked his Choom Gang pals, singling out Kakugawa individually. He also thanked the grandparents who raised him, but omitted mention of his faraway mother. Matters might have been left there, but nearly three decades later, the tabloids thought the presidential candidate's youthful indiscretions could sell more than a few copies. Tipsters in Los Angeles alerted the newsdesk in Florida that the old Choom Gang leader had surfaced after not seeing Obama since 1977. Kakugawa had been busted three times on drug-related charges and spent seven years behind bars on cocaine and theft charges.

Freshly released from prison and living in a beat-up Mazda with another man, he'd called the Obama campaign looking for money. The destitute old pal's reappearance was troublesome for the candidate. Obama had a brief 'Hi, how's things?' conversation, then handed the ex-con over to an aide. She said 'No' to handing over cash but 'Maybe' to getting a social welfare agency to help him. Matters got a bit conflicted, with campaign workers saying Kakugawa threatened to tell what he knew to extort money and

Kakugawa saying that Obama told him to keep quiet around the press. To me, he explained the call simply. "I'm homeless, I sleep in a car. I ask everyone I know for money," he said. And he wanted to earn cash for talking some more. There wasn't too much to hear about the young Obama's wild times, I soon found out. Some youthful booze and drugs, joyriding in a 'borrowed' car, some descriptions of looking for girls at university parties, nothing much, but it was enough to make supermarket checkout headlines. Globe sent Kakugawa a small amount of money, someone, probably at Obama's urging, arranged for him to be housed and he stopped Telling All. My contacts with him after that were more or less fruitless. Other high school friends were a little more forthcoming, and digging deeper in Hawaii resulted in a semi-scandal, even if it was a bit long in the tooth. Back in 1979, Obama had ditched his regular girlfriend to take a teenage beach beauty to his senior prom. She'd caught his eye in a wet tee shirt contest, and was striking enough to land a bit part in a 'Magnum PI' episode.

The girl was now a 42 years old woman, living modestly in Beverly Hills and following a sketchy sort of life. The Globe reinforced my solo efforts with a couple more reporters, and we collected accounts of the woman's criminal past and recent history as an escort. There was even talk of a madam ticked off that her clients had been poached.

Two of the woman's men friends spoke to us about drugs, three-way sex and bailing her out of jail. Globe's editors licked their lips. They were dreaming up headlines about the Candidate And The Hooker, even if she hadn't been anything like that 28 years before, when Obama dated her. Instructions came to send a reporter to check police records. Did this woman have convictions, say, for prostitution? Someone seemed to have beaten the tabs to the punch. Just as Obama's half-sister's online profile had been wiped from the Honolulu school where she worked, no arrest or other criminal records for the onetime bikini girl were to be found. The word came to me from Florida: buy her up. I called her at home, and got a giddy, mercurial, brief interview before she excused herself to go back to her 'meeting.' I offered her $35,000 for an interview and assistance to obtain photographs, putting it to her verbally, as well as in a written offer I had to leave under the windshield wiper of her car, as she wouldn't come to the door. It was moderately serious money for the tabs, and an indication of the importance they attached to the tale, but my flighty subject skipped out for a short visit to Hawaii.

Still slogging around Los Angeles, I heard from one source that the woman had a photo on her cell phone, showing her with Obama at his prom night. Then there were the snapshots she'd been displaying around a Hollywood health club that showed a young Obama, in boxers, on a bed with her and another teenage girl. I didn't see them, as I had to leave California, and a staff reporter took over, disastrously, when our target returned from the islands. He allowed the woman to tape record him while he incautiously advised her: "The paper will use the story, anyway, without your help." She ignored it all, didn't take the money, didn't cooperate further and didn't hand over any photographs. The story ran. A lawyer she hired listened to her tape, and said the reporter's advice amounted to extortion. He wanted a settlement. Eventually, it was a Mexican stand-off. Tabloid lawyers used a proven tactic and wrote to the woman's legal rep to tell him the paper had an ongoing investigation into her criminal past and recent activities as an escort-for-hire. The woman, understandably reluctant to be painted as a prostitute, faded from the scene. It was just another dirty-pool day at the office for a tabloid editor or two, but it was a wracking experience for me. I felt we'd persecuted the woman over something that was no more than a teenage adventure from three decades ago. It should have remained buried.

It wasn't the only time I was pushed into doing negative stories about Obama, though, and one of those times caused ructions but left me smirking. The publisher of a respected watchdog website, Pamela Geller spent a year pursuing what 'birthers' said was an Obama cover-up about his eligibility to be president. Briefly, they asked if he really was a citizen, and they wanted to see his full birth certificate, saying there was evidence he was born in Kenya. During the election campaign of 2008, Obama's people posted a document on his 'Fight the Smears' website, saying it was a Certificate of Live Birth issued by the Hawaiian authorities that showed he met the citizenship requirements mandatory for a president of the United States of America. "The document," said Geller, "was supposed to be a short form of his detailed birth certificate, but what we actually got was a horrible forgery." A forensic examiner concluded that either a real COLB was scanned into PhotoShop and digitally edited, or a genuine COLB was washed blank with solvent to remove the toner, and new editing applied. "There's something in his birth certificate he doesn't want us to see," concluded Geller, adding that Obama hired five law firms and spent $680,000 to fight the release of the 'vault copy' of his birth certificate.

Birth certificate conspiracy theorists also point out that Obama's kindergarten, Punahou School, Occidental College and Columbia University records, his Columbia thesis, Harvard Law School records, Harvard Law review articles, University of Chicago scholarly articles, passport, medical records, Illinois state senate files, Illinois state Bar Association records, baptism records and adoption records have also been made unavailable, or have been purged. Within a year of the ruckus, lawsuits by a leader of the birthers movement had been dismissed on a couple of grounds. One was that they were merely a vehicle for 'political rhetoric and insults," the other, that federal courts didn't have the power to overthrow a sitting president. Globe, undeterred by the rulings, came to me in 2009 to get more experts to comment on what the president could be hiding. It was the usual tabloid dilemma. Few academics will venture their names and reputations in the popular press, fearing either ridicule or more likely, being misquoted. But when the assigning editor is pressing for a named source, the foot soldier at the sharp end of things does what he can. To this end, several years before, I'd enlisted the help of a friend. Will Silvestri had worked on political campaigns in northern California. When I was writing a series on White House scandals, his historical knowledge helped me immensely, and it was useful to have a named source, one unembarrassed to appear in a scandal sheet.

In fact, he was comfortable enough to joke about it to colleagues, and I made sure his quotes were accurate, pithy and appropriate. In the case of the missing birth certificate, Silvestri sensibly pointed out that you need to produce a birth certificate just to get a driver's license, never mind to become president of the United States of America. It was the sort of practical comment I needed in that story, and it was the type of enlightenment that had sent Will from political pundit to historian, and even, I confess, for stories about the cocaine trade, to crime historian. The shorthand term 'political historian' fitted him well. In three years, he'd become a valued resource with just the right Dolly Madison anecdote or Jackie Onassis tale for whatever angle I was standing up. He could explain how George W Bush needed Laura's image to boost his own slumping approval rate, or why Hillary Clinton alienated so many voters. So, when I needed the money quote "What is Obama hiding?" and an explanation that the president's now-redacted kindergarten records alone would have contained his real birth certificate, legal name, parents or guardians' names and place and date of birth, Will stepped up, and said it. On the record. As a political historian.

A suddenly-alert attorney at Globe Google'd Will, and blew a gasket. The lawyer exploded on the Globe editor who'd happily rubberstamped Will for three years, and who'd often made demands like: 'Have Silvestri say 'will be' rather than 'could be' to inflate some invented claim or other. Silvestri had no qualifications, no academic papers, no scholarly history he could find, the lawyer charged. How on earth? All I could say was the truth. Will wasn't a professor, but he did have a political activist background, and his accurate contact numbers had always been included with the file. He was real, but not totally an academic.... It was no matter that his material was accurate and to the point. He didn't have the sheepskin. A tabloid source was burned. I'd have to find another of my poker-playing friends for the next story. You didn't really think that every single reportage in the tabloids was well, New York Times quality, did you?

Praying for Patrick

The tabloids fight an uphill battle for credibility, and even when they're doing no harm, they face barriers. Here's an example I worked on a couple of years ago. When the actor Patrick Swayze was diagnosed with the pancreatic cancer that ended his life, someone at Globe thought it would be a tasteful idea to invite a noted member of the clergy to compose a prayer for him. Our readers would diligently repeat the prayer, which requested peace, tranquility and God's grace for Patrick and his wife Lisa, Globe would look responsible and caring, and maybe Patrick would be helped or comforted. Globe's editors cast around for someone to do the job, and called me. "Get someone famous, someone we know," I was instructed. I started with Billy Graham's organization, now run by his son Franklin. Once, Billy was a friend of the Enquirer, happy to pass on God's instructions via my pal Lee Harrison to the magazine's claimed 15 million readers and potential tithe donors. The televangelist's organization swiftly handed me off to its public relations firm. They didn't even say 'No.' They just emailed me succinctly that 'unfortunately' Franklin was preparing for an upcoming festival.

Next to 'decline involvement' to me was Robert Schuller's Crystal Cathedral team, closely followed over the refusal line first by Joel Osteen's spokesperson and then by fellow televangelist Benny Hinn's mouthpiece. The California priest who performed Charlton Heston's funeral also backed away, pointing out that although Patrick was once a Catholic, he had become Buddhist and had dabbled in Scientology. That cleric was probably sprinkling holy water over the phone, while he hunted for a garlic wreath to hang around his neck, or maybe a stake to drive through my heart.

Next, I approached the parish priest of St Didacus Church, the closest to Swayze's Sylmar, California home. All I got there was a blank wall of silence. Ditto from Father Clint at Houston's St Rose of Lima, where Patrick went to school. You'd have thought I'd accused the Pope of ignoring child molestation charges. By now, I was grinding enamel from my molars. Didn't even one of these professional God-botherers have a minute to offer a simple prayer for an actor admired as a decent man?

I considered approaching a couple of stuntwomen Swayze had worked with, who'd separately become ordained ministers and I put out a call to one of the Grateful Dead's former spiritual advisers. Still no results. Finally, my prayers for a prayer were answered. I came across the Hollywood Prayer Network, a non-denominational group headed by ordained minister and TV producer Karen Covell whose mission is to minister to the entertainment industry. She told me she'd sent Patrick a Bible a couple of weeks earlier, "to bring him comfort and strength.' Unlike her more famous ministerial colleagues—do I sound bitter?—she took time to compose a graceful prayer and did more than just send it to Globe. She also circulated it to HPN's 5,000 'prayer warriors' in four countries who regularly pray for showbiz workers. The story ran, innocent of the help of

110 | TABLOID MAN

organized religionists, and maybe it helped a little. Patrick survived for more than a year before slipping away. That story did earn me a couple of grumbles from an editorial grouch that I hadn't talked some leading religious luminary, at least a cardinal, into cooperating, but my source was genuine.

Then the same whiner, who'd protested that Globe would be discredited if word ever got out that our sources were fake—yeah, right—dove deep into the muck for his next story. That editor had no qualms about spinning gold from straw with one source that few reasonable citizens would credit, telling the tale of Obama's Gay Sex Scandal. Sometime Chicago limo driver Larry Sinclair slithered into public view on a YouTube video in which he claimed he'd smoked crack cocaine with Obama and had twice performed oral sex on the then-state senator. No matter his unattractive self was peddling a book about his claims, had no evidence to support them and had a history of prison time on fraud and other charges. No matter that he admitted dealing drugs and smuggling illegal aliens. The tabloids had no problems in finding this exemplary citizen fully credible, and in suitably shocked terms printed every licentious detail under a 'World Exclusive' banner. The New York Times would have been proud. The tabs' Obama-bashing didn't end with a hoked-up gay sex claim. We had Michelle mad at him over Oprah – too adoring, too controlling was the tabs' claim; we had love child rumors; Muslim connections, hook-ups to terrorists and criminals, murder links, anything and everything negative. We could rely on backup from spurious sources to appease the libel attorneys, and the headline writers were masters of the misleading, with tiny 'sources say' disclaimers supporting the more outrageous page one splashes.

Oddly enough, during the 2008 presidential campaign, I landed a real and unflattering story about Senator John McCain, and the tabs virtually ignored it. McCain and his troubled wife Cindy boasted that they were adoptive parents who knew 'what a treasure and joy it is to have an adopted child.' What they didn't broadcast was that they'd booted out a young girl they were in process of adopting, and her life had descended into hardship, drugs and crime. Cari Paulene Clark McCain was Cindy's first cousin. In 1989, when Cari was 15, her mom Jamie Clark was going through a divorce and asked her wealthy cousin for help. Cindy not only became Cari's legal guardian but in 1992, when Cari changed her name to McCain, documented that the McCains 'intend to pursue the legal adoption of Cari.' That Christmas, the pair quarreled, Cari was banned from the McCain home, cut off financially and found herself living with her grandmother. She told me:" I can't talk about the McCains. I was going to be adopted, that was why I took the McCain name. It just didn't happen."

The story, which was highly relevant as an insight into the mind of a man who wanted to be president, made no splash. Given a real scandal, the tabs didn't know what to do with it.

Shot Down by Brooke and Oprah

However, some maligned celebrities knew what to do when the headlines were stretched too far. They fought back. Even a mention of Oprah was banned for some months in 2008 after her attorneys tired of a barrage of tabloid nonsense that 'revealed' everything from her alleged bid to be the kingmaker behind Obama, through gay rumors, to reported strife with her longtime beau, Stedman Graham. When I suggested some angle for a new Oprah story, the news editor panicked. "We've been told we're strictly not to touch her," he whispered down the phone. Miss Winfrey, ticked off at the latest outrageous rubbish, had set her dogs on the tabs. On the one hand, you had a failing magazine with a billion-dollar debt to service, and on the other you had a ticked-off billionaire capable of sinking the ship. That clout kept Oprah out of the headlines for a while, and Brooke Shields did something similar a year later. She took her outrage public in 2009 when a tabloids' freelancer checked her Alzheimer's-affected mom Teri out of a care home. He said he was a longtime friend, signed the old lady out and took her to lunch, handily escorted by a photographer. All the protestations that Teri and the journo were old friends sounded pretty hollow when you found that he'd needed a snapper along for the 'social' outing. I'm unconvinced he would have kept everything to himself if Brooke's mom spilled a secret or two. Just a year previously, she'd complained publicly that Brooke didn't have time for her any more, a story the Enquirer gratefully ran, although anyone who looked at it objectively would see that an old lady with dementia, living in a care home, was likely to say something similar about not seeing her grandkids every day. Indignant Brooke went public to protest the unsavory intrusion, and turned her attorney loose. The entertainment media delightedly professed pious disgust, the police considered their options, and the Enquirer rapidly retreated. First it distanced itself from the freelancer—Standard Operating Procedure—then Enq editors agreed not to publish the story, apologized and made a 'substantial' donation to dementia research. And Brooke went onto the Don't Touch list.

Inside the 'World Exclusives'

Writing about presidents was safer, and of all of America's presidents, Number 43, George W Bush easily topped the tabs' popularity poll. Even though the Chronicles of Clinton, through MonicaGate, WhitewaterGate, HillaryGate and other tribulations sold millions of copies, the Difficulties of Dubyah capped the lot. Bush's trials provided a glittering spectrum of stories, with 'world exclusives' awash with titivating details and secret delight in the troubles of others. Week after week, for eight years, the tabloids ignored the heavyweight stories of the president's headaches over Iraq and Katrina, Afghanistan and corrupt White House aides. Instead, they ran juicy accounts of Dubyah's battles with the bottle, suicide fears, divorce rumors, gay sex innuendoes, health problems, terror of being prosecuted for war crimes, crumbling marriage, romance with the Secretary of State, ultimatums from Laura and any other Sky-Is-Falling drama they could invent. Even the Bushes' twin daughters caught flak in the ongoing soap opera that kept copies flying off the checkout racks, and I was behind much of it. Phrases like 'devastating blow" and 'beleaguered president' jostled on my desktop's screen with 'medical meltdown,' 'booze problems' and 'sex cheat confession.' Week after week, the tabs travelled the same well-worn route. They reported over and over how the Bushes were ending their marriage, planned to end it, were doing secret divorce deals, were in nasty fights, were giving each other the cold shoulder, were in counseling, or faced a showdown.

Laura was jealous of Condi Rice, was bitter at George, was

spending nights away from the White House or was issuing another ultimatum of: 'It's Jim Beam or me.' Week after week, 'sources close to the family' or 'White House insiders' were talking of secret break-downs, or telling how Laura was icy cold, was seeking a divorce when Dubyah's term of office ended, or was sobbing out her heart over George's confessed secret lusts for other women. Pennyslvania Avenue must have echoed along its length to the guffaws of disbelief from Number 1600. Perhaps there was a grain of truth in tales of the president's drinking. Maybe Laura really did walk out of the White House and spent a night or two at the Mayflower Hotel, after a marital spat. What I know is that there was a pattern. I'd get a Tuesday morning call from Florida, a murmured briefing on the headline some muppet had conceived and an admonition to get supporting copy on the latest World Exclusive to them by Wednesday, because the paper was locking up early this week.

I'd call my fifth-hand sources to bolster the third-hand source another reporter was allegedly interviewing on the latest 'marriage breakup' or George's Gay Sex scandal. Once upon a time, the tabloids actually paid those sources, usually a few hundred dollars, but with the arrival of the 21st century and tighter budgets, that largesse vanished. The onetime tipsters who really knew what was happening drifted away. They probably rationalized that there was no point jeopardizing their position by giving away for free information that may be traced back to them. Those sources dried up, leaving just the few who enjoyed the feeling of being an insider, even an unnamed one, plus those whose goodwill would bail me out with a few scraps of information, if I called them and wheedled. It was like being a spymaster with no funds. You often had to rely on people with an axe to grind, or lift and spin a gossip item from another paper, and that's not the best way to get unbiased, accurate information, but oddly enough, these embellished tales often struck closer to the truth than any respectable reportage ever did.

As a reporter, I tried to get as close to the real core of the story as possible. The editors, on the other hand, simply wanted mate-rial to justify the headlines they'd dreamed up beforehand. It was a constant conflict. I'd scour the internet for web logs, commentaries, or published stories relevant to this week's headline. I'd extract telling quotes or useful facts. For instance, it helped to know that the

Bush ranch in Crawford, Texas was on Rainey Creek, or that Dubyah liked to watch the History Channel. Some source who claimed to know the Bush family might be quoted saying he'd come across the amazing shrinking president sitting glumly contemplating Rainey Creek, staring blankly, or that he sloshed down Jim Beam while watching the History Channel. It added a note of authenticity to the package. Rumors, innuendoes and hints gathered, I'd write it into a story and file it. As required, I carefully noted a source at the end of each paragraph. For example, a paragraph saying how afraid George was that Laura's revelations would destroy his legacy might be attributed to a Texas informant not identified in print, but whose confidential name and phone number were included in a list of sources. In copy, he'd be labeled, perhaps as PB1, PB2 or PB3. The relevant quote would be noted as from 'PB3,' just as a quote taken from, say, a New York Times story might be my fifth source, PB5. I'd fax over the relevant clippings from other newspapers or magazines, marked and identified by source code so that fact checkers – ha! – could see that someone really did say it.

Often, the editorial genius who'd thought up the headline would come back to require me to file an add with a stronger quote about how this would 'definitely' destroy the presidency, not just 'might' destroy it. All the while, a listener could hear the distant sound of a bluster of editors chanting their mantra that 'sources' had provided the story's integrity and truthfulness, so it must be real. Actually, there was very little fact checking at Globe, evidenced by the several years it took for someone to realize that my named 'political historian' source quoted week after week (and whose accurate phone number was in the source list every time) was no academic. The shout of outrage from one editor wasn't about inaccuracy. It was what might happen to him if the lawyers found out he'd turned a Nelsonian blind eye to the makeup artistry involved. "I could lose my job!" he spluttered. Talk about the emperor wearing close-fitting transparent garments...

Nobody at the tabloids ever joked about inventing anything, or shaping anything. A straight face was the rule, and any hint that we all knew it was a fabrication would be angrily denied. And that's a genuine fact. Heckuva job, Brownie! Oddly, when the tabs actually got one right, it didn't seem to matter. In July 2007, I uncovered one fact-based story about Bush and it made curiously little impact. The president's heart was giving out, and nobody really seemed to care. Bush secretly wore a shock harness designed for patients "at high risk for sudden cardiac death" to re-start his ticker if it stopped. He made clandestine visits to America's top cardiac hospital and was treated discreetly at the White House, too. Bush made more than 50 trips to Ohio to sneak into the Cleveland Clinic for repair work on his damaged heart, and wore a defibrillator in a sort of chest holster, to monitor any irregular heart activity. The instrument was to detect any life-threatening arrhythmia, sound an alarm and allow the president to press a couple of buttons to restart his own heart, if he was able. Bush wore the shock box during a debate with John Kerry, when his handlers feared the stress might induce an attack, and the defibrillator showed under his tee shirt during a photo op at the Crawford ranch, too. Ironically, when Globe ran the story, it was virtually ignored. Maybe that's why they preferred 'world exclusives' about marital difficulties from less-documented sources...

GHOSTLY MATTERS

The Spook That Spoke

My visit to Thirsk, North Yorkshire, was in the nature of a pilgrimage, a nod to the past. I was in the UK on assignment and I thought I'd visit the scene of the crime, as it were. I'd look in on the Busby Stoop Inn and visit the Baffling Chair of Death, whose story had led to my moving to America some years before. The chair, said the legend, was a public house seat claimed as his own nearly 300 years before by a murderer, Tom Busby. He'd been hanged from a gibbet at the crossroads by the tavern, and locals said he'd cursed all who sat in 'his' seat. Few took up the challenge, as a series of fatal accidents was linked to Busby's chair. I'd written about the fatal furniture for the National Enquirer, and gone on to report other stories of the paranormal.

It was a sort of homecoming, to revisit the chair and pay my respects, but it didn't work out as planned. Landlord Tony Earnshaw had gone from the Busby Stoop, and the chair was no longer in the place, new incumbent Brenda Barnes told me, adding that the pub's sense of malevolent foreboding had vanished with the chair's departure. Gone too, was the nearby RAF station at Skipton-on-Swale. Its three long runways now served as the foundations for commercial poultry houses, the vale's chief industry.

I spoke to Tony by phone. He had been unsettled by mysterious incidents in the tavern, he told me. One night, he'd gone into York for a meeting of the Licenced Victuallers' Association, a publicans' trade group. His wife had gone to bed and woke around 12.45am when she heard a noise downstairs in the shuttered pub. "She heard a man's footsteps stumbling about, looked at her alarm clock and decided it was me, back from a boozy night out, and probably a bit kettled," he said. When she heard the door latch at the bottom of the stairs click open, she turned over and pretended to be asleep, not wanting to have to deal with a tipsy husband. "She told me the next morning: 'I heard you stumbling up every stair, you drunken lout. You thudded across the bedroom and I heard your heavy snorting as you stood over me, looking down. I wasn't going to wake up for a boozer like you! You took your time turning around and thumping back downstairs, too, didn't you?' " Tony said he went tense. "What time did you say I came in?" he asked. "It was a quarter to one, I looked at the clock," said his wife. Tony never told his wife the truth, he didn't have the heart to frighten her with it. He hadn't come home until 2.30am, and had tiptoed in quietly so as not to wake her. "I even asked my pal, who'd driven down with me, and he confirmed the time I dropped him off three minutes away. That wasn't me inside a locked pub who was walking about after midnight." That incident and others, made Tony wary of the chair, and he donated it to the Thirsk Museum, on condition that nobody be allowed to sit in it. The curator, Cooper Harding, took no chances. He mounted the chair high on a wall alongside a framed account of its history. I drove to Thirsk to see for myself, wondering if I should debunk the legend, as I now knew the chair wasn't even made when Busby was alive.

The museum turned out to be a pleasing stone house on Kirkgate, near the onetime surgery of the world's most famous vet. 'James Herriott,' author of the best-selling 'All Creatures Great and Small,' was actually former Thirsk veterinarian Alf Wight. His surgery, now a storefront dedicated to his work, is across the market square from the museum, which itself is dedicated to the heritage and culture of the beautiful Dales that Wight loved and described so faithfully.

I wasn't there as a tourist, I wasn't tempted to look in on the vet's showplace. My mission was to look at Busby's chair, and I failed. The museum was closed, time was pressing, and I had to be content with learning from a shopkeeper pulling down shutters for half-day closing that yes, the chair was now safely where nobody could sit on it. "That's the old vitnery's house," the shopkeeper nodded. "Aye, him that wrote 'All Creatures Grunt and Smell.' But t'chair's in that museum over there, on't wall." I thanked him for the information, glanced at the clock tower, built to commemorate the marriage in 1896 of the Duke of York, later to be King George V, and realized that I had to be elsewhere. No debunking today. Let sleeping legends lie, I thought.

My busy-ness was to hurry down to London, to meet the invisible residents of Britain's most haunted house, a modest two-bedroom terraced home in Enfield, north London. The Society for Psychical Research had sent a team to live with the tormented occupants and over five months there saw and recorded some startling and inexplicable events. As the Enquirer's senior reporter on the psychic, I was eager to see for myself, and it was not a disappointment. Maurice Grosse of the SPR met me at 284 Green Street, home of Peggy Hodgson and three of her children. The fourth child boarded at a school for the learning-handicapped. Their father had left the family two years before the hauntings began, and Mrs Hodgson supported her family on welfare payments. Maurice had already recounted how the family was besieged by threatening, guttural voices that cursed and growled, by the apparition of a big man walking through the house and by unexplained energies which bombarded the occupants with marbles, Lego bricks and small objects, spun furniture and even threw people around the rooms.

The children had been seen levitating and witnesses told of seeing solid-seeming doubles of them and even of the researchers in one part of the house while they were physically elsewhere. No one, said Grosse, knew what had triggered the phenomena. The Sunday Mirror newspaper had sent in a team which set up motion-triggered cameras, but the electronics went on the fritz, as often happens in energy cases like this one, and although they got a couple of odd pictures, there was no medieval ghost smiling at the camera from the head it held under its arm.

What was happening was classic poltergeist (German for 'noisy ghost') activity that the scientists called RSPK, for recurring spontaneous psychokinesis. Some people theorize it isn't caused by a ghost at all, but comes from the emotions or mental energy of a living human agent, often an adolescent. The agent seems unable to control the phenomena but somehow wishes to cause it. It's hard to quantify or induce, so many scientists regard it with suspicion, a matter of 'If you believe in RSPK, raise my hand.' This case was highly unusual because of the voice phenomena, but it also had the full package—apparitions, movement of objects, footsteps and knocking, with a side serving of levitation. That modest terraced house in Enfield was a world-class psychic site.

As I walked into Number 284, I was startled by a deep growling voice that said 'Ghost hunter!' It came from close to my right ear, but nobody was there. The hairs on the nape of my neck went electric in best novelette fashion, but I said, steadily, I hope: "What are you trying to do?" The voice growled: "Kill you." My instinctive reaction was to sneer back, saying I'd get it dog food: "You'll have to try harder. You sound like a dog. I'll get you some Kennomeat, puppy dog!" For the rest of the evening the voice plagued me with 'Kennomeat!' but never actually swore at me, which was good, as it called Maurice 'fucker' several times. It was a lively evening. From the door where I was leaning, looking into the kitchen, I saw an armchair spin through 180 degrees and shoot 66 inches into the center of the living room, which was empty except for a child sitting 10 feet away. The motion caught my eye and I turned my head in time to see the upholstered chair finish its movement. The child was still, and there was no device I could find that caused the chair to move. Privately, I doubted that the grindingly-poor family had the resource or wit to set up any stunts.

In the kitchen, I witnessed a small pool of what turned out to be cat-like urine (yes, I took a sample for testing) form on the linoleum. Three times the urine appeared, three times we cleaned it up. Later, after a violent cracking noise in the kitchen, a small, still-steaming turd was found in the plughole of the sink, which was a difficult place to drop it as the fixed faucet was right above. Nobody was in the kitchen, nobody could have gone in without my seeing them. The sharp noise seemed to have been produced by a scrubbing brush, which was lying under a dent in the wall. The brush, said the mother, had been on the sink eight feet away, a few minutes before. I looked closely at the stool, without actually picking it up. There were no impressions to show it had been handled. It smelled authentic, I could see steam rising, it looked to have been deposited in a natural way, and I was glad to leave the collection and disposal to someone else. Upstairs, I saw an empty bed dented with the impression of a man's body, which moved as Grosse and I looked on, as if an invisible someone was turning over. That made my nape hairs prickle again, I admit.

Gratefully downstairs again, I saw a sideboard door swing open about a foot, acting against its spring, but nobody was near. Next up, my tape recorder clicked off in mid-tape and would not work again until the next day. I did get recordings of the voices, which seemed to emanate from somewhere around the children (aged 14, 12 and 8) and took them to Imperial College, where the mystery deepened. The voices, said the friendly analyst, seemed to come not from human vocal chords, but from the throat's false vocal fold. Producing those sounds for just a few minutes can give you a sore throat. It is painful to create the sound for an extended time, yet the voices sometimes went on for 10 or 12 hours. The children, who were diffident and polite, spoke normally and without strain during and after the vocal phenomena. Researcher Guy Playfair told of looking into the middle child's mouth, which was full of mashed potato, as she cursed foully in the growling, coarse, old man's voice. "I can't help it, it takes over me," she said. My own notes from the time say: "When the voice comes out, the children seem faintly embarrassed. They hear what it is saying, often lower their heads as the growling begins. They never seem to look challengingly at the person the voice is reviling and sometimes, as soon as the voice has finished, will speak in their own childish voices, politely, about some unrelated subject, just as if the voices never happened." Maurice Grosse, a careful and intelligent researcher, was convinced the phenomena were real, although the children admitted to faking some incidents to see if they could catch him out. He always detected their efforts, they said.

Maurice died in 2006, convinced that the phenomena at the Enfield house were caused by a previous occupant, Bill, who had died of a brain hemorrhage in the back bedroom there. He felt that the children were possessed by one or more entities, adding that the voice had claimed there were eight of them in there. It was, said Grosse, the first time voice contact had been established with some entity from elsewhere since the 1840s. "It's the voice of a devil," said a neighbor. For myself, I don't think it was fraud. I personally witnessed some strange happenings and I heard from too many neighbors and others of a long series of events from the year or so that the family was under its mysterious siege. I heard later that one child died, and that paranormal noises were heard during the funeral and at the graveside, but never could confirm it. The Enfield poltergeist, that noisy ghost, went quiet as mysteriously as it had started, but at least I had the satisfaction of having spoken to a ghost, and hearing it, or something, respond to me.

The Professor and the Spoonbenders

One of the investigators involved in the Enfield case was Birkbeck College experimental physics professor, John Hasted, whose silver hair, leather-patched tweeds and cut-glass Received Pronunciation accent could all have come from Central Casting's idea of an English academic. Prof Hasted was deeply involved in researching psychic phenomena and told me when we met at a conference in Holland that yes, he'd personally witnessed dematerialization of objects, in his own laboratory, and under test conditions. He'd tested the Israeli metal bender Uri Geller with mixed results, but felt he had some genuine abilities that couldn't easily be explained. The professor took me to meet one of his test subjects, teenager Julie Knowles, in Trowbridge, a small Wiltshire town not far from Stonehenge. She'd seen Geller on television and had tried spoon bending for herself. So good were the results, she'd come to the professor's attention. He'd even been able to measure the force she could apply by mind power, using a strain gauge. It showed Julie exerting four ounces of pressure on a brass key, without touching it, under test conditions. I watched one test, when, never approaching closer than 18 inches, Julie bent the key, which was in a glass bowl. She also moved a mobile made of non-magnetic plastic and protected under a large Bell jar just by using mind power and once, she bent a brass bar sealed in a glass tube that prevented her from touching the metal.

Remarkable as these abilities seemed, they were not unique, and other investigators, including George Owen, were trying to measure and harness them. I went to see Dr Owen, a mathematics professor at the University of Toronto, when he was doing early trials at table levitating, and his group made a table float and slide around a room, replicating some Victorian experiments that I've personally done as a party game. Then they went for the jackpot. Owen and seven friends set about making a ghost. The bare bones are that they chose a name, a personality, a life story and a period of history they had researched carefully to ensure that the Philip Aylesford they created could not have been a real person. "We didn't want to tap into a genuine ghost," said Owen, whose script placed Philip in the real Diddington Manor, Warwickshire during a well-documented part of the 17th century. The tone of the experiment was cheery, and the group found that Philip who never was could communicate with them by rapping on a wooden table, loudly when the group felt strongly about something, scratching weakly for indecisive questions. Philip went along with historical inaccuracies, made the table levitate and on occasions caught on film made the table, untouched by the group, shadow people around the room and even jam in the doorway as it tried to follow them out. "The experiment is to demonstrate the power of concentrated thought," explained Dr Owen, who compared the group's efforts to those of table-tipping Victorian seances.

The group never succeeded in creating an apparition of Philip, but they did inspire an Australian group to create a similar, 14 years old girl entity, Skippy Cartman, and in 2003, a Liverpool university group to attempt to create a sailor ghost called Humphrey. The Skippy experiment was reasonably successful, with some communication through rapping and knocking, but Humphrey returned only some anomalous readings in the monitoring equipment. Once again, psychic functioning proved elusive to pin down and created more questions than answers.

All of my work wasn't about psychics and ghosts, but it was about questions. My first chief reporter, my boss at the Eccles Journal in Lancashire, would berate me with it. "Do you know how old this man is?" he'd ask as he looked through the sad apology I'd turned in as copy. "Er, no, Cyril, he didn't say.""Didn't say? " he'd screech. "You mean you didn't ask!" So I learned to ask questions. It didn't matter how arcane the subject, asking questions and actually listening to the interviewee tell what he knows is a wonderful and fascinating thing. You can learn that there are seven grades of wool, ranging from Fair to Middling Fair; or that medieval printers were only assured of two days off each year: Good Friday and Christmas Day, because there was no publishing allowed on those days. Ask, and you'll find that the first printer to set up shop in Fleet Street was the wonderfully-named Wynkyn de Worde (originally called Jan van Wynkyn) who on William Caxton's death in 1491 took over his printing work and gave us such refinements as italic and moveable type. Questions can reveal fascinating material. And, people asked me questions all the time about the stories I wrote. Are there REALLY ghosts? Are those stories really true? All I can answer is that I've seen convincing evidence that some of it seems to be real, some of it is probably faked. The Baffling Chair of Death and the Enfield house infested with poltergeist phenomena had something in common. The fabric of the chair and the rooms of the house were inanimate, but seemed somehow to affect human minds.

The chair couldn't possibly have had the history its legend claims, but it had a presence tangible enough that the landlord of the Busby Stoop spoke of a lightening of the atmosphere after the chair was moved out. Similarly, the mother who lived in the Enfield house said she and the children would not sleep in the back bedroom, where they later found out a previous occupant had died. Investigators suspect that the energy that allows Uri Geller and others to move objects or bend metal by mindpower might also be a cause of other episodes of the paranormal. If there's a still-unknown energy that is some kind of basic building block of the beautiful blue sphere called Earth, can we affect it? Can we understand its workings? Psychics say they can, and they're terrible witnesses. Many professional seers are well-meaning charlatans, making a living from the gullible. They might look into crystal balls or Tarot cards to tell fortunes, but they seem mostly to use their skill at reading human nature to make their most plausible predictions. A few sometimes do have flashes of insight, but getting those flashes on demand seems to be outside the abilities of virtually every seer I ever encountered. Most of the psychics I met, and that was a number in the scores, were pleasant people without any special abilities. They acted best as a sympathetic ear, or as another viewpoint to help their client resolve a situation, and I suspect that's the real worth of the crystal-ball reading trade. Once in a rare while though, along comes somebody like Colorado psychic Howard Starkel.

Custer's Battlefield

There's an area of parapsychology which is classified as psychometry, and concerns reliving experiences or emotions locked into inanimate objects. The psychic reader of objects seems able to somehow extract information that was imprinted on a place or thing. "I can hold an object and pick up vibrations from it," Starkel told me. Starkel demonstrated that he could do more than that modest claim, and he convinced historians with whom he worked on a number of projects that his psychic powers were genuine. The most persuasive evidence he presented concerned the Custer Battlefield, and I'll provide some detail of what went on to underscore Starkel's remarkable readings and to provide a sense of how much research went into a simple 'psychic' story.

The grassy ridges above the Little Bighorn River in southeastern Montana were the scene of Lt Col George Armstrong Custer's disastrous encounter with 3,000 Sioux, Sans Arc, Santee and Cheyenne warriors led by the great chief Sitting Bull in June 1876. Custer and 209 ill-fated troopers of the 7th Cavalry died on those ridges and dry gullies. Another 56 of his command, which he'd divided, were killed in a two-day siege on a hilltop five miles away. No white man survived to tell of the battle that Custer fought at Medicine Tail Coulee. Key parts of the battlefield were preserved by the US War Department, and 257 marble headstones were set out to mark where the troopers were supposed to have fallen (the extra 47 were never explained). Some of those battlefield markers were misplaced, possibly for dramatic effect. Custer and the 50 men immediately around him were killed on the grassy 'Last Stand Hill' but most likely were not the last to die. The real last stand probably occurred in Deep Ravine, where 28 troopers from Company E were found dead. They were supposed to have been buried hastily, post-battle, by a relief column, but in one of the many mysteries about the battle, when the Army went to exhume those bodies for more proper burial elsewhere, they were never found. Modern archeologists with metal detectors have systematically combed and plotted the killing ground and although they have not been able to reconstruct the events of the day in the usual way from survivors' battle reports, diaries and witnesses, they have reached some conclusions. For example, they found numerous spent shells from US Army-issue Springfield carbines that told of a rearguard skirmish line being formed. Because the Indians used widely different types of rifles and pistols, the researchers could also detect where the Indians overran the military position. The history detectives also concluded that soldiers and Indians alike fought on foot, mostly from fixed positions, and not as romantic film makers suggest, with whooping warriors circling on horseback. The reconstructionists knew there were three distinct engagements. Custer, in his white buckskin battledress, had a one-hour fight on the ridge, where he and his men killed their horses to use as cover. They were picked off by Indians firing down from a higher knoll 140 yards away. There was a second battle down in the valley where Major Marcus Reno attacked the Indian village from the south, and a third, two-day siege on bluffs five miles away, where Reno retreated and Capt Frederick Benteen joined him.

"We wanted to know more," said Dr Donald G Rickey, former senior historian at the national monument and assistant director of the US Army Military History Institute. So when Dr Rickey met Howard Starkel at a psychic symposium, he was intrigued. "Starkel was demonstrating psychometry. He'd hold personal objects such as the watch of someone's dead uncle, and talk about the deceased person." Dr Rickey asked if the psychic would experiment with historical material and set up a test. The psychic handled seven nondescript items including a piece of barbed wire and a tin can and was 'amazingly accurate' about their use and origins, said the historian. After a second successful test, Rickey handed Starkel a rusty spur. "It was not military issue. It had been found near the valley of Little Bighorn and had been tossed out of a collection for lack of storage space. Dr Rickey retrieved the old spur from the trash and knew nothing of it except the vaguely-recorded place of find. "I wanted Starkel to describe what he thought was happening after he held the object. It surprised me how consistent he was with historic accounts." What Starkel described fitted the actions of a civilian doctor, killed after crossing the Little Big Horn River.

"He was a big man, someone in medicine, and was wounded in the foot. He was struggling to climb a hill with a small group of cavalrymen," said Starkel as he held the old spur. He described the man's thoughts: "I saw the Indians killing our horses by the stream. Our group of soldiers wasn't the main group, with Custer. The Indians killed some of us, then backed away. They don't have time to play with us. They set fire to the grass around us as they left. I was hatless, hurting, in a panic. I lost my spur below the ridge. My boot is full of blood. It's hard, struggling up the hill. There is an Indian with a big bulls-eye painted on his chest. He is on horseback and he is riding me down. At any second, I may be cut down. I shoot at him but there is a crushing pain in my chest and I know I am mortally hit. I am dying now, the noise seems very far away."

Rickey and Dr Neil Mangum, chief historian at the battlefield, were stunned. "What he told us is historically accurate, but he could not have known it normally," said Dr Mangum. "It sent chills up my spine." The spur, said the historian, was iron, not military-issue brass, and almost certainly belonged to Army contract surgeon James DeWolf, who was probably the only man on the battlefield with non-issue spurs. It was found where Starkel said, just below the ridge where DeWolf's body was found. He was with Reno's battalion, a small part of Custer's force. The scene the psychic described was also confirmed: the Sioux and Cheyenne did kill cavalry horses by the stream—their bones were found eroding from the right back of the Little Bighorn in 1956—and they did fire the grass as they moved off after Custer. "Starkel's description coincided exactly with the Reno valley fight—the valley attack, the river crossing, the bluffs beyond, were all historically-accurate episodes encountered by Major Reno's forces in the fight. He gave us technical details of weapons and tactics he could not have known," said Dr Mangum. In further experiments, the historians were even more astounded. They gave the psychic some different cartridge shells from the killing grounds. He accurately described where they were found, and replayed the thoughts of the long-dead men who'd fired them. One shell puzzled him. "How could this be?" he asked as he duplicated an Indian's action of loading his carbine. Starkel was trying to slap the bullet into the rifle butt. "It was a Spencer cartridge that is loaded through a tubular magazine, through the rifle's butt plate," said Dr Mangum. "The psychic was correct!" A Martin .50 shell case brought a flood of memories of an Indian warrior who'd fired it in the battle and who thought of his squaw, killed 18 months before. "She was trapped against some cliffs and the soldiers shot her," he said. From Starkel's details, the historians pieced together the tale of the Bates Fight at Snake Creek, Wyoming, where three squaws were killed just as Starkel described. Now, the psychic recounted the warrior's thoughts at Little Big Horn. "I was kneeling and shooting. The soldiers were mounted and on foot. Mounted Indians attacked them, running up and parting around the soldiers, who were in an arc. We formed a line to divide the arc of kneeling soldier-skirmishers from the horse soldiers who were behind them. The mounted soldiers were in confusion. Crazy Horse led a flanking movement and the soldiers were overwhelmed." Starkel explained: "When I handle an artifact, I experience the feelings of its long-ago owner. It is as if I am inside that person. I feel his fear, confusion, pain. I can see through his eyes and I experience what was happening to him. It is like a TV set in my mind."

Dr Rickey gave the psychic the shoe part of a cavalry boot. Starkel said it was found in a pit, which it was, along with other trash. Starkel described the boot owner's death. "The main body of cavalry was almost opposite the big river bend to the west. They intended to circle northwest then sweep down on the Indian camp but an Indian manoever separated the group. This soldier was wounded, knocked off his horse. He was crawling, firing his carbine. It was very confused, no one to give orders, no firing line. He dies in pain but his main thought is: 'I don't care.' The screams and hollering are one loud roar. I can't explain losing the boot," said the psychic. "It has to do with the hostiles, but not in combat. It happened at a much calmer time." The academic explained it. "Most soldier bodies were stripped of equipment after the battle. Indians would cut off the boot legs for the leather but had no use for the shoe part. This was found buried in a cache of bones, trash and shoe parts."

Said Dr Mangum: "I doubted the validity of Starkel's claims when I first heard about him. Historians deal with fact, but after these experiments, I feel there is some inexplicable truth to Starkel's approach. His revelations were shocking. He was able to draw maps of the area, a site he had never seen. I'm convinced, based on what I have observed, that psychometry cannot be merely passed off as fake and fraudulent."

Today, the silence and the shadows of the Greasy Grass are best experienced at the Reno-Benteen section of the battlefield, because there are too many visitors to the iron-fenced monument at the top of Last Stand Hill where Custer's unmutilated body was found two days after the firefight. There, 300,000 visitors each year pay their respects to the troopers who are buried in a common grave, without their commanding officer. Custer himself lies at West Point Military Academy, on the other side of the continent. "There are ghosts here," battlefield guide Mardell Plainsfeather told me. "There are strong vibrations from the bloody deaths that took place here. The Crow name for the battlefield superintendent is Ghost Herder and we believe that the purpose of running up the flag every morning is to warn the ghosts it's time to go back to their spirit places."

Ghost on Tape

The Custer Battlefield is just one of the US National Parks Service sites associated with the supernatural, and another Parks site gave me a piece of powerful evidence for the post-mortem survival of consciousness. I made a tape recording that may be a voice from the dead. In Washington DC, the Old Stone House on M Street is the city's oldest building, and is plagued with ghosts, including a the apparition of an angry, bull-like man who tries to push people down the stairs. Over the years dozens, maybe hundreds of visitors have reported feeling unseen hands pushing on their backs and shoulders, or have had encounters with the angry man, whom they invariably reported as being real, not ghostly at all. They've also reported hearing a child's footsteps running along the landing, even on rare occasions sighting the boy himself, and have spotted misty, half-formed figures of other ghosts around the place.

The house's history is reasonably documented, and several English families sequentially owned it in its earliest days, a fact of some significance for my other-wordly tape recording. When I did a

1982 phone interview with Rea X, the curator there, I tape-recorded our conversation. Later, playing back the tape, I heard a voice that I certainly did not hear during the talk, and as it over-rode the curator's voice could not have been hers. I'd just asked her how many ghosts were there, and said "Six, isn't it?" As she enumerated the seven ghosts in the Stone House, a whispery male voice corrected me. "Four, two and a kid," it said. There were four male ghosts, two female ones and the spirit boy who ran along the landing. I have that tape still, and it is good for a back-of-the-neck prickle whenever I listen to it. What's so convincing to me is that the accent of that whispery voice is English. It's a South Midlands accent to my ear, a breathy exhalation. It's clear, definite, but not energetic. It gave me the sense it was the voice of someone not living. Yet the voice not only intruded on our conversation—and I can't think this was a crossed line because I certainly did not hear the interruption—but it displayed intelligence and new information. That voice corrected my statement and provided accurate data that relatively few people possess, which would eliminate a chance prankster who happened on the call. Yes, I called Rea back to report the voice and she was very matter-of-fact about it. I suppose when you get people reporting ghostly events on a near-daily basis that one more incident won't excite you. Skeptics may scoff, and are entitled so to do, but it flat-out convinced me that consciousness may survive death. As the poet Thackeray said: "It is all very well for you who have never seen a ghost to talk as you do, but had you seen what I have witnessed, you would hold a different opinion." Well, I have my opinion, and I have an audiotape, too.

Haunted Gettysburg

Some famous ghosts surfaced at another National Parks site. At the Eisenhower farm in Gettysburg, where 51,000 soldiers died in the wheatfields in one of the bloodiest battles of the American Civil War, staff reported seeing the ghosts of Mamie Eisenhower and her mother, so Virginia psychic Anne Gehman went along. A credible psychic, Anne taught half a dozen congressmen as clients to use their intuition, and had an impressive track record of psi success when she worked with police to solve murder cases. She mentioned the readings to me, and I approached the contact at the NPS, Priscilla Baker, special assistant to the director of the Parks Service, who confirmed matters, and provided some corrections. "It's true, " she said. "It should be told." She later had cause to regret her integrity, as her superiors felt such matters 'sensationalist' and wanted them kept under wraps. It made me wonder how many other National Parks sites have untold stories, how many other pieces of evidence of an afterlife are covered up by bureaucrats, but here's one that got away from them.

"At the Eisenhower farm, people had seen or heard a great many weird things – footsteps in empty rooms, music, doors opening and closing, lights going on and off," said Baker. "I invited Anne to see if she could explain matters. She was enormously successful and uncovered a lot. She walked the battlefield, pinpointing troop movements, describing uniforms, accurately giving exact names. The historians were astonished." At an old house in the park, Gehman asked to be taken to the oldest fireplace. The ranger showed her a brick wall and said the fireplace was behind it. Not this one, said the psychic, the oldest fireplace. In the cellar, a crumbling pile of bricks proved to be the original fireplace. Gehman instructed the ranger to put his hand up the chimney, to go up three bricks and back two. He should remove the loose brick he found there, she said. "It took the ranger a long time to wriggle the brick out of the place it had occupied for 150 years, but when he did so, he found a picture of a man behind it," said Baker, who has been unable to identify the painting or its significance.

Next, Gehman visited the Eisenhower farm, a onetime log cabin built in 1749 and faced with brick before the Civil War. It is the only home the Eisenhowers ever owned, and rangers and other staff insisted they'd frequently seen Mamie's ghost and that of her mother, Elivera Doud, moving about the place. The supernatural activity had become worse recently, with bangings and knockings. Gehman came up with eight or ten names associated with the house. One of them was Quentin, who said that Mamie was annoyed at plans to build something alongside 'her' home that would disturb the peace there. The Parks Service boss was stunned. Quentin owned the farm in 1840, records showed, and it was not public knowledge that officials were considering plans to build a parking lot alongside the place. Rangers told me of hearing the rustle of taffeta and of seeing Mamie in a rosy-colored long robe-like garment, or in a dark blue mid-calf length dress. They reported maid board lights that go on and off although the wiring is disconnected and the pushbutton in the master bedroom is now inaccessible behind a heavy headboard, and they said that doors and drawers 'frequently' opened without human help. The hauntings still go on, but with a different tone. "The place feels peaceful, again," one ranger told me. "We still see odd things, but the parking lot plan got dropped and Mamie's happy again."

CELEBRITIES AS PREY

Bitter Bob Hope

Celebrities are a large part of any tabloid's mix of stories, so it's a meaningful coincidence that American Media Inc, which owns the tabloids that made Hollywood gossip a mega-industry, is headquartered in a town called Mouth of the Rat (Boca Raton, Florida.) As a tabloid reporter, I didn't care much for stories involving celebs, because most of my dealings with them convinced me they were insufferably self-centered and self-important. When I was working in Britain, before the cult of celebrity took the world by the throat, actors and actresses were, well, normal if slightly glamorous people. In the 1970s, I could call such luminaries as Peter Sellers and enjoy a telephone interview (Sellers told me frankly he wasn't sure who the inner Sellers was, he was much more comfortable in character as someone else). By the 21st century, a washed-up character from TV's 'Love Boat' wanted $2000 for an interview, and wouldn't even tell me what the subject would be. It was best, I found, to steer clear of actors in person. I'd long admired Phil Silvers, but meeting the comic genius whose Sergeant Bilko character was a classic of television, was a disappointment. He was readying for a London run of

'A Funny Thing Happened on the Way to the Forum' and appeared less than youthful. In fact, 'well-aged' would be accurate. Worse, his vest was visible under his toga and he had a most unheroic potbelly. The interview did yield a good line, though. The brilliant comedy director Joe McGrath visited Silvers on set, and added a line to the script, Silvers said. The actor, in full Roman toga and laurel leaves, had to call for a drink, and was handed a flagon of wine by a slave. He studied the label for a moment and asked: "Was 'One' a good year?"

I told the story to Bob Hope and he didn't get it. I was at Hope's house in Burbank. A mansion in extensive and beautifully-groomed grounds, it was surrounded by what seemed to be a crumbling industrial estate. Bob had been there a long time and said he hadn't met a neighbor in years. The assignment was a fishing expedition, to see what story I could come up with from a Hope interview. He told me how he kept fit by hanging from an overhead bar each morning and rambled on about how he was popular with young people. It was an oddly dull interview with an old gent in startling baby-blue cashmere sweater and canary-yellow open-necked shirt. He hardly heard my questions, and rambled on contentedly about nothing very much, then, every so often, his conversation would kick up two or three gears and he'd tell a joke. The astonishing thing was that the jokes were very funny, and the telling of each was a polished, perfected delivery straight from one of his routines. "I ruined my hands in the ring," he mused about giving up his early career as a boxer. "The referee kept stepping on them." He chose showbiz, he deadpanned: "Because when I was born, the doctor told my mother she had an eight pound ham." He recalled his family's poverty and his six brothers with: "Four of us slept in the one bed. When it was cold, mother threw on another brother. It's also how I learned to dance: waiting for the bathroom." I genuinely laughed out loud, he gave a half-smile that he'd done his professional duty and then he relapsed, continuing his uninspiring monologue of diet, exercise and positive thought. After a couple of hours, I dragged myself away, drained. Another hero had turned out to be backside-numbingly boring. I felt there was a half-truth in his patter that he'd performed for 12 presidents and entertained only six of them.

In time, I discovered that Hope was more than an old bore with a fine memory for his younger days and deliveries. He had a bitter streak. Billionaire Bob had turned his back on his daughter, Nora, whom I found living on welfare in a tiny wooden shack in Walnut Creek, California. Nora was adopted by the Hopes as a baby, and was Bob's favorite. In her early 20s, she let her father know she felt she should have a greater share of the trust funds Hope was setting up for his kids. Hope took offense, words were spoken, Nora went off and married Suzanne Somers' ex and she and her father stubbornly ignored each other for decades. Hope died in 2003, a stranger to his adopted daughter and her child. Bob's longtime publicist Ward Grant told me regretfully: "Neither Nora nor her daughter, Bob's granddaughter, made it to the funeral." It was a sad situation. Here was a man with every material thing he could wish for, but his daughter disliked him so much she'd rather live in poverty than reconcile with the parent who'd positively chosen her.

Curing Tony Curtis

Family troubles can beset anyone, famous or not, and when my Hollywood assignment was to interview actor Tony Curtis, I reflected that he'd had troubles, too. My 1997 assignment was to get the story of the teenage beauty queen and the twins she said she'd had with Curtis. I didn't think Tony would be talking to me, because I'd added to his woes when he was in a rehab clinic in Pasadena, California, battling depression. The Enquirer, scenting scandal, had told me to get down there and get the goods. My assignment took me to the psychiatric facilities offered by Las Encinas Hospital, Pasadena, where a tipster told us the actor was recovering from a stressful time. I called the hospital and told them I was 'strung out' and needed to check in for a few days' rest. They took me in, a tabloid hyena in patient's clothing. I found Las Encinas to be a 17-acre compound, a pleasant collection of small cabins, a popular refuge for Californians and others in need of time to dry out from drugs or booze, or who wanted a restful time for whatever reason. The receptionist who spoke to me before I flew down from San Francisco told me: "Don't bring in any alcohol, and leave your car elsewhere." I parked on a nearby street and checked in, smug in the knowledge that, as a patient, I wasn't trespassing. That night, I scaled the wall and drove to a bar. The next morning, after my blood work showed alcohol, orderlies searched my room for contraband booze. Nothing. I went out again the next night. Another morning blood test, another search. The third night, in the early hours of Sunday, they were waiting for me as I climbed the wall. They told me I'd be booted out when the administrator came back after the weekend. I didn't care. I'd been busy in the daylight hours and had the story, except for one thing. I hadn't yet spoken to Curtis. He'd been in the hospital for two weeks, following a solitary routine, not mingling with the other patients. Each day, the actor would get a morning massage, take a walk and eat breakfast. By mid-morning, he'd be collected by an intimidating-looking chauffeur, who spent his time punching one leather-gloved fist into the other, and staring challengingly at the frails who were ambling around the place. Around dusk, Curtis would check in again for the night, then depart again come daylight.

That Sunday I was up early and over the wall to load my car before I went to Curtis' room. 'Mr Allen,' whom the staff had been cautioned on pain of firing not to acknowledge recognizing, and certainly not to pester with autograph requests, was sitting on the edge of his bed. "Morning, doctor," he greeted me. "Well, Mr Curtis," I said. "I'm not your doctor. I'm actually from the National Enquirer, and I was wondering how you're doing?" Curtis went from listless to ballistic and ran at me, then changed his mind. He's not a very large man and I'm a rugby prop forward. He turned back to the bed and picked up the phone, waving a hand at me. "Sometimes, you've gotta get away from it all," he said. "It's nothing I want to talk about." "Thank you," I nodded. 'Goodbye." He was dialing as I left for the front desk, to get my bill. Before I got there, the loudspeaker system was on Boost Over-Ride. "Dr Finkelbein! Dr Hammond! Dr Page-Morton!" I decided to call them later, to sort out the bill. Sometimes, it pays to be discreet, and as an almost-doctor, I didn't want to raise the poor fellow's blood pressure. It wouldn't be professional etiquette.

Later, when a very nice lady called to tell us she had 30-years old twin sons by Curtis, I went to tiny Coarsegold, California to interview her. All was as it seemed, she had birth certificates and other evidence and wanted nothing from Curtis except the chance for her sons to meet their natural father. One of the now-successful young men called Curtis and had an hour's chat. The actor, he reported, was intrigued but non-committal. At the end, he said the Hollywood thing. "Let's do lunch one day." And that was that. The twin shrugged. Another hero had clay feet.

Locating Loretta

Around that same time, actress Loretta Swit showed me her feet, and pretty they were, too, in open-toed sandals. Word came to me in California that M*A*S*H's Hotlips was romancing someone in Acapulco, Mexico. I was told to get there, pronto, and snuffle out the facts. I flew in, checked into a hotel, heard that super-photographer Alec Byrne was on his way and would be with me in the morning, and wandered out into the town to find a pleasant place for dinner. The restaurant was good, but I had to wait for a table. I settled happily in the foyer under a large mural, sipping a glass of wine, wondering where I'd start the Loretta hunt in the morning. Acapulco's a big bustling place and actors know about preserving their privacy, so I was expecting a long and probably fruitless search. A woman was standing in front of me, hand in hand with two young girls, admiring the mural above my head. I did a double take. Ash blonde, in a sleeveless, simple, white, subtly-patterned dress, bead necklace. Tan legs, sandals. When she laughed, the dazzling smile confirmed it. In a city of a million people, the one person I wanted to find was standing in front of me. I couldn't have been more surprised if she'd stood up in my soup. A moment later, her gallant showed up. He was the brother of the two girls whose hands she was holding. The maitre d' ushered them to a prime table outside on the stone-flagged patio. It overlooked red bougainvillea, a sapphire-blue pool and one jubilant reporter, who'd just bribed the manager for an adjacent table. Next, I needed a photograph of Loretta and her beau, but my camera was back at the hotel. No worries, the magic continued. The manager heard my pleas, I folded another $50 into his palm and soon a plump girl photographer was wandering between the tables, taking souvenir Polaroids. I explained to the photographer that I was a Hot Lips Houlihan fan and would love a picture of her. Please, provide a complimentary picture for her, and a copy for me and here's $100. Oh yes, don't mention my involvement, it's a gift from the restaurant. The strolling photographer did something else for me, too. She re-seated the group to place the two young girls on the outside of the picture, where they could be cropped out. A ten-minute chat with the maitre d' later established the identity of Loretta's date, an hotelier at the lavish Acapulco Princess resort six miles down the road. My job was almost done. Alex flew in the next day to be met by smug me. "Don't really need you, mate," I said. "Got everything already." We checked into the Princess and enjoyed a very pleasant few days dotting the I's and crossing the T's. We intercepted the hotelier as he walked through the grounds and took a good picture, and the job was done, like dinner. We never did see Loretta again, which was a pity. I'd like to have told her this story in person.

Joni's Sung Secret

One celebrity whom I'll probably never get to tell in person how I got her story is the ultra-private singer Joni Mitchell. It was 1997, and I landed a world exclusive by luck and hard work, but an upset Joni wrongly believed a friend had betrayed her, and maybe still does. The facts are that we had a tip that she'd employed detectives to find the baby girl she'd given up 31 years before. I was given the task of sorting a story out of it. It took me to Saskatoon, Saskatchewan and back to Victoria, British Columbia and it didn't really have much of a happy ending. The tale began when Joni was 19 years old, an art student away from home. She got pregnant by a fellow student and had a baby girl. She tried to keep her, but after a few months surrendered the child, whom she'd christened Kelly, to an adoption agency. They in turn gave her to a pair of Toronto schoolteachers who brought the child up in a comfortable, loving home. Amazingly, although Joni kept the secret from her parents for decades, she sang it to the world in the coded lyrics of her songs and even had the baby's picture on the sleeve of one of her albums.

When a Hollywood tipster heard she'd hired detectives to find the baby, he alerted Globe magazine and I went to Joni's hometown of Saskatoon. There, I went through the high school records of Roberta Joan Anderson, which an obliging administrator turned up, checked her report card (mostly Cs and Ds and no credit for music) and pored over the yearbooks for names of possible friends. I tracked down and interviewed people who knew her in the late 1950s, had some luck and pieced the story together. A great help came by chance. When I mentioned to a friend who was a Joni fan that I was looking for her baby, the story burst open. My late rugby pal Norm Marshall lived in Parksville, British Columbia, across the water from Joni's BC hideaway. A musician who considered Joni the late 20th century's most important female vocalist, he was an expert who'd puzzled for years over some of her mysterious song lyrics. With the baby information, he joined the dots and extracted the vital clues she'd confessed in song.

It couldn't be plainer, once you knew. "Child with a child pretending, weary of lies you are sending home, so you sign all the papers in the family name, you're sad and you're sorry but you're not ashamed," she sang in 'Little Green.' Joni also sang of her Kelly to the unknown adoptive mother: "Choose her a name she will answer to, call her Green and the winters cannot fade her. Call her Green for the children who have made her." My story ran and, I found out later, Joni raged at the old friends she thought had 'betrayed' her. I wrote to Joni to tell her exactly what had happened, that it was not a secret given away by friends, but something I'd uncovered without their help. She didn't reply. Meanwhile, Joni still had not found her daughter, Toronto model girl Kilauren Gibb, who had been seeking her birth mother for five years. My story caused a firestorm of questions for Joni, who admitted to her search and took it public. Kilauren effected a reunion, but it was not all to be wine and roses. The reunion soured, mother and daughter were estranged, and Kilauren has even turned away form her adoptive parents. It was Rain and Snow on Everyone.

Demanding Stefanie

Rain and snow certainly fell on me when I had to deal with actress Stefanie Powers. I'd come across a couple of glossy Hollywood designers, two nicely-groomed men who'd designed the red, bugle-bead dress Joan Collins wore so suggestively on the cover of Playboy magazine. Their public relations (read 'blocker') person was eager to get their dresses on show in a few magazines, and I had bites from the Enquirer as well as mags in London and Italy.The selling point was not the dresses, but who was wearing them: the designers' famous friend Stefanie Powers, who'd agreed to help them out. It took eight months of back and forth, as Miss Powers was always seemingly in Africa tending to a game preserve, but her flack, with the guarantee of a women's magazine cover in the UK, greenlighted the project, and I lined up super-snapper Alex Byrne. We were planning on doing the shoot at Miss Powers' home, but just one day before the agreed-on date, the PR person called me with some new conditions. We could not use Miss Powers' home, but she would cooperate for photographs at a nearby convent which she knew of from a previous fashion shoot. The nuns rented it out, she said. Miss Powers would also require us to pick up the tab for makeup ($300-plus) hair ($150 an hour, four hour minimum) lighting assistant (unknown), stylist, ($150 an hour, and the usual minimums). Oh yes, refreshments for the crew, plus limo transport. I didn't even know what a stylist did, but found out it was someone who matched Miss Powers' shoes, handbag and so forth to the dress. I also quickly established that the good nuns wanted $1,200 for only a half-day's use of their scenic stairway and courtyard and even an extra half-hour qualified us for the full $2,400 day rate. Already the bill to prep this 44 years old actress for a modest photo session was more than the fees Alex and I would get from the European magazines, but I could maybe, just barely, break even if the Enquirer offered an unusually handsome payment.

"Oh no, you can't use these pictures anywhere in North America. Miss Powers is under exclusive contract to Sears to wear only their clothes in publicity work here," said the PR flack. I passed on the news to Miss Powers' designer friends that we couldn't afford to pay more than we'd earn to publicize their frocks, and told the flack it was all off. "But nobody, nobody, stands up Miss Powers!" she gasped at me. I took sour delight in that. Rain and snow on everyone, I thought. I'd had more than precipitation on my head over this one, and nobody even paid my phone bills, much less for my time.

Good Guy Grizzly

Some celebrities are like sunshine on everyone, though. Meet Dan Haggerty, the actor who played second fiddle to a grizzly bear, as TV mountain man Grizzly Adams. Today, he's concerned with charity work, his grandkids and the occasional movie project. His TV series days are long past, but he's instantly recognizable everywhere, and is as popular as free ice cream. An animal trainer before his first big screen foray (in the 1969 cult flick 'Easy Rider' as a campfire hippie) Dan was working in Central America on a B-movie Tarzan-style epic, handling chimps, horses, snakes and a tiger. The hero, the 'talent' as those who appear in front of camera are called, slightingly suggesting that those who do the skilled, hard work, not just playacting, are the Untalented, was a prickly egocentric who humiliated one actor too many. "He gave his stand-in, an actor who was desperate for work, such a hard time the guy broke down and quit," said Dan. "I liked the stand-in and felt that the big star needed a lesson." The next day's shooting called for the jungle hero to swing on a rope from one tall tree to another, landing on a concealed platform 45 feet up the trunk of the second tree. He wouldn't swing alone, though. He'd do it with his chimpanzee costar riding piggyback, holding onto his shoulders from behind. "I went over the swing with the chimp, and taught him what to do," grinned Dan. Came the day, cameras rolling, chimp on shoulders, the jungle hero hiked up his tiger skin drawers, let out a ferocious whoop and swung for the next tree. In mid-jump, as he'd been taught to do, the chimp clapped both hands over the hero's eyes. Flying blind and panicked, the hero obeyed Johnny Weissmuller's basic rule of Tarzanhood: The important thing is never let go of the rope.

He hit the tree trunk at about 20 mph and clattered to the ground, where he was found to have a busted nose and a broken leg. He not only couldn't continue filming, he didn't even look like himself any more. The understudy was quickly re-hired and did a fine job of taking over the now-vacant role, once he and Haggerty stopped laughing.

Dan is my favorite Hollywood celeb, down to earth, droll and a charmer. He's had a rollercoaster ride through life, sampled everything Tinseltown has to offer, and seen the dark side of fame, too.

He's been busted in a drugs sting, his two daughters were once heroin addicts but he helped them to battle out of that hell hole, and he kept his second marriage to Samantha and their family together for decades. He's an exception in Los Angeles, a big-screen actor who's not in the Gone Hollywood mode. We first met in the mid 1980s, when Dan was filming in Merlin, Oregon, near the admirable wildlife refuge Wild Images, where they had bears and eagles used in the film. Dan told me a tale of working on 'Easy Rider' with Peter Fonda, Dennis Hopper and Jack Nicholson. "We had good times making the movie," Dan confided. "I built and painted all the motorcycles, including the Captain America bike Peter rode and the Billy the Kid bike that was Dennis'. We filmed in the desert, and we'd all get together around the campfire at night, to drink and yarn. Well, Dennis kept bugging me to find some dope, so I quietly scooped up some dried-up mule dung and rolled a huge joint. Dennis saw me with it, and the joint pretty quickly went around the whole crew. 'This is good!' they agreed, dragging deep. 'Well,' I said, 'there's lots more out there,' and I pointed to the ground where the mules were tethered."

In 2004, I was on set with Dan near Banff, Alberta. He was playing a Mongolian warrior and the scene called for him to be out on a frozen lake and be 'attacked' by a couple of trained Siberian snow tigers. The sight was magnificent, and we watched and filmed from inside the trees as Dan and the tigers wrestled on the frozen lake. That evening, a women's social group called the Bitch and Stitch Club met at the crew's hotel, and a woman joined us, to talk to Dan. He said he'd been filming at Lake Kananaskis. "She said: 'That's funny, my husband was there today, ice fishing. He came home in total shock. He was smoking weed while he was fishing, and said he'll never, ever do that again. The dope made him hallucinate, and he saw a vision of Siberian tigers attacking an ancient Mongolian peasant. He said it was so real he couldn't believe his eyes. It shook him up terribly. He vows he'll never smoke dope again and he'll never go back to that lake!" Haggerty, spluttering with laughter, enlightened the woman to his afternoon's costume and activities. She thanked him, and added: "I won't tell David any of this just yet. Or maybe, not at all...."

Jackson High Five

I never did tell Janet Jackson how honorably the tabs had treated her. Well, I had. For six years, the supermarket sleuths had been on the trail of Janet's supposed love child. Star magazine had twice sent a reporter to Kokomo, Indiana, to track down Amy X, who was supposedly the illegitimate child Janet gave away. The paper had carried stories in 1996 and 1998, identifying the 'beautiful little girl that sexy Janet Jackson gave up at birth, two months before she became a runaway teenage bride." The first of those stories came two years after the magazine had reported 'exclusively' how Janet's ex-husband and his mother were trying to find the girl the singing superstar had hidden from them. Now, in June 2000, Star told me, Amy's stepbrother wanted to spill secrets. Amy, grown into a teenager, was under the legal guardianship of Shirley X, who lived in Kokomo, but the girl lived elsewhere with her grandparents, address unknown. I was required and requested to go to Indiana and Get The Story. Like the Baffling Chair of Death tale, it proved to be just that, a story.

When I met Amy's stepbrother, Alan, alarm bells went off. He seemed devious, and he certainly wasn't helpful, despite the promise of bundles of money. I did some checking, and found that he had done time for forgery, when he was part of a car theft ring. Alan promised much, but wasn't eager to take me to meet his stepsister, and his mother was conveniently out of town. Under pressure, he agreed to provide some proof that Janet's baby was adopted, and that his mother, Shirley, had brought her up.

The alleged 16 years old document he provided was suspicious. It looked computer-generated, an unlikely event in 1984, when typewriters were still in vogue. Under the letterhead of a Kokomo attorney was a mis-typed letter replete with spelling errors and unlikely capitalizations that made me wonder at the education level of the attorney, or at her ability to check what her assistant had written. The letter confirmed the adoption and said $10,000 would be paid quarterly into Shirley's savings account. Additionally, more would go into a college fund. The payments seemed as unlikely as rocking horse apples. I'd seen the clapboard shack Shirley lived in. She certainly wasn't receiving an extra $40,000 a year in child support, if she was living so humbly. I called the attorney's office. Number invalid, which was reasonable, as the letter was dated July 1984. I went to the address after finding no listing for the attorney. The street number didn't exist. There WAS an attorney of that name, but she was now deceased. She'd been killed months earlier, in an accident that had made news. A call to the local bar association determined that she'd not begun practicing law until 1986, two years after she was supposed to have handled the adoption. Just to nail matters down a little more, I stopped by city hall, and found examples of the attorney's signature. They bore no resemblance to the scribble on the fake adoption letter. Stepbrother Alan didn't show to the rendezvous, and was even more evasive when I called him. I found out that the quotes in the original story attributed to a friend of Shirley's came from Shirley herself, who claimed she couldn't speak publicly because of a confidentiality agreement signed at the time of the 'adoption.'

Killing the story of Janet's love child was an easy decision. A convicted forger and a woman who claimed to be under a confidentiality agreement would not be the best witnesses to stand up in a lawsuit and testify credibly. The tale went on the spike. Janet, after the tabs had it going for six years, I knocked that rumor on the head for you. No love child secretly given away and disowned. You're exonerated. No thanks, that's fine, you're welcome.

Doris' Frequent Last Days

There's no secret about it. The tabloids follow A-List stars like jackals trail lions, as the stars' most trivial activities are of interest to readers who evidently regard actors as part of their extended family. It leads to some bizarre categories of stories, and a favorite (for the tabs, anyway) is the 'Tragic Last Days' headline. What usually happens is that some fan or ambitious pap takes a picture of an ageing star looking especially wrinkly or tired, and the tab editors scramble to cobble together a story to fit the pictorial bill. Clint Eastwood, Doris Day, Rock Hudson, Liz Taylor have all been frequent fliers on the 'Last Days' shuttle, as was 'Candid Camera' prankster Allen Funt. Like Clint and Doris, poor Allen lived on the Monterey peninsula, a place where expensive homes around the Pebble Beach golf courses offer privacy from snooping paps. Allen was wheelchair-bound for the last part of his life and the tabs had a standing offer of $2,000 for the right picture of him looking frail. They did get one fuzzy shot published and felt it was a successful venture, so several times sent me to try for pieces about the reclusive Doris and the fiercely-private Clint. Insiders offered me verbal glimpses of them both, and I was able to file stories about their everyday doings around Carmel, where Clint served a term as mayor, seemingly so he could ramrod his own development project through the council. In my bid for results, I even went so far as to deliver sacks of dog food to Doris' home. My hopes of softening her heart into an interview didn't work. In summer, 2008, I was told: "Try again, Bannister."

I flew into San Jose, rented a car and drove to Carmel, where I checked into the 1930s inn that was still partly owned by Doris. My room was up a short flight from the noisy bar and boasted a gap under the door that would entice a limbo dancer, so I got full value of the locals' social chatter. My window, a period piece that would take the average teen burglar no more than a few seconds to push open, was conveniently at chest height to an alley that would make great cover for him. I resolved not to leave valuables around, and strolled out to check on the social scene. A dozen or so pastel-clad retirees, many of them with pet dogs at foot, were enjoying an extended happy hour. I'd soon learn that most of them appeared daily, that they all claimed close friendships with Miss Day and they were all lying. Fact is, the still-bubbly star lives with her dozen or so dogs behind high gates and dense thickets of privacy-making rhododendrons several miles away, and rarely comes out. Her rustic home is in Carmel Valley, not Carmel by the Sea, and is perched castle-like, on top of a limestone bluff that overlooks the Quail Ridge golf course. Needless to say, after one draughty night in her inn, I was checked out, installed in a modern place in Monterey where my laptop worked, and back to the golf course. Your Correspondent could be found avidly photographing wildlife there, raising the lens optimistically towards Doris' deck and pool 100 feet above, but she didn't emerge. The trip wasn't wasted, though I got anecdotal material from the rummies at the bar, and I learned of the extensive renovations Doris was having done to her run-down home. She plunged about $300,000 into it, and in 2010 the ingrates at Globe used my material again, saying Doris was ready to die, and she'd had the house upgraded just to keep her doggies happy.

Ironically, I got my best story when Doris delivered it herself. She went fully public in a 2009 radio interview with a local DJ and bubbled on happily about her Hollywood life for all the world, and one tabloid journo, to hear from the comfort of their own homes, no golf course commando tactics required. I took a shorthand note and made a recording right at my desk, wrote the piece and sat back satisfied. Mission, I felt was Accomplished, at least until the next time her Tragic Last Days pop up again. Long may they be delayed.

Meeting Jacko

It was the same way with Michael Jackson. After all the digging and delving, one of the Enquirer's most memorable scoops came with his full cooperation. Fact is, A-Listers themselves profess to hate the tabs, but if they're ignored, they'll struggle to get back onto the gossip pages. The late MJ has been lashed as a horrible pervert, and could be thought of as a media victim, but it isn't necessarily so. He's a victim who cooperated with his oppressors in a sort of publicist's version of Stockholm Syndrome. Back in the 1970s, during a lull in the hysteria that was Jacko's career, his agent sent along a Polaroid of the Gloved One lying in a hyperbaric chamber, telling us it had been taken secretly while Jackson was asleep, and we weren't to reveal the source etc. Photographer Vince Eckersley got the image and called the man. "The picture quality's absolute rubbish," he told him, tactfully not revealing what he really felt. "We need to do it again." Vince showed up at MJ's mansion and waited while the singer climbed back into the chamber, then he took a sharp image of the scene. It went out as the 'secretly-shot' photo, the mag sold millions, and Jacko was back in the news. Of course, the Gloved One made a terrible fuss about invasion of his privacy, the game went on and both sides were pleased.

I witnessed at first hand MJ's odd behavior when he went to San Francisco in to open a waxworks exhibit of himself. The waxworks was a smallish storefront on Fishermen's Wharf and Jackson, his handful of minders and several photographers and I were crowded in to witness the unveiling of the popster's waxy alter ego. Outside, a surging mob of 4,000 fans had the building surrounded and were climbing on cars to get a better look. They crushed the roofs of five cars, including a new Jaguar, right down to the window line, which cost the Jackson organisation some serious dollars. Jacko's personal photographer, Michael Leslie, told me:"In the limo as we arrived, we were battered around like a ship in a storm. Fans were climbing on the car, and twice, the chauffeur had to gun it away." The singer finally got into the waxworks by ditching his noticeable white limo and arriving at the building's back door in a small Toyota. Inside, the manager had taken the precaution of covering the display window with butcher paper so the fans, who were being held back by just three San Francisco cops, couldn't see the singer. I'd heard him crooning through some vocal exercises in a stall in the bathroom beforehand, but he hardly had a word to say when he came out to meet the media. He thanked us, said how hard it was to have the wax impression made of his face, undraped the waxwork and had his picture taken with it. Then, in an act of utter, careless folly, the mental Michael leaned over and ripped the butcher paper from the window so the fans could see him. We all looked in horror as the mob outside yelled and surged forward. The three police uniforms were backed up against the glass, which I expected to burst inwards at any second. I saw several young girls at the front, pushed up against the window by the press of the crowd, tears streaming down their faces, mouths open as they shouted for help. And Jacko slipped out of the back door, unheeding. Somehow, the cops got the crowd to retreat a fraction. Somehow, order was restored, but no thanks to the stupid superstar's reckless behavior. I still don't know how those three officers saved their own—and who knows how many of the crowd's—lives.

Princess Di's Pics

Once, though, I was responsible for likely saving a British police-man's life. No joke. Here's how it happened: a year or so after Princess Diana died, I had a call in California from a UK contact. "I can get you pictures of Di during counter-terrorism training," he said. Was the Enquirer interested? When I put the pitch to them, talking in six figure numbers, it was yes, emphatically yes, they were interested.

The princess had gone to the Special Air Services' training facility in Hereford where important people are tutored in hostage recovery situations. Get kidnapped, and the SAS will burst in and save you. Just do as we tell you and you won't be the one shot. One of the training aids at the barracks is a room whose interior walls absorb bullets, so live-firing exercises can be conducted in there without danger of ricochets. Diana and Charles, who'd already been through the course and who knew what to expect, were taken into the facility by 'kidnappers.' In pitch darkness, the couple went through a live-fire 'rescue' by troopers who blasted off their weaponry less than 24 inches from the princess' head. A military photographer recorded the moment when terrified Di reacted as the bullets sprayed by her. A laughing Charles was pictured, enjoying her shocked discomfort. He'd known what to expect. That photograph, plus others that showed her with fully tooled-up troopers, with her boys, on an armored vehicle and so forth, were on display on a sort of Wall of Fame of the heads of state and other glitterati who'd been through the course. Some cunning people had managed to photograph the wall of pictures and were asking me to broker their images. I was on a plane to the UK within a day to meet them. They wouldn't allow me to fax the images themselves back to Florida, but I was allowed to see and sketch them, then send that rendering back for the Enquirer editors to view. Much of the business took place in a country pub, with me scuttling back and forth to my hotel to use the fax machine. The result by closing time was that the photographer was blitzed, I was sober and the intermediary was somewhere in between. I drove the photographer back to our hotel around 2am to find we were locked out.

While I roused the night staff, the photographer, whom you'll not be surprised to know was once an SAS trooper responsible for assassinations in places like Bosnia and Africa, decided to go to his car in the hotel courtyard. I was alone outside the hotel's front door when a police patrol car pulled up. Someone had called us in as acting suspiciously. As I explained matters to one of the officers, the other moved away to investigate the courtyard, which was accessed through a longish and very dark archway. Something exploded in my brain and I ran away from the cop I was talking to, and into the arch. The other cop turned to my running footsteps and didn't see the silent shadow rise up from the ground. The drunken SAS man was about to commit mayhem on the cop, purely on instinct. I think I shrieked girlishly, diverting the trained killer enough that he didn't lay hands on the uniform, and then we needed to begin the explanations... After it all, the Enquirer opted not to buy the photographs, making the trip, the hangover and the fright just another tabloid disappointment and loss. At least I'd saved a Bobby from being brutalized. Or worse.

Celeb Files

Libel and celebrity headlines go together like a horse and carriage, is the popular perception. In fact, suits are relatively rare, even in the adversarial relationship between celeb hunters and their quarry. Comic Carol Burnett started a fashion when she sued the Enquirer for a brief gossip mention that seemed to suggest she was inebriated in a restaurant. Carol sobbed in court as she told the jury how being portrayed as a drunk hurt her so much, as her mother was an alcoholic, and the very thought of it...The actress got a then-huge $1.6 million judgement, which was trumpeted with triumphant virtue by the regular press. On appeal, the judgement reduced the award to $200,000 or so. That hardly got a mention, as did the fact that one of Carol's regular comic characters was a drunken housewife. It seemed that not just the tabs had double standards, but Burnett wasn't alone in hating us. Johnny Carson despised the tabloids, too. When he was approached to see if he'd cooperate for a cover photograph one Christmas, he had a short but pointed response. "I'd rather be photographed looking up Mother Teresa's skirt than appear on the front page of the National Enquirer," he said. Tom Hanks, however, is low-key, amiable and cooperative. I even came across an incident where he'd given an unhappy kid his own iPod. When I called to check, his agent told me he'd rather not have his good deed advertised, in case people thought it was a publicity gimmick. Another Tom, Selleck, found the tabs too intrusive but did little about it until a couple of Hollywood freelancers who for 18 months made up Tinseltown stories, filed a piece that had him in a romance with Victoria Principal. As he was in Hawaii and she was in Germany at the time, he had a case. The freelancers went elsewhere, Tom's favorite charity got a payoff and no Selleck stories ran for ages. It was deal time. It happens, from time to time, a celeb's lawyers will broker a deal with a tabloid. It might be that the magazine has their actress client's prostitution rap sheet and she will cooperate on another story or two to suppress it. Or it might be that a published story was too strong and they want the actor left in peace for a while, or else. Oprah was untroubled under such a hands-off policy in 2007 after some spurious article about her and her beau, Stedman Graham.

Oprah's Death Plans

Through the 1990s and into the 2000s, I did a few Oprah stories, and found Chicago a very difficult place to work, as every employee of her vast Harpo empire is under a strict confidentiality agreement. After Hollywood, where every waiter, valet parker, florist and caterer is on the phone with the latest, this can be tough. Even students who took the business course Oprah and Stedman conducted at Kellogg College had to sign a non-disclosure agreement and couldn't even discuss course work or their famous tutors' comments on it, much less anything of interest to the tabloids' readers. You can call Oprah a control freak, but she built it and she keeps her billion-dollar media empire the way she wants it: tightly held. She sees every proof, every storyboard before it goes out, and only she can sign any corporate cheque for more than $5,000. It's grief for news-sniffing journos, but it's the way Oprah works. I think of all the Oprah stories I did, the one I liked best, the one that underscored her detail-oriented approach, was the planning she's put into her own funeral.

My insider sources, and they were few and precious and very, very cautious, had told me of other things. I'd heard of her food binges and how she'd eat an entire fried chicken at one go. I even knew of her search for spirituality, her effort to be the power behind the Obama throne, of the baby she lost at age 14, of the sex abuse she suffered and how she'd felt valueless as a child. But what knocked me out was the final farewell she has planned. Insiders told me she's picked the casket, gravesite, flowers, music and even the perfume she'll wear to the grave. But the shocker for mourners will be Oprah's post-mortem video appearance at her own memorial service. "Mourners will watch giant TV screens to watch as she tells family and friends how much she loves them. "She even starts with 'If you think this is weird, imagine how it feels for me to be making this tape,' and makes a joke about being 'cancelled,'" said the source at her Harpo HQ. The 'secret' video has gushy goodbyes and memory lane musical selections and the billionaire media queen has updated it every year or so since she first hit on the idea in 1993. Sources say she's made dozens of amendments to her own eulogy, altering the order in which people are mentioned, or amending what she has to say about each, although nobody is put down or criticized. "She gets as excited about planning her own funeral as other women get about planning their wedding. It's like a hobby with her," said one insider. "She's just very particular, very demanding, about what is going to happen." I understood. Super-private Oprah's always been one of the hardest celebs to follow, and my dozen or more trips to Chicago to dig up material about her have always been difficult. Not to wish her ill, but I hope to attend her funeral, because I'm really looking forward to watching that video.

Pop Tarts and Me

Another demanding diva to cause me grief was Britney Spears. I'd been to the remote Oregon home of her then husband-to-be, dancer Kevin Federline, and been given the brush-off by his suddenly-important stepdad. A telephone lineman, he wasn't impressed that I wanted to write a piece about K-Fed's down-home background. The shaven-headed ol' boy gave me some sagebrush editorial advice. "Come back to Pendleton in the fall, to see the bull-riding at the rodeo. Now that's a good story," he said. Thank you, I said. Ouch. Kevin's younger brother Cameron was a little more positive, we chatted briefly, and I got some sort of angle. Months later, that didn't help. Britney's handlers were already unthrilled with me. I'd written about her foundation to help inner-city kids and pointed out that of the million dollars' worth of donations sent for the kids' summer camp, she'd shelled out a measly $4,571. In 2007, I tried to get into Kevin and Britney's Studio City wedding, which was held in a modest back yard under a canopy, and wasn't eminently crash-able, as the 15 guests wore warm-up suits and I didn't. My trip to

TABLOID MAN | 151

Pendleton paid off against me. I was recognized and shown the gate. Still, I did get a couple of details: Kevin and his pals wore white sweats embroidered 'Pimp' and 'Pimp Daddy' and Britney's friends wore pink suits, with the new bride's outfit emblazed 'Mrs Federline.' Oh yes, they served chicken strips and mini-cheeseburgers at the reception. I'd expected pop tarts.

Two other pop tarts, of a different kind to the pastry ones, don't like me, either. Christina Aguilera spent years claiming that her father beat her mother and once punched her out, too, when she was just a toddler, but her uncle and father, decent men both, angrily told me several times that was a flat-out lie. Her uncle Johann was almost in tears, protesting how his brother, Christina's dad, had been maligned. "It's a message that's been vindictively planted in her head," Johann Aguilera told me, saying that friction between his brother and his ex, a German-Irish woman, was the source of the poison that had turned Christina against her father. Of course, the tabs ate up the explanation in my story, and Christina's mom was livid. She used her web site to tell fans that everything the media wrote was fiction, then stormed that she was closing the site because she was fed up with being accused of lying.

At least, in Jennifer Lopez' case, I had her almost mother-in-law on my side, even if her staff refused to talk. Details of J Lo's lifestyle intrigue people. She insists, for example, that her fake eyelashes be made from red fox fur, and that her toilet seat must be the $100,000 bejewelled one, and her hair has to be done by Oribe, at $15,000 a day. So when she and Ben Affleck were such a hot item they'd built matching mansions on an exclusive Georgia island, I called Ben's mom to talk. You can't get much closer to a star than to her likely mother-in-law, as Chris Affleck was in 2004. "Is it true that Jennie from the Block insists that her coffee is stirred counter-clockwise or she won't drink it? Does she really have a professional coat holder who follows her around? Are her staff really told to lower their eyes and not look at her directly?" Enquiring minds, I suggested, were thirsting to know.

Chris Affleck is an elementary school teacher in Cambridge, Massachusetts who raised Ben and his younger brother Casey solo after she and the boys' actor dad divorced. She's gentle, approachable and courteous and still lives in the same modest house she's had for almost three decades. "You'll have to talk to David Pollick about my son," she said, naming the actor's publicist."All I can say is that I taught my boys to be considerate, mannerly and unpretentious." A nice, classy way of conveying an opinion about J Lo, I thought. A few months later, Ben and the demanding diva broke up. Actions speak louder than words, sometimes.

Darryl's Depression

Another famous person's mom who was very helpful to me was Sue Wexler, mother of Darryl Hannah, the willowy blonde who entranced the world as a mermaid, and who nearly married JFK Jr. Sue spent hours telling me in a phone interview how seven years old Darryl went into deep depression when her father left them, and how she became 'semi-autistic' and had to be taken out of school and away to heal. "After three months in the Bahamas when she'd talk only to her teddy bear, she one day announced that she was ready to go home now," said Sue. The anecdote and others made a fine story, and the photo editor arranged for a photographer to go to Sue's Chicago penthouse to copy pics from the family album. Monkeys with cameras, I should have remembered. The mentally-adrift moron opted to rent a complicated duplicating lens, then imposed himself on Sue Wexler for six or seven hours while he carefully clicked off frame after frame, copying photographs of Darryl.

Here she is as a girl on horseback, here as a child at the beach; playing soccer; acting as Kermit in a school production. Finally, the snapper was done and no doubt Mrs Wexler heaved a sigh of relief at getting him out of the house. He developed his film and everything was black. He'd not attached the special lens correctly and light had leaked in. So he called the Wexlers and asked if he could come back and do it again, please. Not today, said Sue, I'm busy. The next day she was chatting to Darryl in Colorado and mentioned the episode. "Oh no," said Darryl. "I don't want those pictures going out there." The noise I heard was the door slamming. The London magazine for whom I was writing did manage to retrieve a couple of images from the shoot by some expensive computer enhancements, but the spread my wonderful story deserved was kaput. I have not had contact with that photographer since then. He wrecked my show, but something different wrecked my next story.

Dee and the Tiger

An old time Hollywood actress, Dee Arlen was living in Oregon with a 330 lbs tiger called Babe. "He's completely tame, he even sleeps on her bed with her," said the crazed news editor who put me onto the story. "We have a picture of him sitting on the bed with her. Update it, can you?" I went to Grants Pass on a rainy 2008 day with cameras, notebook and my yellow Labrador dog Molly, whom I left in the car, a short walk away from the rural cottage where I was greeted by Dee and a Great Dane called Thor. Dee is a tiny person, trim at 78 years old and still recognizable as the Sinatra costar she was in 'Oceans 11' Babe was another matter altogether. I could hear what sounded like a Saturn V rocket's first stage rumbling from elsewhere in the house. "That's just Babe," said Dee airily. She motioned through a door to show me a 20 yards square, muddy compound with a 15ft wire fence. "That's where Babe goes to exercise when it isn't raining," she explained. Oregon, I thought. Maybe he's an indoor cat.

We went through into a smallish bedroom where the double bed took up much of the space. By the bed head was a flimsy-looking door with a clear-ish plastic pane in the top half. The rumbling turned to very loud roaring, as if someone at Cape Canaveral had called for liftoff. Babe, it seemed, was behind the door. I was keeping Thor in front of me and was anxiously eyeing the skimpy hook and eye latch that kept the door closed. Dee, all 4ft 11in of her, moved past me and picked up an aerosol the size of a lipstick. Pepper spray. She opened the door and a striped head bigger than a small fridge appeared. Where the door would have been was a very fine set of gleaming dentistry. Dee said something like 'Oh phooey!' and squirted a tiny amount of pepper spray into the tiger's face. He never even blinked. Dee closed the door so we had a chance to hear each other, and sat expectantly on the bed. How, she asked, did I want to handle this photo op? I explained that the news editor had a ludicrous idea that Babe would sit next to her on the bed while I took pictures. Even Dee looked doubtful. "Well," she said. "He used to go everywhere with me, but that was 10 years ago. These days, he's a bit

edgy with strangers. If you'd brought that nice photographer Eddie Sanderson, he'd know what to do. Babe would do anything for him."
Fast Eddie, I reflected sourly, had made a wonderful image of tiger and mistress sitting on her bed when the beast was a couple of years old and tractable. Today, this mad menace would probably devour him and his motor drive, too. Dan Haggerty, actor and animal trainer, had told me before I left on the assignment that tigers go crazy after about age five. "He'll not only be unpredictable, he's probably de-socialized from not getting much human interaction," Dan had warned. Babe, at 15 years old, was about ten years past his sell-by. He wasn't only mad with age, but was also stir-crazy from being in solitary. Dee reassured me that Babe had been declawed, though I knew he'd escaped a year or so before and had mauled a cow. No claws, but plenty of fangs, I noted. Finally, I opted to shoot a picture of Babe from the doorway of his pen. Dee opened the door and Babe bellowed at me, moving closer. I was absolutely convinced by his actions. There was no need to call 'Kitty, kitty.' I hastily closed the door. My editorial judgment told me it would be a much better story if I just got a picture of Dee with the dog Thor. Back at the car, my poor Labrador was trembling. She'd heard the tiger, too. I told her: "I know what you mean." That little old lady chose to keep a crazed, wild animal in her house, and nobody, even the authorities, seemed able to do anything for her. (Since then, Babe has been taken to a big cat refuge in Colorado and Dee is concentrating on horses.)

Some of the biggest names in Hollywood can walk on the wild side, too. At a strip club, in sober, midwestern Lincoln, Nebraska, I went to talk to the manager about Harrison Ford. What Lincoln knew about Ford was surprising. The Sexiest Man Alive visited a strip joint there, flying in for an eyeful. Moviedom's Indiana Jones has six aircraft, including a Gulfstream jet and a helicopter, and was a stalwart of the search and rescue squad based in Jackson, Wyoming, near his ranch.

He'd stopped in Lincoln to refuel and had dropped by the Night Before strip joint for female visual stimulation, said manager Ken Semler. I talked to the stripper, a girl working her way through college, and she told me how Harrison had given her his megawatt smile and a proposition. Maybe it was because of the story I sent to the Star tabloid, maybe it was previous activities, but it was Temple of Doom time for Harrison's marriage very soon afterwards. His reps didn't have much to say to me, either, when I asked about the strip club visit and the stage name he suggested for himself when he first went to Hollywood: Kurt Affair.

Unfriendly Dog

Curt was a good adjective for the way Dog the Bounty Hunter became with me, after he Went Hollywood. Back in 2002, when Duane Lee Chapman was first easing himself into public view, with his snakeskin cowboy boots, handcuffs and fire extinguisher-sized canister of military-grade Mace, he answered my calls eagerly, happy for the publicity. Over the next couple of years, I wrote about him and his longtime girlfriend, later fourth wife, Beth for the tabloids and for more respectable magazines. He called me 'Brother' and tearfully said he'd pray for me. The Hawaii-based bounty hunter in the wife-beater tank top, scrubby blond beard and pompador'ed mullet haircut told me he'd had 18 arrests for armed robbery and served a couple of years for murder. He told me he couldn't carry a gun: because he was a convicted felon, and he got his nickname, a reversal of 'God,' from fellow biker gang members.. He even admitted he wore built-up cowboy boots because he's a mini-sized 5ft 7 inches tall. Dog revealed his technique if a suspect pulled a gun. He'd call 911 and shout: "Officer down!" because that's what police respond to quickest. His best source of fugitive info is hookers, and after he tells them the quarry is a child molester, "they always call. They hate pedophiles," he explained. I wrote it all down and got profiles of a Dog's seamy life published. Dog practically wept when he told me how grateful he was for my help. "You've made me famous, you've changed my life, brother," he said.

I denied it as hyperbole but secretly, I thought maybe I HAD helped a little. Maybe this budding TV star did owe me a little credit. But when it came to Dog's biggest case, I had to get the inside story without canine help. The ardent self-promoter clammed up on me and wouldn't return my calls. I soon found out why. He was ticked at the tabloids, who'd bought a tape recording of his racist rant to one of his sons. The fellow sold the tape, the Enquirer ran the story,

Dog almost lost his TV show. He wasn't pleased with anyone associated with the tabs. Well, I had other sources.

The case concerned Andrew Luster, the 6ft 4ins handsome heir to the Max Factor cosmetics empire, a playboy with a $40 million personal fortune and a taste for date rape drugs. Luster had a history of drugging unsuspecting college girls, then video'ing himself having sex with them while they were unconscious. Caught, he fled California in mid-trial, through the efforts of a gay celebrity's lover, forfeiting his million-dollar bail. In his absence, he was found guilty on 86 criminal counts of sodomy, rape, drugs and weapons possession and poisoning. He was sentenced to 124 years in prison.

Dog went after him, mindful of a $100,000 bail reward and some excellent footage for his TV show. He rummaged through Luster's garbage and found his mobile phone bills. He called Luster's mother every day to taunt her and prod her conscience. Until Luster changed phones, Dog even called him to declare his determination to catch the fugitive. Luster's mother provided a vital clue in one chat. She mentioned that her son spoke fluent Spanish. Mexico, thought Dog, might be a convenient destination for the fugitive. He called Luster's mother pretending to be from the coroner's office. He told the maid: "We have a body. It might be Andrew's." "Oh no," said the girl, "we heard from him two days ago." Finally a tipster in Thailand alerted the bounty hunter to sighting Luster in the Mona Lisa bar. Chapman went on Bangkok TV to chant "Fee Fi Fo Fum, look out Luster, here I come." The fugitive skipped to Mexico, where an alert American student recognized him at the Motel de los Angeles. Dog and a film crew headed to Puerto Vallarta.

Luster's Last Stand came after six months on the lam, and happened outside the El Zoo bar as he exited his white VW Jetta. Dog, his son Leland and his brother Tim cornered their quarry as the crew filmed them. Dog went face to face, swearing at Luster then Mace'ing him. Leland came from behind and put Luster in a chokehold. The trio took him to the ground. Luster spat and fought, promising to dance on Chapman's grave, but was quickly handcuffed and bundled into the crew's truck. Witnesses to what they thought was a kidnapping called the cops as the manhunters headed for the border. The federales set up road blocks and the team in its two-car caravan was nailed. They spent the next four days in jail before being allowed to post bond, on their promise to stay in the country for trial. Released, they promptly fled. Furious Mexican authorities tried for months to get Dog back, but the bounty hunter was aware he could face up to 20 years inside for his vigilante actions, and wouldn't return. Back in the US, Dog was dismayed to learn that he wouldn't be getting a reward for catching Luster, either. A judge ruled that the million bucks' bail money should go to Luster's victims and the county. Dog wasn't acting officially, the judge ruled, and there would be no bone for him. He was wrong. Dog's phone began ringing off the hook with TV offers, agents, and writers all eager to exploit his image, fame and operations. Playboy came calling and Ozzie and Sharon Osbourne showed up for a barbeque, the bounty hunter's new kennel mates. The Dog was having his day, and even bumps in the road like his brother's arrest for indecent exposure, or the more serious time when his show was yanked off air for Chapman's racist rants on a tape recording didn't derail the Dog cart. He did penance, got reinstated and made more money. My calls and emails go unanswered to this day. I still don't know why, but I'm in the doghouse.

Alicia the Porn Queen

It was a different story when I went to see one of the world's most famous porn stars. Lisa Ferreire was a beautiful, blue-eyed brunette known best by her working name: Alicia Monet, a porn queen who starred in more than 100 films with titles like 'The Slut.' She was a stripper at 17, a prostitute at 19, the star of hard-core porno videos at 23 and is now featured on 570 website vids. She was a queen of Internet sex so celebrated that 'X Files' tv star David Duchovny once announced that his secret wish was to meet her and thank her for his lurid daydreams.

My daughter and photographer Rachel and I drove south of Reno, Nevada to meet Lisa at her desert home one winter day in 1999. Our assignment: chronicle a day in the life of a porn star. We had some difficulty finding the place: it was down a remote and icy desert road and was an unprepossessing clapboard, single-storey house. No car outside, I noted. But Lisa was there, pale, tired-looking, with a cheerful toddler on her hip. She had startlingly lovely eyes, but her body tone looked neglected. She looked like a washed-out housewife, not a glamorous porn star. As I'd expected to find an affluent actress who could inject a bit of glamor into the story, this looked difficult, but Rachel started setting up cameras and Lisa and I talked. "Sex is just my job," said Lisa, as she gave us coffee. "I juggle home, work and motherhood just like many other women. I have my workout, my housework, my little boy to collect from nursery school. The babysitter might take over while I drive to San Francisco to film a sex video in a private home," she told me. Privately, I made that 'nanny' and 'fly' if it was going into copy. "While I'm there," she added, "I'll shop for material for my costumes, discuss a possible Las Vegas show and photo shoot, and come back the next evening." My mental amendments included the thought that there was little chance of shopping for glitzy showbiz fabric in Weed Heights, Nevada, and no wonder the girl looked tired, if she had to finish filming then face a six-hour drive across Donner Pass to get home. Her ex-husband had left her broke, her new manager was doing a half-hearted job of finding work for her, she was living on welfare. It was a low point, she was demoralized, stuck in the middle of nowhere with no resources and a small child.

But Lisa's life story was interesting. A rebellious teen who left home at 16, she'd started stripping to pay the rent. Within two years she was working at the Mustang Ranch brothel. "It was nice," she said. "They looked after me. It was safe, warm, comfortable, friendly." At 20 she was married, and with her husband's management was touring as a nude dancer, doing five half-hour shows a day. Some states allow dildo shows, so she did that. In Canada she had to wear a G-string, but the law doesn't specify exactly where to wear it. "Some of the girls use it as a garter," she confided.

I wasn't happy at the idea of photographing a tired housewife and explaining how she was a big time porn star, and the interior of her small house was cramped. Best focus on making her look good in everyday situations and use pickup pictures she could provide of her skin-show days. We wheeled her outside. Winter, cold and icy. No, she didn't have any warm coat other than this casual down jacket. She looked good in it, but it wasn't the image we wanted. Rachel went to the car, came back with her stylish, black wool overcoat. Lisa put it on, and her star quality started to shine out. She went from tired housewife to fashion model.

Now for a picture with her son, taking him to nursery school. Some small difficulty here: she had no car. She was stranded in the desert, as her manager was off somewhere with her vehicle and she'd been dependent on her teenage babysitter's occasional visits for transport. My Mercedes looked sufficiently Hollywood, I thought, so Lisa suddenly became its new, if temporary, owner. Only for the pictures, I told her. The atmosphere lightened, we were all in the conspiracy. Lisa's smile broke out, a bit of cosmetic aid (supplied by my Girl Friday) and she was a film star again. Forgive me, but I stretched the story. Or at least, I turned back the clock to where Lisa used to be before she was broke. "I'll be working again soon," she said earnestly. "It's just my new manager..." her voice trailed off. Then the old Lisa, the one we'd not met when she was a star, kicked in. "I'll do a few more years of this, make some money, get married, get out of the business. There's plenty to be made," she said. "You can make two or three movies in three or four days," she explained. "The producers get someone's big house, and the cast all stay there, together. It's OK, I don't think I've ever done a scene I didn't enjoy, except once, where a German guy was hurting me and I bit him." In fact, she nearly bit off the guy's penis, and was arrested running naked down a San Francisco street to escape his handlers.

Lisa was living in sex-industry-tolerant Nevada where prostitution is legal. She visited the doctor monthly, was meticulous about personal hygiene and liked performing for internet sex. "You do it in front of a camera and charge people $50 to watch. They log on, give us a credit card number and watch the action. It's just sex, it's perfectly natural." Still mildly stunned, Rachel and I told jokes to each other all the way home to California. From then on, she's called that coat her porn queen outfit. Porn queen she might have been, but at least Lisa was cooperative, and that's not always the case with interviewees.

Inside a $100k Buy-Up

When a British national newspaper called in 2008 to have me buy up an interview with someone, I assumed I'd get cooperation. After all, they told me I could go high – maybe as much as $100,000 for a world exclusive. The story concerned a smalltime Florida wannabe gangster and bodybuilder, David Bieber, who had cold-bloodedly executed an unarmed Yorkshire police officer after a traffic stop. Bieber was on trial—he eventually got a life sentence—and word had leaked out about his life in Florida, where he was wanted for the contract killing of a drugs supplier in 1995. He was also accused of attempting to murder his live-in lover, Michelle Marsh. She was so afraid of Bieber's steroid-fuelled rages she'd applied for a restraining order, and had fled Florida to live with her parents in Ohio.

My task was to find her and persuade her into an interview that she'd have to agree would be exclusive to my paper. The major difficulties involved rival Brit newspapers, as the story was huge in the UK, and they were equally eager to do a buy-up. One other hurdle was that while the trial was ongoing, no Brit news outlet could carry Michelle's story, so the whole thing would have to be done and kept under wraps, maybe for months, until a verdict was reached. In turn, this meant that the paper asking me to set it up didn't want free-lance me to do the interview, in case I sold it elsewhere. The actual recounting of her 'sensitive story of international significance' as the paper's bureau chief described it, would be made by Michelle to a staff journalist. So, in the humble role of fixer, I set off to Ohio to meet one of the world's most mule-headed people.

Michelle's father, Joe Stanforth, was a retired delivery company manager living in some affluence. I noted a Lexus and a Cadillac in the garage, and an expensive pickup truck outside their large home on a new development 20 miles out of Dayton. Not that I noticed the garaged vehicles on my first visit. Then, Joe answered the door, and regarded me with hostility even when I mentioned large sums of money. He closed the door in my face with a curt admonition to come back another time because he was going to see an attorney. So I went back to my drab motel and waited a day. After a tentative phone call, I arranged a return. Joe was as bullheaded as ever, Michelle turned out to be a photogenic, platinum blonde wearing nice clothes, an expensive gold necklace and a vacant look. Her father hardly let her speak. As bluntly and rudely as he could, he told me he would be the negotiator because he was as smart as any lawyer and I'd better not think about trying to pull the wool over HIS eyes, no sir. "I have the smarts," he told me. He'd seen the attorney and he'd handle all negotiations himself. He'd had good, damn good, offers from other papers and I'd better pay close attention to him, and he was going to get money up front because none of you newspaper people can be trusted. Overwhelmed by such grace and tact, I kept smiling, nodding like a demented bobble-head doll and trying to get a word in to ask Michelle what did she have to tell us?

Finally, some of it came out. She'd had a two-year relationship with Bieber, they'd lived together for four months, they'd gone on a cruise together, she'd try to find photographs of them both from friends in Florida, and there were other things she couldn't talk about. "And won't until we get that money first," Joe interposed. I gritted my teeth and laid out a first offer. We'd pay $75,000 on publication for her exclusive story. We'd give her $1,000 cash just to hear what she'd have to tell us. That money would be hers what-ever happened. If her story warranted it, we'd need to spend a day with her, taking photographs, copying her own photos with Bieber, interviewing her. At the end of that session, we'd hand over another $9,000 for her agreement not to talk to any other media. The balance of $65,000 would be hers within three days of the paper publishing her story.

Joe grunted and demanded we pay him, not Michelle, as he was retired and had minimal income, so the tax bill would be lower. This, I felt, was an encouraging sign. Then he floored me. The News of the World was offering $100,000 and the Sunday Mirror had put a $90,000 offer on the table. I made a call or two, and our offer went to $10k up front and $90k on publication. No, said Joe, taking three days to get around to it while I froze my buns in wintry Ohio (though I did sneak in a visit to the USAF air museum, killing time). His new demand was $25k up front, $50k on publication and $25k more for the follow-up story, and no negligee pictures of his daughter, either. He was inclined to deal with us, he said, because "You're the ones who have been bugging me the most." I was beginning to enjoy the wrangling, and countered with a demand to see these generous offers from the other papers. How, I asked, did my editors know he wasn't just making up all these numbers? Why should we believe him? Surly Joe floored me again. He went and produced the emails. I laid them on the kitchen table and took out a small digital camera. Joe promptly put his fingers over the address line, covering up his

162 | TABLOID MAN

own name, but allowed me to photograph the offers. That safely done, I looked to see what the rivals were up to.

The News of the World, I told him, had a track record of making extravagant offers that never quite panned out. Their offer was for three $33,000 payments, one for each of three parts, payable "at the editor's approval." "They'll only carry one part, Joe," I warned. "You'll likely get just $33,000." The Mirror offer was $2k up front, and two $44k payments for the first and second parts of Michelle's story. Again, I pointed out he'd probably only get $46k, as the follow-up tale would probably never see the light of day. (They later upped the total offer to $100k, not specifying how it would be paid). I mentioned second rights, movie rights, book signings, TV interviews, all possible revenue sources that would entirely belong to Michelle. Joe saw visions of sugar plums and the light, and agreed to our bid. We danced around the amount of up-front money and London emailed a contract to him. Then they pulled off a coup. They sold a half-interest in the bid to the rival Mirror, I fled to the airport and the interviewing angel flew in a couple of days later to do the easy part: sit down and chat to Michelle. Months later, while I was still wrangling to get my meager day rates from the paper for whom I'd saved tens of thousands of dollars, the Interviewing Angel called me about another story. "How'd you find Joe?" I asked her. "What a stubborn, difficult man," she said.

Tonya Time

And then, there was Tonya. Most celebrities enjoy fan adulation they don't deserve. One or two get fan opprobrium they don't deserve, and I stand witness for the much-maligned Olympic ice skater Tonya Harding that she doesn't deserve all the bad press she's had. I say she's just someone who's made poor choices of partners. The skater is notorious for l'Affaire Kerrigan, in which blue collar Tonya's preppy rival ice queen Nancy Kerrigan got whacked across the knee. It all went down just before the US championships, which Nancy missed while Tonya went on to win. Many believe that Tonya did the whack job herself, but that's not true. Her then-husband Jeff Gillooly, who's now Jeff Stone to dodge the negativity associated with his former name, hired a hitman to do the job with a retractable metal baton. Tonya was nailed for covering up for her husband. She lost her crown and her career. She was slapped with a $160,000 fine and did 500 hours of community service. Figure skating boomed, but she got no part of the rich new dividends she'd created.

After a time wandering in the wilderness, when she was most famous for a sex video of their honeymoon that was sold by her ex to a skin magazine, Tonya began efforts to revive her career. Her Las Vegas publicist offered us a world exclusive interview for 'only' $35,000. Tabloid editors told me: "Go and find her and have a chat. We're not paying 35 grand, though!"

I met photographer Rochelle Law Wagener at the Portland airport. I'd found an address for Tonya, so although it was around 7pm on a Saturday, we thought we'd drive by for a look at the situation. Double bingo. The house was for sale, Tonya, her dad and her new husband were outside. Before we knew it, we were a married couple looking to buy a house. Tonya was showing Rochelle over the place and hearing 'No, that was lightning' when the camera flash went off as Tonya demonstrated the drapes. I was chatting to her gormless husband Mike in the kitchen, where he had an array of tee shirts and baseball caps embroidered with a 'Tonya II' slogan. He obligingly explained that she was famous, and instantly, I was shouting upstairs to Honey that did she know who she was with? A Hollywood Person! Tonya hiked up her thigh-length sweater to show me her powerful legs—Honey gasped—and agreed to have her picture taken with me, and wearing a TII hat. She was warm and friendly and told us all about her hopes and her training regimen, which had dropped her weight to 111 lbs, or 5 lbs lighter than when she won her first national title. She talked about how she wanted to become eligible for the Olympics again, how it was her new start. Mike Tyson and OJ Simpson, she said, had paid their debts and begun again, why couldn't she?

I really felt she wasn't anywhere close in the notoriety table to that pair, but I saw her point. Yet, she entranced us. Clear eyed, with a healthy glow and curly hair, she was an All-American Girl. We came away without any inclination to buy the house, but we did like Tonya. The story ran, and was so sympathetic that Mike didn't resent not getting the $35k, and even offered me another tale. But, sympathetic though we found her, Tonya's reinstatement bid was turned down by the US Figure Skating Association. She became a boxer, famously TKO'ing Bill Clinton inamorata Paula Jones, who seemed to spend most of her time protecting her nose job. Tonya also worked at detailing cars, signing autographs at a car dealership and teaching small children to skate. Her attempt to make a skating comeback was booed off the ice, her singing career flopped when she and her band were pelted with plastic bottles and even the New York strip clubs turned down her offer to display her enhanced boobs. The last time I spoke to her dad Al Harding—Tonya had dropped off the radar for a while—he told me: "She's doing anything and everything to be a success. She knows what it is to hit rock bottom on a county jail work crew, but her spirit's unbroken. I'm proud of her!" Today, she's married again to a 'good guy' and is living quietly. Maybe one day, we'll see her skate again. Life dealt her a poor hand, she made it to the top, suffered some bad luck and worse judgement, and paid a heavy price. It was ironic. One of the few celebs I found to admire was seen by almost everyone else as a Bad Girl.

STORIES OF FEAR

Death by Python

The variety of stories a general reporter gets to do is engagingly large, and although I suffer from comprehensive areas of ignorance, most interviewees are disarmingly happy to reduce their subject's arcane mysteries to everyday terms. It gives me an ongoing education for which I am deeply grateful. When a steel mill operator spells out the need for different kinds of sand to make molds for molten metal, or a Pilkington explains the principles of float glass, even a hack retains something of the tutorial. Tabloids have little use for the details of industrial reporting, but the wildlife expert who deals with grizzly bears, the parachutist who survives a fall with a malfunctioning canopy or the forensics expert who examines crime scenes all have absorbing tales to tell. Those who survive dangerous events tell gripping, vivid stories of facing death or injury, and their experiences add to a reporter's education and store of memories. I have my favorites—more on those later—but some stories stay with me because their subjects touch primal horrors in me. I'm cautious about snakes, underground places, large wild animals, leaping from aircraft and getting married. Yes, the last is just a joke. I've been married to the same excellent person for decades, but one couple whose secrets I'll reveal were so gun-shy about leaping into commitment, they devised a formula.

Here's a sampling of tabloid tales on subjects to make your skin crawl: snakes, caves, lions and parachutes, And marriage. They're just as I wrote them, and I might immodestly add, in better form than the dog's breakfast of rewrites they chose to print, so here's another tabloid secret: they don't always give readers the full version of a story.

Lou Daddono vividly remembers the day he died, his life squeezed out by a giant python. "I believe I am the only person in the world who has been seized by a 23 foot python and lived to tell how I was crushed to death. I was technically dead for five minutes," he said. "I didn't have a pulse until they restarted my heart in the ambulance. Yet, dying saved my life!" Pythons have an internal organ that detects their victims' pulse and breathing. When the heart stops, the python stops crushing. When Daddono 'died,' the snake released him and turned on another handler.

It was a routine day in 1998 at America's biggest reptile zoo, Serpent Safari, near Madison, Wisconsin, where Daddono, 44, was the owner. He and his ex-Marine partner Paul Keeler were cleaning cages of the snakes, alligators, lizards and other reptiles kept there. Through the inch-thick, bulletproof glass of the cage of a 275 lbs Southeast Asian reticulated python, they noticed a burned-out light bulb. "The python had been caught in Thailand a month earlier, and was still a wild creature who had survived 18 years in a jungle where the rule is eat or be eaten," said Daddono. "I knew she could devour a 50 lbs pig in one swallow, so I took care." Daddono also knew the snake's power: he'd seen it hurl itself at the glass. The impact 'was like a car hitting the building,' he said. Daddono entered the cage cautiously, carrying a snake hook to pin down the reptile's head, with its 200-plus barbed teeth. Keeler followed, carrying a piece of heavy canvas. He had a cell phone and a 10-inch military knife strapped to his belt. On cue, the snake struck at Daddono and missed. The two men threw the canvas over its head. "If you block out the light, a snake lies still," the zookeeper explained. Keeler kept watch as Daddono cleaned the cage, then reached up to change the light bulb. What the ex-Marine couldn't see was that the canvas that covered the reptile's head had ruckered up, forming a place through which she could see. Daddono was stretched tall, changing the light bulb. "My left hand was down, about five feet from her and she must have sensed the heat. I saw her eyes glitter as she peeked from under the canvas and my mind registered an 'Oh no, she can see.' Before I could even flinch, she grabbed my hand, lacerating and breaking it, but she released me," said Daddono.

As he retreated in pain, the keeper stumbled and knocked the canvas away. The snake struck like a blacksmith's hammer and backed Daddono into a corner of the 12ft x 5ft cage. He pinned her head with the snake hook, then dropped it and grabbed her behind the head with both hands. "She thrashed, and a coil as big, solid and hard as a bus tire went over my neck and shoulder. Instantly, she threw another coil around my ribs and I heard them breaking."My head was between my knees. She threw me to the floor. Another coil went around my waist, then a fourth around my head. My eyes, nose and mouth were covered. I felt the coils moving, working against each other, crushing with incredible force. My head was bursting, the noise of my ribs breaking sounded like a fire crackling. My eyes seemed certain to burst right out of my head, and my chest felt as if someone had parked a truck on it. I knew I was going to die and I welcomed it, to relieve the terrible pain. I could feel the snake slashing at my legs and buttocks, so I dimly knew I'd released her head. The world was red and roaring. Suddenly it became a place of calm and quiet. I felt a sense of great happiness because the pain had ended. My heart had stopped."

Keeler, who dialed for help during the three-minute attack, was wrestling and slashing at the snake with his knife, trying to decapitate it. The python turned from Daddono's limp body and bit into Keeler's arm, then coiled itself around him. With a superhuman effort, the burly, 220 lbs keeper dragged the python out of the cage, still slashing at its head. The snake lunged, disentangled itself from him, then retreated. Keeler desperately gave his partner CPR. "I couldn't revive him. He didn't even have a pulse," he said. "Lou was dead for five minutes until they re-started his heart."

Doctors said the oxygen Keeler blew into Daddono saved him from death or brain injury. An ambulance crew restarted the unconscious man's heart on the way to the emergency room, where both men had their lacerations treated and Daddono's broken ribs and hand were reset. "It took me months to move without pain, and my eyes were full of blood for more than a month, but I got off lightly," said Daddono. A veterinary team spent seven hours sewing up the reptile's wounds, and for weeks Daddono gave the python daily antibiotics, but despite the medical care, it died several months later. Daddono replaced the snake with the world's largest captive python, a 27 foot monster called Baby, and he handles it cautiously. "I don't blame the snake that that attacked me," he explained. "It was her nature to attack, but I take no chances now." And, Daddono now gives his reptiles only pre-killed pigs. "I was almost a python's meal myself," he said. "It was such a painful death I will never put anything else through that." Lou Daddono told me during our interview facts that stayed with me: that constrictors can detect heartbeats, and stop squeezing once their prey is dead, and that the body wrapped around him "was as big, solid and hard as a bus tire." With graphic, informational ammunition like that, I can bore into stupefaction anyone brave enough to talk to me, no squeezing needed. The story went on my mental A-list.

Trapped Underground

Another story that made an impression on me, partly because I dislike being confined in underground places, was about the rescue of a caver who'd managed to get himself into a nightmare situation. Again, here's the piece I wrote: Rob Gillespie was looking into the darkness of hell. He was jammed fast, upside down in a vee-shaped fissure 300 feet underground. He was vomiting, half-frozen and dying of thirst. For 20 hours, the Colorado caver had been fighting to free himself, but his efforts and those of 28 highly-trained rescuers had failed. "Time was ebbing away," rescue leader Carl Bern, 31, said. Bern and his team had fought for hours with drills and electric hammers to free the 38 years old cave explorer, and were losing hope. "He was alternating between calm and despondency. He was chilled right through. The freezing rock was sucking the warmth from his body, he was weak and in great pain." "It was a nightmare," said Gillespie. One arm was trapped under him, he was wedged pain-fully by his hips, face down on a 50-degree downhill slope. He could hardly breathe in the cramped fissure, his legs were doubled up and his body twisted sideways. He had been vomiting for eight hours. "I was going to die and I didn't want to."

Gillespie had started the expedition as just another day under Iron Mountain, where his Durango caving club had been prying and scraping for years, hoping to break into a complex of limestone caverns. "We'd found Farside Cave in a rubble field in the mountain, right underneath Glenwood Caverns, an incredible complex of stalactite and stalagmite-filled chambers," said Bern. "Over the years, cavers have been tunneling through the rubble, clearing passages filled with sand and rock by ancient water flows. We're looking for a way into the caverns above, or to discover new cave systems below." In March 2005, Gillespie and two other cavers went the length of a couple of football fields into the cave to make the 200 foot crawl through the twisting tunnel to the new limit of the dig. The caver dropped about eight feet into the entrance, then followed a downhill chute another 35 yards. He wriggled through a squeeze, elbowed into a tunnel 20 inches high in a dug-out breakdown of rubble, and emerged into a man-sized cube of a room the cavers had cleared. In its opposite wall, he squeezed through another fissure and into a series of narrow twisting passageways. Near the end of the painfully-cleared tunnel was an awkward squeeze: an 11 inch wide, vee-shaped tapering fissure in the solid limestone. Only two feet high, it required the caver to edge in head first with left shoulder down, then turn abruptly right and sharply down a steep slope to slide past the obstruction and reach the working face of the tunnel 30 feet ahead. Gillespie had twice been to the face of the excavation and was wriggling backwards up the slope to come back out when disaster struck. "I'd wriggled mostly around the squeeze corner and was almost to the top of the slope when something shifted, I put my hand back to free myself, slipped and fell headfirst."

In the inky blackness the highly-experienced caver had twisted like a corkscrew, and jammed himself by the hips in the vee crack. At first, rescue seemed routine. With help, he could be pulled back up and out, but the turns of the passageway made access nearly impossible for his partners. Teams from the Colorado Cave Rescue Network were called in. "Rob was jammed stuck and he'd fallen so awkwardly he just couldn't help himself," said Bern, of the Denver

Grotto caving club. "We'd have to chisel him out with feather and wedge techniques, drilling then removing flakes of rock a little at a time until he was free." The problem: Gillespie's body was pressed against icy rock that sapped his core heat. The race was to save the caver before he suffocated, died of cold or became fatally weak. "Our first concerns were dehydration and hypothermia. We could see his lower legs, doubled back painfully, and we got a down jacket and a space blanket on them. We got electric heaters in there, but the dust made it stinkingly unbreathable, so they were junked."

Working in desperate relays, the teams dug a staging room, but the solid rock where Gillespie was trapped made it impossible to enlarge the passage there. The rock was removed painfully slowly, as only one caver at a time could work near the trapped man. "He was screaming, he went from being calm to being despondent, to being panicked, he was scared," said Bern. "I knew that in time we should be able to get him out, but he'd been vomiting for hours and I didn't know if we had enough time left." Back at the surface, anxious rescuers debated strategy. The trapped man was in a blind tunnel. He couldn't be pulled out by one man, but if they could get another caver somehow past him, to help push from the front.... Daniel Laos got the call 15 hours into Gillespie's ordeal. The 31 years old rescue caver who has explored caves on two continents had carried out five successful underground saves. A pocket rocket at just over five feet tall, and a wiry steel-and-sinew 120 lbs, Laos is a floor tile setter during the week and a human mole at weekends."I'm a little guy and I can get where the big guys can't," he explained. "If there is a six and a half inch gap, I can get through it. The plan was for me to get underneath Rob, get past him, turn around and push him while someone else pulled." Laos drove for four hours from his home in Colorado Springs, ran to the cave, clambered into his rescue gear and starting wriggling through the cramped passageways.

Bern moved back to a 40-inch high dugout a few feet from the limestone fissure that held Gillespie and Laos wriggled forward to the tormented, moaning man. "There was a lot of stuff to get out of the way—drills, heaters, cords, lights, so I had to shift those back. They'd been trying to bust the rock around him, but there was no room to drill. They'd been tapping in wedges to crack off flakes. It was going to take a long time. I took a look from up top, by his feet.

There was a 4½ inch gap under his right side. I wedged under him to look, talking to him. He was telling me: 'It hurts, it's painful, stop it!' I told him who I was and that there was no way I was going to leave him there, I was going to get him out, he had to just work with me," Laos told me. "I said: 'I'll do my damnedest. You're coming out with me.' Then I set about finding out how to do it." Laos groped under the trapped man's body and coaxed an extra two-inch gap near Rob's right hip. It was the edge he needed.

Face down in the limestone rubble, Laos pulled Gillespie's left leg into his own right armpit and eased Gillespie's right leg over his shoulder by his head. Then, with a steady, muscle-wrenching effort, the tiny caver forced himself backwards and upwards, twisting the agonized man clockwise and pulling him out like a wine cork. "Rob was screaming: 'You're killing me!' "said Bern, "but Daniel was quiet and patient and determined." He was also successful. "I spun him out of there, corkscrewed him out," he said. But the rescue was not over. The first twisting, wrenching pull had dragged Gillespie out of the fissure's vee-grasp and moved him 24 inches up the slope, but the greatest danger was now."I had him, but I had to hold him while I moved back to pull him to safety. If I slipped now, he'd fall back worse into the locked position and we might never get him out alive," said Laos. Scrabbling one-handedly at the rubble, the smaller man used his other hand to draw the sobbing, helpless 175 lbs caver backwards and upwards to safety, then fell face down and gasping. "I was excited and a little bit teary," he confessed. "It was a happy moment for all of us." The rest of the extraction was routine. Gillespie was checked over by Bern's team, given water and hot drinks, and led out of the narrow twisting passageways to the sunlight. "He had some cuts and bruises and was dehydrated and very cold, but didn't need to go to hospital," said Bern. Three days later, Gillespie was on a plane headed for a caving expedition in China. "Things happen," he shrugged, unconcernedly. "I'm just glad Daniel was there to unscrew me."

Cougar Attack

My spine seemed to be still tingling from reliving the horror when I came across another story of a life and death struggle. Canadian

Dave Parker lives in woodsy Vancouver Island, British Columbia. It's a place of beautiful forest and water views, of clean air and water, skyscapes, stunning ocean and mountain vistas. It's a beautiful place to enjoy the outdoors, and Dave was doing just that. He was out for a stroll when he found himself in a bloody battle for his life, with a mountain lion. It took him a couple of years to come to terms with it, but he was able to tell me about the day he should have died: "I watched my eyeball bobbling about on my cheek, hanging from the optic nerve, then my scalp, which had been torn loose, flapped across my good eye and I couldn't see."

Dave fought a cougar almost as big as himself for ten long minutes, hugging it like a wrestler as it crunched its huge fangs into his head and tried to snap his neck. Finally, despite terrible wounds and blood loss, the retired draftsman managed to slash the big cat's throat. "I survived," he said. "I didn't think I would, then I got boiling mad at the cat for taking my life, and I thought I'd cripple him so he couldn't attack someone else." Dave, 64, once won about $50 in an ice curling contest and thought he'd spend it on a trophy of some kind. He chose a Schrade Old Timer folding knife. That curling win memento saved his life.

The deadly attack came just after Dave took shelter from rain while walking near his home in Port Alice, British Columbia. He relaxed, and sprawled, arms outstretched, under a rocky overhang. "I heard a 'tap tap' and looked left. A foot away, inside the curl of my arm, a 95 lbs mountain lion was sitting there, so still he looked just like a painting. All of a sudden he opened his big jaws and a howl came out. I was in deep trouble." Parker rolled right, the cat pounced. "I could feel this horrible pain of his claws going through my scalp, ripping me apart, ripping the scalp and my face. The cat slammed me face down, breaking my left cheekbone, temple, jaw and eye socket. The pain was amazing, as if someone had parked a truck on my head. He dug into my skull with his fangs and I thought he'd crush my head. His lower jaw was on the back of my head and he took a big bite. He was going for my spine."

The lion almost swallowed the man's head. "The lower jaw went in just short of the spine. His top jaw came in at my nose and crushed back everything. He even took my ear off in one bite. He took out the cheekbone and the right eye socket and the eye with it. The eye was dangling by the optic nerve. I was spilling blood like a fountain and I felt a tearing sensation. My scalp was loose, and slid across my left eye, blinding me for a moment." Dave, struggling to get to his knife, swore. " 'The bastard's killed me!' I was so mad at the cat for taking my life. When I saw that eye come out of my head and bobble, I thought: 'My life's over. The best I can do is injure this animal so he can't injure anyone else.' I was ticked." His face still in the lion's mouth, Parker did a pushup, got his feet under him and pushed backwards. The cat hit the ground backwards, under the man, and released him. On his back, Dave kicked out at the circling cat. "It went on for minutes. He'd run in, I'd kick him off. I was lying on my knife, struggling to get at it. The cat charged through my legs and I got his front paw and grabbed him in a scissors with my legs." The cat easily rolled out of it. On another lunge, Dave grabbed the lion's jaw muscle. "That is a big muscle, and he just shook himself loose, though I was trying hard to hang on. Then I grabbed him around the chest and rolled over. I was on top of him, my head buried in his chest. He was screaming, howling, on his back. He didn't like being held. I put all my weight on him, trying to tire him, and hung on as tight as I could. I tried again for my knife, but every time my grip shifted, he'd thrash around again." Twice, Dave reached his knife. Twice, blood-slick, it slipped to the ground. By chance, the second time, it bounced back into the man's grip. "He was tiring but he was still clawing at my shoulder. I smelled the dank fur, and the smell of blood. I thought I'd take a couple of toes off him. I got my knife open and stabbed, but it went through his toes and into my own shoulder.

"The cat went really wild again. After that, I just sought the territory above his shoulders and stabbed. He went berserk and I just held on as best I could. Somehow, my blade found his throat and I sawed and slashed. Blood was spraying everywhere, mine and his, then he slowed but I held on for a couple more minutes. There seemed no life in him, so I started to let go. He kicked again, in his death throes." Dave relaxed his bear hug, staggered upright and walked a few feet. He turned and threw his knife at the dead lion. "I thought: 'I don't need this again.' " Dave flipped his scalp back onto his skull with a wet 'slap,' and started for help. His right eyeball dangling, face torn, blood dripping from his head and coagulating on his belt, he managed a handful of steps before lying down in the roadway to rest. Then he stumbled to a lumber mill for help. At Port Alice Hospital, surgeon Dr Keith Symon was appalled. "I've seen people before with injuries that bad," he said, "but they were all dead." Dave had 350 staples and 250 sutures put into his head and face, has had bone and skin grafts and a titanium plate and screws inserted into his skull. His right eye still has vision, but the destroyed muscles and scar tissue mean it is virtually useless. "I still have a hate for that cat," he said. "I've cleared the trees back from my property so I can see what's there—we have had three mountain lions killed within 600 yards of my house in the past decade and I never go outside now without my knife, and I wear it in front of me. I've had plenty of nightmares and I'm apprehensive of the bush. I killed that lion, but there are plenty of others. It's still tough to think how hard that cat fought me. They're serial killers, and once he focuses on you, he will keep coming. Well, I survived. I didn't want to be dinner."

The image of Dave, scarred face, black eyepatch, tranquilly looking out across the beautiful forest where he nearly died, is burned into my mind's eye. Sometimes, you take a small part of a story with you for a long, long time.

Falling a Mile

When I interviewed the girl parachutist who survived a horrifying plunge to earth, I came away with the memory of her cool assessment of whether or not she could climb the shrouds of her failed 'chute in mid-air to release the tangle, or whether it was better to…. Well, read what she had to say: "I looked down at my miracle baby and I just cried and cried with joy. My new son, Richard Tanner West, all 7 lbs 13 oz of him, should have died with me the day my parachute failed in a skydive. From more than two miles high, I landed facedown on an asphalt car park at about 50 mph. I shattered my face bones like an eggshell, smashed my teeth, broke my arm and crushed my pelvis, but I survived. So did the two-weeks-old fetus I didn't know I was carrying. So, the day my perfect baby was born last June, I knew he was also a special gift to go with the miracle of my own survival."

Travel agent Shayna West, 22, loves parachuting. Her husband Rick is a professional skydive instructor and that bright October day in 2005, the couple from Republic, Missouri were working towards the 25 jumps that would get Shayna her full skydiving licence. "I'd made ten jumps already, and I was on my sixth solo jump, an Accelerated Free Fall where the instructor stays with you until you pull the ripcord after you've skydived free for a while."

Shayna, whose name means 'beautiful' in Hebrew, had readied for the day and was eager to go, but waited while Rick made several jumps with clients. Finally, it was her turn to climb into the four-seater Cessna 182 and take off from the airfield at Siloam Springs, Arkansas, for the first of the three jumps she hoped to make that day. "I'd spent all my money on a $5,000 pink and purple 'chute – I love pink – but it was smaller and too fast for a novice, so I was using a friend's neon green and blue canopy for my main chute, and had a white reserve 'chute, too. I was wearing one of Rick's jump suits, a blue and purple one, over my pink tee shirt and blue jeans. I had on a black helmet, pink lace-up tennis shoes, pink goggles and a pink backpack rig." The Cessna took 20 minutes to grind up to altitude at 11,000ft, then Rick climbed out of the plane and held onto an exterior strut as instructor and pupil began a carefully-rehearsed routine. When he was satisfied with his stance in the 80 mph slip-stream, he gave Shayna the OK to clamber out. "We'd practiced and practiced on the ground and perfected the freefall routine. I had some jitters, but I wasn't afraid, I was eager to go," said Shayna.

On the wing, the duo began the jump cadence. Shouting to be heard above the slipstream, Shayna called out 'Prop' as she went up on her toes and readied for the jump. 'Up' came next as she teetered, then a shouted 'Down' as she launched and both pupil and instructor simultaneously released their grips and were pulled away from the plane. "There's no roller-coaster stomach-swooping as you go, it's like floating," Shayna explained. "Later as you reach terminal velocity of 120 mph, you can tell you're falling, but at first, it's just a lovely floating feeling." Rick was holding onto Shayna's harness on her right hand side as the couple followed the freefall cadence of checking first the horizon, then the altimeters strapped to their left wrists and then each other, for hand signals. Falling for 45 seconds, Shayna watched the clock hands of her altimeter unwind from 11,000 to 5,000 feet, then it was time to signal Rick that she was about to deploy her main parachute. She used the correct signal, waving her hands over her head to signify: the 'chute is coming out.' Rick let go of her harness. Shayna reached back and with her ungloved hand tugged the release. "There was a jolt, I was sitting there in my harness and I looked up. I asked myself: 'Is it there? Is it square?' The canopy had deployed perfectly, a rectangle of colourful nylon above my head." Rick was above, his orange jump suit silhouetted against the bright blue sky. Then things started to go wrong. Shayna reached for the two toggles that allowed her to steer her canopy by tugging on them to spill air from the umbrella. There was a sharp 'crack' and one of the toggles came loose. Shayna started to spin in growing circles.

"An experienced skydiver would not have been bothered. You can still steer without the toggles, but my first thought was to remember the horror stories the instructors had been telling each other. One had told how he'd heard a sharp crack and found his parachute lines had snapped and he was not being supported. He'd cut his main 'chute loose and deployed his reserve, safety 'chute." Shayna heard the 'snap' with horror. "I still hear it, in my mind," she said. "I thought my parachute lines had snapped and I was falling to my death. I fought the panic. I was flustered, paralyzed for a moment, but not panicked yet. I thought, 'OK, I have 5,000 feet yet, but don't waste any time. I've got a back-up 'chute, I'll use that.'"

She fumbled at the right side of her harness, where a hook and loop fastener held down a red canvas tab—the emergency release for her main parachute. Calmly, Shayna tugged the fastener free, pulled the tab and released her main 'chute to float to the ground without her. Then she reached for the left side of her harness, where a silver 'D' ring would release her back-up canopy. "I wasn't thinking about another safety feature. When I ditched my main 'chute, it automatically tugged my reserve 'chute free without me having to release it." The second canopy, which skydivers call the Guaranteed Open, blossomed above Shayna's head, but a million-to-one accident happened. A slider intended to separate the lines and open the 'chute properly had snagged on a knot caused by tension in the parachute lines and the canopy had not filled properly. One side of the parachute was fluttering, collapsed, and the half-filled canopy was swinging Shayna around in circles as she descended.

The walkie-talkie clipped to Shayna's collar squawked into life. Her controller on the ground saw her spinning like a sycamore seed and was shouting instructions to her. Above her, anguished Rick was calling out the same advice. "They were telling me to pump the brakes! Pump the brakes! " Shayna told me. "They meant to tug the steerer toggles to spill air and make the slider come down so the canopy could re-inflate." Said Shayna. "I looked up and could see the problem, six or eight feet above my head, but however much I pumped and hauled at it, that slider didn't even think about coming down. I told myself, 'Stay calm and focused. Let's try to fix this.' I wasn't scared, it was just 'Oh, shoot, as if there wasn't enough drama already!' Nothing would dislodge that knot, there was too much tension in the line. I was doing 360's, circling around as I fell, and everything seemed to be going in slow motion. I honestly thought about climbing up the line to try to release it, but I reasoned that if I put too much weight on one side of the 'chute, I could collapse the whole thing. I thought I'd be better off riding out what I had, with half a 'chute, rather than having nothing at all and hitting the ground at 120 mph."

Shayna continued her spiralling descent for three long minutes as Rick hovered above, screaming himself hoarse as he desperately tried to help his wife. "I was in despair, I could not believe what I was seeing, watching the girl I love plummeting to her death. I think I was crying, I just do not know what was in my mind, I was crazed," he said. As Shayna approached the ground, a sense of calm washed over her. "I knew I was going to hit. There was nothing I could do to fix it. I told myself, 'I'm going to die.' I wasn't afraid, my life didn't pass before my eyes, anything like that. I'm a religious person and I don't fear dying. I'm afraid of snakes and needles, but my faith has taught me not to fear death. About the last thing I remember was talking to God. I said: 'Lord, I'm coming home. Please don't make it hurt.' I stopped fighting the 'chute. I reasoned that I didn't want my last few seconds to be fighting, I wanted to be at peace." Shayna released the useless steering toggles and instinctively arched her back, hard, to assume the belly-down position of the skydiver. Then, as the G-force of the circles she was describing as she pendulum'ed under her 'chute drained the blood from her brain, she blacked out.

"We estimate she was doing 50 mph when she hit the ground, face down," said Rick. It was probably the only way she could have survived. Not only did Shayna land in the one clear spot in the area, a parking lot sandwiched between power lines, trees, a busy highway and buildings, but impacting unconscious, flat-out and relaxed spread the force through her whole body.

"If I'd landed head down, I'd have been killed. If I'd landed feet first, I'd have been killed. If I'd landed on grass, the infections in my wounds would have killed me." Far above her, Rick's helmet-mounted camera recorded the whole horror. He landed a quarter mile away at the drop zone and raced to his wife. Incredibly, she rolled over and started talking to the rescuers. "Am I alive? Am I dreaming? Am I in heaven?" she wanted to know. When the ambulance arrived, she fought the crew. "I'm fine," she told them. Leave me alone. I don't want any needles!" In hospital, she resisted the doctors until her blood tests came back that afternoon. Shayna was in the ER, strapped down as doctors worked on her wounds. "They told me I was two weeks pregnant, I didn't know, or I wouldn't have jumped. At once, I stopped fighting them. I knew I had to do anything to save my baby," Shayna said.

A team of surgeons worked on Shayna's shattered body. From her eyebrows to her upper jaw, every bone was shattered like an eggshell. It took 15 steel plates to rebuild her face. Five of her top teeth were broken beyond repair; her pelvis was broken in three places, she had fractured bones in her feet and her right leg was smashed. After a month in hospital, Shayna left with her jaw wired shut to let it set accurately, and suffered through painful months of rehab. When the time came, she opted for natural childbirth, without painkillers, though doctors warned the birth could break her once-fractured pelvis. One hour and 11 minutes after she was induced, Shayna gave birth to healthy, 19 inches long Tanner, and 'cried and cried.' "I was waiting for him for so long, it was an awesome day. God saved me, and he saved Tanner, too."

Shayna had one last thing to do to close the circle. Six weeks after Tanner's birth, she left her baby with her mother and climbed into an aircraft. At 10,000 feet she and Rick skydived again. "It was just fine, but I hated being apart from Tanner. All the time, I was fretting for him. He was all I could think of. I haven't skydived since, maybe I will one day when he's old enough to understand that I'm coming back soon. For now, I'm just happy being a mommy. I had my miracle. In fact, I got two for the price of one!"The story went worldwide, a happy ending, feel-good tale that made your fingers tingle as you fell with Shayna, and women's magazines loved it.

Marriage Lines

Then I came across another woman's story that went world wide. No animal attack, no fear of falling, fear of being trapped underground, but certainly a sort of fear of being trapped. This is the tale two intelligent people told me, of their by-the-book marriage that has confounded the critics, and more than a decade later is going very strongly indeed. It's one couple's roadmap to romance, their business plan for matrimony that clarifies what each expects on almost every issue. And I have to say, I really liked this couple, who were charming, droll and patient. Here's their story:

When her first marriage ended after three years, Teresa Garpstas vowed she'd "never let someone tear my heart out again." So when she met twice-divorced Rex LeGalley at a sales meeting and found they were mutually attracted, the detail-oriented computer engineer laid down her meticulous rules for by-the-book love and marriage. "We didn't want to fail again," explained Teresa. "In our first marriages, we didn't communicate properly. Only later do you realize just what someone means by a certain phrase. My first marriage ended when I found to my surprise my husband didn't want children, and I did." The second time around, Teresa took no chances.

During their cautious, 15-month courtship, 30 years old Teresa and Rex,38, drew up a detailed prenuptial agreement that covered all eventualities. They spelled out everything, from how often they'd have sex (three to five times a week) to what kind of petrol they'd buy (Chevron Supreme). Putting it on paper worked. After 15 years of scripted wedlock, the couple happily say their marriage is a success. "We both had cold feet about marrying again, and we wanted no surprises. We attended parenting classes and we read advice books on marriage, together, to discuss things they brought up," said Teresa. "We talked about everything, I took notes and we drew up a blueprint for our lives," she said. Some blueprint. The agreement that started as a budget exercise turned into 16 single-spaced pages that spell out their intentions on everything from finances to family planning. Then, to make it official, they filed the agreement at the local courthouse in Albuquerque, New Mexico before their marriage in July 1995. "Someone there sent a copy to a magazine, who printed excerpts without even calling us, and we found ourselves in the public eye without wanting or trying to get there," said Teresa. "We were ridiculed, we were told you can't regulate life or marriage, we were accused of doing it as a stunt to sell a book and we were asked for advice by about 50 couples, but the agreement was only for us, not for anyone else. Rex is an engineer like me. We're planners. We were both hurt in previous marriages, and we wanted to remarry with our eyes open. It's healthy to see what you are committing to. After all, it's for the rest of your life. You don't want the honeymoon to end and then reality to hit. We made the effort to communicate, to have a strategy and goals and to remove as much of the unknown as possible before we married."

In her first marriage, Teresa confessed, she didn't communicate well. "I was naïve," she said. "We'd talked about children, and said we'd have some, but within a very short time, he was saying no, he didn't want kids. It had never really been addressed properly." When Teresa met Rex, they held wide-ranging discussions. On long car trips, she'd take notes of their opinions and hopes. "Writing it down solidifies things," she explained. "It spells out expectations, it's a foundation and a benchmark." Rex, 48, said: "Today, things couldn't be better. We worked out so many things before we married, we didn't have the transition period so many couple have in the first year of marriage. We decided to prepare, and we did."

Take a look at some of the pre-nup clauses, from the section 'Personal Conduct' "On weekdays, we will turn out the lights by 11.30pm and wake up at 6.30am. When driving, we will stay one car length away from other cars for every 10 mph. We will buy supreme unleaded fuel (Chevron) and won't let the fuel gauge get lower than half a tank." Teresa explained: "Rex hated my tailgating style of driving, so I changed it. As for the fuel, a car runs best on the same fuel after five tanks full. I did once leave my car almost empty, so I filled up and later I filled up his car too, and took him to a Monster Car show." Under 'Sex and Child Care,' the couple specified: "We will engage in healthy sex three to five times per week. Teresa will stay on birth control for two years after we are married and then will try to get pregnant. When both of us are working, Teresa can have only one child. When one parent is free, Teresa can have another child. After the third pregnancy, we will both get sterilized." Said Teresa: "We have two beautiful children, John Walter, 8, and Mary Kathleen, 6. We've decided not to have another child."

By agreement, the duo count to ten when angry, provide 'unconditional love,' and make themselves available for discussion up to 30 minutes a day. They each draw a personal allowance of about $80 a week for haircuts, gifts etc. Rex maintains the outside of the house and Teresa does the laundry and grocery shopping. When their children go to high school, they will be given a six years old car —if they can pay for insurance and fuel. "Upon college graduation, we will buy each child a reasonably-priced car as a present," says the pre-nup. With everything so precisely planned, has the union had any friction? "We have had problems with Rex's two sons from a previous marriage. They're in their early 20s, and when they come here, they don't abide by our rules," said Teresa. "He has to fix that. Also, sometimes, Rex makes comments about my driving!" So, if the pre-nup is broken, what then? "It's our agreement, not a contract. It's not legally binding, but it is LeGalley binding!" joked Teresa. "We've agreed to do what it says. It's up to the offender to put things right. We don't act as policemen for each other, we just wrote down what we wanted from our marriage. It's up to us individually to make it work."

OTHER SPOOKY STORIES

The Psychic Detectives

Crime is a top feeder in the tabloid food chain, and one area of crime-solving that draws readers isn't hard-boiled, flatfoot detectives or know-all, nice-hair TV forensics folk, but psychics who can pull clues from the air.

I accept that many psychics are frauds, and a few are downright criminal, but I've seen the elephant, and there are a very few who seem able to control their psychic talents in a meaningful way. Of that elite, a handful have shown they're capable of switching on some inner vision. They can tune into information that even skeptical police detectives have admitted is useful, accurate and occasionally stunning.

It was no surprise that when these stories started showing up in the Enquirer newsroom, my editor looked at the somnolent figure of the reporter who'd brought in the tale of the Baffling Chair of Death and rudely prodded me awake. "Check this out," he demanded. What follows isn't a stunning revelation of shocking secrets, but it does attempt to tell in some detail what people always ask about the tabloids: "Are those stories really true?" Short answer: well, yes, some of them. The magazines won't give up the space to explain everything fully, and the skeptics may believe it's because they don't have the full facts, but here, for a short time only, and wait, there's more: here's a sampling of the psychic stories I did, unvarnished and complete. Doors to manual, I was arriving in Cupertino, California, heart of Silicon Valley, birthplace of the modern computer and home of Kathlyn 'Kay' Rhea, Navy widow, psychic visionary and future breeder of goats with colored fur. Kay was already well-established in a crime-solving career when Reno, Nevada attorney Larry McNabney needed to track down a vital witness in a murder case. He called on Kay to find April Barber, a friend of the man the client was later convicted of murdering. He hoped to uncover evidence favorable to his client, but it didn't happen that way.

Kay travelled to the attorney's office, talked for a short while, then induced her mental self to visit the murder scene. "Kay told me April was dead," the attorney told me. "She'd been taken into the desert by a man and stabbed a number of times in the back. She told me the body was in a shallow grave in sandy, rugged terrain where two streams came together east of Reno. The site was near a road and a radio tower, near a billboard. She was exactly right. When the body was found, the description matched perfectly." Kay also detailed where April's knife-torn clothes would be found in a garbage can, and how the girl would be found, naked and face-up. Kay told me: "I felt I was in April's mind before she died and during the attack. She was in a car with her murderer, and she knew she was in great danger. Then she was standing by the car. It was dark. I felt thudding blows on my back, under the shoulder blade. There wasn't great pain, just dull thuds, another and another. Suddenly she was dead. Then, I was back in the lawyer's office, drained and feeling hollow inside."

In other cases, Kay described a renegade police captain who killed a woman, describing details as small as his badge, and worked numerous times with a police sketch artist to describe suspects in murders. I'll not spell out chapter and verse here, Kay has that. It's enough to say that almost always when the killer was caught he/she matched the sketches. When a 72 years old man went missing on California's Mount Diablo, Kay psychically saw him descending after topping out his hike. She told the search and rescue organizers:

"He's fallen into a ravine below a big rock and was sitting with his back to a tree. There was a yellow tag next to him. The place had an echo, so there were walls near him, not open space. He has brush scratches on his face and he'd lost his glasses and his backpack. You could see city lights from the big rock above him and a green helicopter had passed overhead."

The searchers had been out for five days with dogs, choppers and on horseback, and thought the man must have walked out of the area. They also said they had no green helicopters, but later corrected themselves. One had joined the search that day. The next morning, they found the man, dead, sitting slumped as Kay had described him. His face was scratched by brush, the ravine echoed, his eyeglasses were lost, as was his backpack. Next to him was a yellow tag from the pack, torn off in the fall. "It was an exact, chilling description," said sheriff's rescue dog handler Judy Robb.

Over the years, as I worked stories with Kay and other psychics, a pattern emerged. The psychic seemed to become one with the missing person, experiencing what they saw and felt. Greta Alexander, of Delevan, Illinois got her powers after being hit by a lightning bolt. When Mary Cousett went missing, police charged her boyfriend with her murder, but were frustrated in their search for Mary's body, so called in the psychic they knew might be able to help. Great ran her hand over a map and told the police where to look. They'd find the body in this area—which the cops had already searched—with the head and a foot separated from the body. A man with a 'bad hand' would be involved in the recovery, as would the letter 'S' be important. The body was found where Alexander indicated, the skull was five feet from the trunk and the left foot was missing. The name of the man who found the corpse began with an 'S' and his left hand was damaged in an accident—all as Alexander predicted.

Ghost Tourists

The cases were impressive and made great copy, but privately I liked the ghost stories best. I'd been the judge of a ghost story contest, once, for Enquirer readers who'd sent us their tales of being spooked by the dead, and had the pleasant task of arranging a three-week ghost tour of Europe for the winners, as their handsome prize. The outline of the trip was simple enough: take the winners and photographer John T. Miller, a wonderful wild man who'd been my co-conspirator on a number of adventures.

I sketched out the trip: the UK first, then France, Italy and Germany. I called Hilton Hotels' publicity people and arranged a tiny discount so I could tell the accounts people that's where we should stay, and arranged flights, a couple of TV appearances and ground transport. The winners were chosen: a 60-something grandmother and feed store owner from West Virginia; a Nebraska housewife (who brought her husband along for the first half of the trip); a 40-ish blonde from Miami; and an Italian-American from New York who admired Benedict Arnold. Finally, worst for last, there was a large-headed, mid-30s New Jerseyite I privately called Tweety Bird who should have been strangled at birth, and that was how I thought of him on good days.

We all met in a lounge at Miami airport a few hours before our London flight. Tweety Bird hadn't brought his passport. I'd told the group to ensure they had passports, told them they would not need visas. Tweety understood that to mean he must have a passport, but didn't need to bring it, as we were travelling in a group. I arranged for his documents to be Fed Ex'ed overnight to the airport hotel, and he followed us, 24 hours later. It was an omen, as he was invariably 40 minutes late to every appointment for the next three weeks.

Other than Tweety's antics, the trip was splendid. We visited haunted sites and met parapsychologists, drank with the locals and made ghost hunting fun. We started at Salisbury Hall, near St Albans, England, where owner Walter Goldsmith, a former RAF fighter pilot, showed us around his 15th century manor house, built on the ruins of a Norman motte and bailey. "We believe that the laughing ghost of Nell Gwynne, the orange-seller mistress of King Charles II, still haunts this house," he said. The place was one of the Merry Monarch's favorite country retreats, and Nell gave birth there, in a cottage by the moat, to the king's bastard. Charles was riding by when the high-spirited Nell jokingly held her baby out of the window and threatened to throw him in the moat. "The king is supposed to have called out: 'By God, Nellie, take care of.... my young Duke of St Albans!' bestowing the title as fast as his eye could light on the church spire of the town," said Goldsmith. "All we know is that we have heard her laughter, in daylight as well as at night, and it is a pleasing, lovely sound." The old hall has other ghosts, one of them tragic. Goldsmith told how he and every member of his family had heard the sounds of a man's dragging footsteps going along a corridor and through a wall where there was once a door. History holds the story of a wounded Royalist who escaped the Parliamentary forces after the battle of St Albans, and took refuge at Salisbury Hall. "He was so despairing and unwilling to be captured, maybe to be cruelly executed, he shot himself with his own horse pistol," said Goldsmith. "When alterations were made to that part of the house, we found an old door with a heavy lock. It was jammed. Jammed by the ball of a heavy, horse pistol....."

In York, not too far from the home of the Baffling Chair of Death that led to my involvement in these adventures, we met one of the most credible witnesses to a ghostly sighting you could wish for, and his story sent chills up our spines. Police constable Harry Martindale is a stalwart of the British police force. Six feet four inches tall, and 250 lbs of prime English beef, he has hands like shovels, a big man's confidence and a careful, ponderous manner. Every instinct tells you: this is no fey hysteric, he's solid, stolid, not prone to flights of imagination, but the story he told was stunning. Before he joined York's Finest, Martindale was a 20 years old heating engineer called in to work on the pipes that ran through the cellar of the town's medieval Treasurer's House. He'd planted his stepladder in the beaten earth floor and was working on the overhead pipes when a noise caused him to turn his head. "I heard a sort of tinny bugle call," he told me as we visited the damp, ancient basement. "I looked around and a smallish soldier wearing a kilt and carrying a sort of trumpet came out of that wall over there. He ignored me and shuffled diagonally across the cellar towards the opposite wall. Before he had time to disappear, another soldier on a ragged-looking pony followed him. I fell from my ladder and cowered in the corner as about 14 or 16 more men, in double file, marched across the cellar. Not one looked my way, they all ignored me."

The oddest thing Martindale realized, was that the spirit soldiers were marching thigh-deep in the floor. Only at one spot, where someone had dug away part of the floor, could he see their feet. Martindale described the phantom soldiers in detail to our enthralled group. They had small round shields and wore hand-dyed woolen kilts of streaky green. The sandals they were wearing had knee-high thongs. They carried an assortment of weapons from short stabbing swords to throwing spears, and most wore leather helmets. The horseback rider had a few plumes on his crested helmet, and the trumpeter's instrument was long and curving and seemed to be made of brass.

Martindale's overall impression of the soldiers was that they were 'seedy.' "They sort of shuffled along dispiritedly. I reckoned they were Roman soldiers, but they didn't look like I'd have imagined, like Charlton Heston in polished armor." For several minutes after the last soldier had vanished through the wall, Martindale remained crouched in his corner, then quickly got out of the cellar and up into daylight. It took him several days to consider the apparition before he confided it to a local historian, who had the wit to write everything down. Back in the cellar, the historian pointed out that the hole had been dug by a couple of archeologists who were excavating the old road through the Roman city of Eboracum, England's then second-largest settlement, now called York. The friendly historian made Martindale frown, though. He told him he must have been mistaken about something he saw: the Roman infantry did not use round shields.

"I knew what I saw," said Martindale. "There was no question. These long-ago soldiers had round shields." The report of the sighting was filed away, Martindale became a police officer, the story became a memory. Seven years later, two archeologists were working in the same cellar when the exact apparition marched through again. The shaken researchers asked questions, Martindale's account was turned up, the stories were matched in every detail, including the round targs carried by the ghostly troop. The archeologists, whose names I never could track down, did more research, and the jigsaw became a little more complete. The Emperor Hadrian's Sixth Legion ('The Victorious') had been in Britain so long it was renamed Britannicus, but it was pulled back from the misty north and out of York late in the fourth century, as the Roman Empire crumbled. The Sixth had been reinforced with native auxiliaries, possibly from the border regions of England, and they carried small round shields.

Martindale took the news with typical phlegm. "I believe I saw the ghosts of a troop of those auxiliaries marching out on some hopeless foray in which they were all to die. They were marching on that Roman road and they knew they would not be coming back."

Nearly two millennia after those soldiers marched out of their camp, they seem still to be trudging through time. Like many ghost stories, it's not proof, but it is compelling and it fits typical elements of the better-documented ghost anecdotes, of someone who died in emotional circumstances, maybe of anger, despair or fear that survives as a sort of psychic echo. This story had extra elements not often found in ghostly reports: sound, color and an undeniably credible witness.

Our bemused group moved on, after a TV talk show appearance on which they had little to say, followed by a tense flight in a private plane with no toilet. That discomfort prepped everyone nicely for our visit to the Museum of Purgatory, in Rome. The museum is just a few hundred yards from the Vatican itself, inside the Church of the Sacred Heart for the Intercession for Dead Souls. That's the Chiesa de Sacro Cuore del Suffragio, on Lungotevere. The place offers an impressive ossuary and a one-room 'museum' which it cheerfully admits is small: the Piccolo Museo delle Anime del Purgatorio. The new, old evidence proudly shown to us by Father Antonio Giorgi were hand and fingerprints burned into clothing, wood and prayer books. The burns, Father Giorgi assured us, were the handprints of long-dead people returned from the grave to plead for prayers to help them escape purgatory. "The authenticity is beyond doubt," he told us.

Photographer Miller raised an eyebrow at me and I agreed. The burn marks looked a bit like Victorian pokerwork. I didn't really expect to see whorls, loops and arches, but I'd hoped for something shaped more like, well, a hand. Father Giorgi presented the evidence, much of it a century old. One woman, Margarette Schaffner, from Baden Wurttemberg, claimed to have spent 68 years in contact with the dead and had handprints burned into her clothes five times. In Lublin, Poland, a handprint was burned into a courtroom table where a woman who felt she wasn't getting fair play asked: "Will it be better to get justice from the Devil himself?" Maria Zaganti, of Rimini, Italy, got three fingerprints burned into her prayer book. She said they came from the former parish priest, Fr Palmira Rastelli, who'd been dead for 26 years and wanted out of Purgatory, though he never said why he was there in the first place. Our ghost story winners liked it, though, and even the Miami blonde whose hand I'd painfully trapped in a car door smiled at me. The Piccolo Museo offered something that wasn't the best evidence for life after death, but it was typical of what's on offer, and I include it as evidence of, well, something. Maybe someone with religious fervor can elevate their own temperature enough to burn fabric, or maybe it was just some mischief-maker with a red hot poker.

The next day, matters with our own private mischief maker came to a head. Tweety Bird's late-for-everything antics made me boil over. We'd arranged a group photo-call in the ruins of the Forum, and everyone showed on time, except Tweety Bird. We couldn't do the pics without him, and he knew it. After waiting for almost an hour at the rendezvous, John and I went hunting for him. I found the clown crouching behind a wall, hiding from us. It was too much. I took Tweety by the throat and shook him into submission. We did the pictures, and back at the hotel—where he'd run up a fortune in pay-per-view TV charges and about six room service meals every day—gave him his air tickets. 'You miss the bus, you find your own way back to Jersey.' He never missed an appointment after that, unfortunately.

The USAF's Haunted Bomber

After that tour of historical hauntings, it was a contrast to move into the modern era and to speak to witnesses in sunny California about ghosts from the recent past. Better yet, they were no-nonsense military men, eyewitnesses who described their experiences without hysteria, but certainly with conviction.

Captain Douglas DeWitt was curator of the museum at Castle Air Force Base near Merced and as we stood in blazing sunlight by the gleaming bomber, he had a powerful story to tell about a Boeing B-29 Superfortress his aircraftsmen were restoring. "We think a long-dead flier still protects his bomber," he said. "We have logged more than 40 supernatural events around it. I myself have seen a shimmering figure in the pilot's seat, I called out the guard, but the still-padlocked plane was empty. We don't know what it is, We know it isn't a hoax. These are genuine events and we cannot rule out that a ghost is causing them." 'Razin' Hell' was the name painted on the nose of the bomber, but its history was complicated. The aircraft was reconstructed from three Superfortresses salvaged from the US Naval Ordnance test range at China Lake, 200 miles south of the central California museum. The mechanics scoured the site, where planes that took the war across the Pacific have been used for decades for naval gunners' target practise.

The museum staff took a wing from one plane, a tailplane from another and the fuselage from a third, enough parts to create a restored whole bomber. "Many of the planes had been so destroyed the squadron and other markings were indecipherable," said Capt DeWitt, "but the recovery crew found a handwritten note in the mid-upper gun turret of the plane which had yielded the tail unit which said 'Bouncing Betty,' Okinawa 1944-45.' " Back at the museum, mechanics building the composite bomber started experiencing uncanny events. Tool boxes as heavy as 60 lbs were moved when there was nobody but the mechanic in the aircraft. A 50 lbs box of rivets moved 10ft as a startled mechanic watched. Two people reported being tapped or feeling a friendly hand on their shoulder when they were in the cockpit and almost all reported having a sense of being watched as they worked. Sgt Rickey Davidson soberly told of a pressurized bulkhead door with bent hinges. "I had to lift and apply considerable force to open it, and it latched shut very firmly, but once, when I was working about 15 feet away, the door opened, then closed. I shook my head, and went to close it. I was working with one other mechanic and we watched as the door opened and closed itself a second time. I tried to swing it open, but had to lift it with quite a bit of force, unlatch it, then open it. I made sure the damn door was locked tight. When I went forward, the goddam door swung open a third time, then clicked shut. We just got the hell out. It really shook me. There was no one else on that ship, and someone can't sneak around a B29 without you knowing!"

At other times, the sergeant's toolbox snapped shut—something that had never happened in 15 years "and should never be possible." Staff Sergeant Robert Klaus found a 14 lbs box of rivets he'd left on the pilot's seat was moved 10 feet away, when nobody was near.

Other mechanics reported that tools or wrenches they'd left on the pilot's seat were moved mysteriously, as was Klaus' toolbox, which 'walked' down to the bombsight ten feet away. "It was an awkward place to put a big heavy thing like that, and there was nobody up that end of the ship to do it," said Klaus.

Two sergeants were working on the wing one evening when all the landing lights came on, said Capt DeWitt. "It flooded the area with light, and they were very badly shaken and ran to call security forces. The plane was in a secure area, MPs and security people combed the place, but nobody was there. We all saw the lights, landing lights, navigation lights, all blazing. What's uncanny is: there was no way the lights could work. They had no batteries, no bulbs and most of the wiring was ripped out when the planes were cannibalized. I've had calls from civilians driving by outside the fences, to report that its lights were on, yet we have never had lights on the plane!" The bomber sat in full view of the Captain's office window and twice, at dusk he saw a man-like shadow sitting in the pilot's seat. "The figure was silhouetted against the lights behind. It was not rock-steady, but shimmering slightly around the edges." Each time, DeWitt called out the base MPs and ran to catch the 'intruder'. Each time, he and the guards found nobody, and the plane was still padlocked, chained, and empty. "We've got photographs taken inside the plane that show odd lights and shapes our photo analysts couldn't explain. A TV crew who spent the night in the bomber fell mysteriously ill after hearing a man's voice warning them: 'Don't use this radio!' The baffled restorers even called in a psychic to try to find out what or who was haunting the old plane. She held a séance, and turned up the name Arthur Pryer, who said he was a waist gunner. USAF records in Alabama and San Francisco that might have tracked him were destroyed in a blaze, and the museum staff found themselves stymied. After the air base was decommissioned, a private group took over the museum, but the old Superfortress still stands in the California sunshine, where the USAF personnel still throw a salute to their long-gone comrades. "We think there's an old crewman still protecting his ship," said DeWitt, simply.

Testimony of Past Lives

The pilot's seat in that old Superfortress was a friendly one, unlike the Baffling Chair of Death, and I found it wasn't unusual. My work for the Enquirer caused me to uncover other mysterious examples of unbreakable loyalties that seem to have defeated the grave. National Enquirer story number 643912T took me to Bathford, in England's beautiful west country, to meet a psychiatrist with a puzzling tale to tell. Dr Arthur Guirdham had a glittering resume that included honors from Oxford, an exhibition scholarship at Charing Cross Hospital, a Royal Medical Psychiatric Association medal and position as senior consultant to the Bath Clinical Area, where he was engaged on an intriguing research project. He was documenting evidence of reincarnation.

It started when a housewife who went to him as a patient recounted dreams and incidents which had plagued her for years. They were filled with intriguing details of people, places and events from a life 700 years ago. The doctor took notes and wondered about the matter, until a second patient, a stranger to the first, began telling him of similar dreams. Guirdham began collecting specifics from the women. In time, he had 70 names, dozens of descriptions, and specifics of distances, places and customs. He began a 15 year odyssey and made a dozen trips to France to verify the dreams. It all fitted. What the women, a housewife and a businesswoman, neither of whom had ever been abroad, were recounting was life as members of the heretic Cathar sect of the Catholic Church in 13th century France. The doctor and researchers he employed searched through medieval manuscripts written in Latin and French that was arcane even to scholars, and confirmed the stories the women were telling. "They recounted their own deaths by burning at the stake, they recalled details of clothing that historians insisted were wrong but later found were accurate," Dr Guirdham told me. "They insisted that the Cathar priests wore dark blue cassocks. For centuries, historians believed the garments were black, but when we checked the contemporary records, the women were right!"

"They accurately drew long-forgotten details of the interior of the castles of Mazerolles and Montsegur, which they had never seen. They correctly sketched religious symbols used by the heretic sect and mentioned that one priest wore his ring on his thumb, which is just what the medieval practice was. They recounted details that only a specialist scholar of the period could know, and offered names and details even the scholar could not know until he had researched them in manuscripts that have laid unopened for hundreds of years." Names like Sicard and Guirard D'Adalo and De Levis surfaced. "They were linked," said the housewife. When Cathar scholar Jean Duvernoy looked into the heretic trial records of the French Inquisition, he found that the Seigneur De Levis had three servants who were brothers. Their names were Sicard, Gaucerand and Guirard D'Adalo. Two of them died during the siege of the castle of Montsegur, the last stronghold of the Cathars.

One of the women told a dramatic dream of her death, at a place she described so closely Guirdham and his researchers could identify it as Montsegur. There, on March 16th 1244, more than 200 captured Cathars chose to be burned alive rather than renounce their faith. "We all walked barefoot through the streets towards a square where they had prepared a pile of sticks all ready to set alight," the 20th century patient told her doctor. "We sang canticles as we walked. There were several monks singing hymns and praying. You should pray to God when you're dying, if you can pray when you're in agony, but in my dream, I thought of Roger, and how dearly I loved him. I didn't know that when you're burned to death you'd bleed. I thought the blood would dry up in the terrible heat, but it was dripping and hissing in the flames. The worst part was my eyes. I was going blind. I tried to close my eyelids but they'd been burned off and now those flames were going to pluck my eyes out. Then I began to feel cold. I wasn't burning, I was freezing to death and I started to laugh." Dr Guirdham's businesswoman subject told of seeing a massacre when a cross-shaped gibbet on which dozens of people were being hanged, collapsed. "The poor people were slaughtered, cut down by the soldiers," she told the therapist. "I was astonished to discover that there was exactly such an incident in May 1211, at Lavaur, when Simon de Montfort hanged 80 Cathar knights. The account was in the Bibliotheque Nationale de France for the archives of Toulouse, and it told how the gibbet collapsed and the knights were put to the sword by soldiers," said Guirdham. The doctor told me: "I learned to read medieval French so I could look through those ancient depositions myself. The Inquisitors worked with ant-like industry and recorded details of only peripheral interest—names of servants or soldiers, for example—which were invaluable in my research. These women had knowledge they should not have had, and relayed accurate information whose source we do not understand!"

A Town Reincarnated?

Those two unnamed Englishwomen did not claim to know each other in their past lives, but another group of believers in reincarnation told me that they certainly did.

I drove to Lake Elsinore, California, on a day of blistering heat, but what I heard was enough to send chills down my backbone, and the story is ongoing today. Dozens of residents of Lake Elsinore have accurately described places, people and details of lives they say they lived 3,000 miles and 150 years distant, in Millboro, Virginia, during the American Civil War. The past-life bonds came to light in the 1990s, when 34 years old Maureen Williamson went to psychotherapist Dr Marge Rieder, after a failed marriage. Under hypnosis, Williamson turned up odd memories. She was, she said, Becky Ashcroft, wife of John, and she lived in Millboro, a town with sulfur-smelling hot springs like Lake Elsinore's. "I described how I was strangled by my husband for having an affair with a Confederate spy. Later I said to myself: 'This is impossible. It can't be real!'

Dr Rieder was intrigued enough to do some research. There is a Millboro, Va., the town constable in the 1860s was John Daniel Ashcroft and the town has hot springs. Like Dorothy awakening in the 'Wizard of Oz' and pointing out the farmhands as the Tin Man, Cowardly Lion and Scarecrow, writer Williamson started seeing other 1860s Millboro people in her 21st century town. Security officer Joe Nazarowski, 44, was skeptical when Williamson said he'd been her past-life lover, but agreed to hypnosis if it would help him stop smoking. Under the influence, he claimed to have been Charles E. Patterson, an 1861 West Point graduate with George Custer. He said he'd been wounded at the battle of Shiloh, which he called by its contemporary name of Pittsburgh Landing. He had become a grey-coat spy and his mission was to prepare Millboro's railroad tunnels for destruction in case Union troops took the town.

Dr Rieder found there was a Charles E Patterson in West Point's class of 1861,who was injured at Shiloh, fighting for the Confederacy, before he disappeared. Joe was down to earth, practical, not fey at all when I interviewed him. He had no idea what was happening, he knew only what he'd revealed under hypnosis. Dr Rieder decided she'd best visit Millboro, to uncover more, verifiable details. Joe detailed the shot holes he'd made in the railroad tunnel, sketching their placement, 14 inches deep, every 30 feet in a tunnel a continent away, in a place he said he'd never visited. Dr Rieder and several of her subjects found the town as they had described it. They even found the shot holes Nazarowski said he'd placed more than a century ago in a now-disused railroad tunnel.

Then, more and more people began to surface with odd links and knowledge of the past. A firefighter said he'd been William O Winston, Union spy and failed West Pointer, who'd written to Jefferson Davis for an officer's commission. Archivists at the military academy confirmed Winston's existence and that he had failed to graduate. Then they found his June 19, 1861 letter to Davis, and said it seemed he had gone on to become a spy for the Union.

The group stunned Millboro locals by pinpointing three previously-undiscovered chambers made by Indians and by providing them with minutiae like the name of the town's commissary officer in 1862, John Orr. That was information Millboro historian Richard Armstrong said he'd searched for years to uncover. But reliving the past wasn't always easy. Williamson, visiting Millboro, couldn't bring herself to visit Becky's grave and felt she'd shared the long-dead woman's fears and grief. "We might never have solid proof we have lived before, but I am content knowing who I am," she said. "We have uncovered a mystery."

CRIME AND ME

JonBenet, OJ and Drug Wars

The Enquirer was originally based on Reader's Digest, and worked to a version of that publication's formulaic mix of stories, so reporters at the Enq tended to work by category, too. Celebrity stories, as I've said, are a big part of the tabloids, but I'm a reluctant celebrity reporter, even though I've worked for all of the gossip sheets: Enquirer, Globe, Star, Examiner and the late Weekly World News, which was affectionately known as The Wacky. Instead, my niche has been mostly in the non-celeb categories of crime, occult and human interest.

Crime stories are big-selling eye-catchers at the supermarket checkouts, and I've had a hand in some iconic stories. There was JonBenet Ramsey, the little beauty queen murdered in her home, and well I remember the locals in Boulder, Colorado, harassing us media to show support for their admired local man, John Ramsey. That case, reopened in 2009, is still unsolved, after a dozen libel actions involving $260 million. The Ramseys sued the tabloids and other media, and authors and the Ramseys' housekeeper sued them in return. Then there was the OJ Simpson murder case, when, in an only-in California coincidence, a onetime Enquirer reporter showed up in court to testify. He was a neighbor who'd heard the thing happening. After the dust settled, I was then called on to crank out the first couple of chapters of an instant book about OJ, and given two days to do it, and that included visiting the crime-wracked Hunters Point region of San Francisco where OJ grew up.

Even more dangerous was covering the Mexican drug wars, where just being a visiting journo in Tijuana or Acapulco was dodgy for your health. It didn't take long to recognize the silk-shirted young men in designer jeans and lizard-skin cowboy boots as dangerous and often coke-fueled pistoleros unafraid to shoot you for any imagined insult, or simply for being in the wrong place, asking the wrong questions. Another time, I had the experience of interviewing Mistress Jill, a tiny black East Orange, New Jersey, dominatrix who counted David Berkowitz, the 'Son of Sam,' killer, among her clients. I took careful notes while her favorite 'slave' knelt humbly in the corner. I was in the scrum in Honolulu for an interview with the wife of John Lennon's killer, Mark David Chapman, I followed the trail of air pirate D.B. Cooper and chronicled serial killers like 'Bind Torture Kill' madman Dennis Rader and woman-hating Green River murderer Gary Ridgway. I've interviewed criminals and their victims, jobs which took me inside Folsom, San Quentin and other forbidding prisons, places which scared me into staying law-abiding. But when I go back to the 'people ask me what's the ... worst/best/most important' line, I have to admit that some crime stories I've done impressed me deeply. One, like the murderer himself, stands head and shoulders above the crowd.

Mafia Hit Man

Richard Kuklinski was The Ice Man, a killing machine and cold-blooded lone-wolf executioner who claimed more than 100 victims. A big man at 6ft 4ins and 270 lbs, Kuklinski led an outwardly blameless life in suburbia with his wife and three children, but secretly worked for the Gambino mob in New Jersey, as an enforcer. He strangled, shot, clubbed, poisoned, bombed and stabbed his way into infamy, getting his nickname because he kept a body in a Mister Softee ice cream truck's freezer for two years to mask the date of death. He blew up one victim with a grenade, he suffocated a chemist who irritated him by stuffing him headfirst into a barrel of fast-setting cement. He even killed the associates who taught him his deadly trade. Nobody was exempt. After feared hit man Roy DeMeo beat Kuklinski for late loan repayments, the Ice Man paid him back in bullets. He left DeMeo's body in the trunk of his car, a chandelier on his chest. "So he could rest in peace," said the Ice Man, sarcastically. His favorite technique was to load a small spray bottle with cyanide solution. He'd spray it in his target's face as he passed him in the street. The Ice Man would cover his own mouth, pretending to sneeze into his handkerchief. The victim inhaled the poison and was dying as he hit the ground. Fifteen seconds after being sprayed, the guy was dead.

Kuklinski, who would be given four life sentences totaling 120 years, started his murderous career young. He clubbed a schoolyard bully to death with a length of wood when he was just 14. He wasn't caught, and he killed again as a teenager, during a pool hall fight. For nearly 40 years, he continued to kill, but his criminal record showed just one conviction, for writing a bad check. The Ice Man claimed he took no pleasure in killing, and did it strictly for money or self-protection, and he had a side business running a car theft ring. His usual MO was to offer stolen goods, and when the mark showed up with the money, Kuklinski would kill him for the cash, varying his techniques so cops wouldn't see a pattern. He wired one victim's car seat with a bomb; he threw another man out of a 14th-floor window and he blew up a third with explosives attached to a remote-controlled toy car he steered under the victim's car.

He liked executing victims with a .22 bullet to the back of the head. "It's neater," he explained. "The bullet stays in the skull and doesn't exit." Kuklinski killed with baseball bats, an ice pick and a garrotte, but he favored poison. "You mix cyanide with gravy or ketchup if you put it in food," he explained. "It hides the powder and the bitter-almond taste." He devised his cyanide spray technique, then coldly tested on an innocent stranger. "I did it on a busy street where they thought the guy had a heart attack," Kuklinski told the undercover cop who arrested him. "I walked right up to him, made like I was sneezing into my handkerchief to protect myself and sprayed him right in the face." The man died in seconds, as

Kuklinski strolled away. He was pleased with the "neat, no-mess" technique that sometimes fooled autopsy doctors, and he used it often.

A pharmacist angered the Iceman by bugging him for stolen drugs, so Kuklinski robbed and killed the man, put his body in a 55-gallon drum filled with concrete, then positioned the drum near his favorite hotdog stand. "I went back there for months. I'd eat a couple hotdogs with sauerkraut and a Coke and look at the drum. It was like visiting the guy," he said. The Ice Man also admitted whacking Peter Calabro, a former NYPD detective suspected of drowning his wife Carmella. The detective should have thought twice. His Italian wife had crime family links. They took out a contract on the cop, and gave it to Kuklinski. The Ice Man waited behind a parked car for Calabro to drive by and blasted him twice with a shotgun. "As he's going by, I fire," Kuklinski later told a TV crew. "I never knew the man, what he looked like or what his job was."

Robert Prongay, the mafioso mentor who helped Kuklinski develop his deadly cyanide spraying technique, helpfully let Kuklinski keep in the freezer of one of his ice cream trucks the body of a businessman the Ice Man had robbed of $100,000. Investigators who examined the corpse after it was dumped in a wood two years later were baffled. Louis Masgay had been missing for months, his body wasn't decomposed, and the heart was frozen solid. Kuklinski exulted to Prongay that the cops would never be able to solve the murder, but Prongay pointed out: "I know where you live." It was a fatal error. Prongay's bullet-riddled body was found hanging out of the ice cream truck. "He threatened me," Kuklinski explained later. The Ice Man even whacked two of his own underlings in his burglary ring. He poisoned Gary Smith, then strangled him with a lamp cord because Smith wanted to go straight. Dan Deppner was there when the Ice Man killed Smith, so Kuklinski poisoned him, too. He wanted no witnesses.

Police investigating a theft ring stumbled across the murders, and the killings caused the Ice Man's meltdown. An undercover cop recalled that Kuklinski asked him to get cyanide. "I need to take care of a couple of rats," he said. The cop taped the killer's boasts of murders, and set up a sting to catch him. The Ice Man was arrested outside his house and, faced with a mass of evidence, confessed to killings he'd done, and ratted out a former Mafia colleague, jailed mobster Sammy Gravano, who himself has admitted murdering 19 people. Kuklinski didn't bother to keep quiet, he knew he was going down, and he didn't care if he made matters worse for his onetime fellow mobsters. In all, the Ice Man claimed more than 100 killings and the cops have confirmed details of 34 of them. Kuklinski shrugged off the huge numbers in a phone interview shortly before he was apparently poisoned in Trenton State Prison, New Jersey. "I only killed men, and they were all involved in criminal deals, so what's the harm?" he told me. The police think he stowed away millions in a Swiss account—he had an air ticket to Switzerland when he was arrested. But, typical of the stone-cold killer, the ticket was for one. The Ice Man didn't plan to take his wife or family with him.

Crime Lord on the Run

At the other end of the scale, another wanted killer would only travel en famille. He killed for pleasure and is noted for his intelligence, and at the end of the first decade of the 21st century, he's still on the loose. James 'Whitey' Bulger is an armed, dangerous killer wanted for 19 murders. He has a million dollar FBI Most Wanted reward on his head, and he's probably living quietly somewhere in the British Isles. The missing mobster who's the model for Jack Nicholson's character in 'The Departed' has been on the run for so long, critics are questioning if the Fibbies even want to catch him. They say that the task force bosses keep getting promoted for not finding him. "The crux of the matter is that the FBI spent decades protecting Whitey," an investigator explained to me. "It might be embarrassing now to hear what he has to say about them. He was their prized Top Echelon informant, and he used the feds to break the Italian Mafia in Boston so his Irish gang could take over. In turn, the feds protected him. They didn't just keep him out of prison, they even turned a blind eye to murder. They tipped him off to snitches who were spying on him so he could whack them. When the state police, the Boston police or the Drug Enforcement Agency bloodhounds got close, Whitey's FBI handlers dropped a dime in a pay phone slot and he vanished. He's stayed uncaught for 12 years, and on their current record, the FBI look like they'll never haul him in. The fact is, there's so much known about Whitey any observant acquaintance could identify and catch him!"

Bulger, 81, has been indicted for 17 murders and his former henchman says he admitted to 18 others, including members of his own gang whom he ratted out to rival mobsters. The crime lord who got the FBI to protect him began as a rent boy in Boston bars. Next, he did nine years for bank robberies, including a spell in Alcatraz that might have turned his brain. "He said while he was on The Rock he was a guinea pig in CIA experiments with truth serum and LSD," said the investigator. "After he got out, he said he found murder to be a great stress reliever. One FBI profiler warned the agency not to employ him, because he was a psychopath."

In Boston, Bulger got mobbed up with Howie Winter's gang and relieved his stresses on the Patriarca crime family, whacking some, and turning others over to the FBI. Bulger's crimes went mostly unreported, partly because of an incident when Boston Herald reporter Paul Corsetti began investigating them. In a bar, a stranger told the journo: "I'm Jimmy Bulger and I kill people." Then he read out Corsetti's address, car details and the name of his young daughter's day care. Corsetti started wearing a .38 revolver to work, and stories about Bulger suddenly omitted his crimes and instead concerned his donations to the poor. The FBI didn't care. They were getting good information from Whitey, who was using them to clean up his rivals. But they went too far in the case of John McIntyre, ratting him out and causing his death.

The Irish-American McIntyre was involved in a 1984 scheme to smuggle seven tons of guns and ammo into Ireland for the Irish Republican Army. The ship was intercepted and searched. To save his skin, McIntyre coughed that Bulger had $14 million worth of marijuana on another cargo boat. The FBI leaked to Bulger who'd grassed him out, and Whitey personally dealt with it. Lured to the killing ground, McIntyre was bound and interrogated, then Whitey tried to garrotte him. The ship's rope he tried to use was too thick, so Whitey pulled out a MAC-10 machine pistol. "Would you like one in the head?" he asked. "Yes please," said McIntyre, unflinching.

It was Whitey's second killing in that cellar and it would not be his last. He'd executed bank robber Bucky Barrett there for not paying protection money, shooting him through the back of the head; and it was there that he strangled stripper Debbie Hussey, 26, with his bare hands. "She was causing trouble," he told associates.

Whitey got away with his killings because, he boasted, he was helping the feds bust other criminals, and he had six FBI agents in his corner. In 2006, a court awarded the relatives of John McIntyre more than $3 million, as compensation for the FBI 'mishandling' of Whitey that led to McIntyre's murder. One of Whitey's rogue FBI men was Special Agent John Connolly, who eventually got 10 years for obstruction of justice. Another agent, Paul Rico died in jail after being charged in 2004 of complicity in a Bulger murder. "During the time he was an FBI informant, Whitey killed at least 11 people," said a Boston police source. "There was a millionaire in Tulsa who suspected Whitey and his crew were skimming from his business; there was a man who happened to be giving a lift home to someone on Whitey's hit list; there were three people who were cooperating with the FBI against him and two women he thought of as threats. One of them was Debra Davis, his partner's girlfriend, who made the mistake of saying she was leaving for another man. Like several other Bulger victims, she knew too much. She had to go." In 1995, state police and the DEA built a racketeering case against Bulger and secretly obtained warrants for him, his partner Steve 'The Rifleman' Flemmi and reputed mafia capo Francis 'Cadillac Frank' Salemme. The Drug Enforcement Agency needed just one day to find and catch Flemmi. They 'cuffed him while they held a gun to his head. Salemme was quickly captured, too, hiding out in Florida. The FBI had the job of arresting Whitey. They told the state cops: "We have him in pocket." There was a hole in that pocket, and some question if the FBI really wanted to sew it up. Whitey was driving back to Boston from New Orleans with his longtime girlfriend when he got a pager alert of the warrant for him. He did a 180 degree turn and holed up for a few days.

He was ready for a life on the run, and the pager green-lighted it. Whitey had an Irish passport, plus fake driver's licences from at least three states. He had offshore bank accounts and several stashes in safe deposit boxes of 'significant' amounts of readies, including one bundle of $1.9 million from a lottery ticket he'd heisted from an unfortunate winner. He left nothing for the FBI investigators but a cold trail.

What's known is that Whitey wears a knife strapped to his ankle, and a waist pouch containing a second, pearl-handed knife and a bundle of crisp high-denomination notes. When he bought a new car the FBI got a tip about his previous vehicle, in which he and his girlfriend had driven 65,000 miles in 18 months. The feds dropped the ball, and didn't bother to check out the used car. Word filtered down to local cops, who three weeks later found Whitey's DNA on a bloody sticking plaster under the seat. Alongside it was a flyer for an Irish festival in Texas that had been held just days before. It looked as if the luck of the Irish had held again, and they'd missed Whitey by two days. Early in 2007, in Ireland's remote Connemara, the Gardai thought they'd caught Whitey, but it was just a looka-like. Since he went on the lam, Whitey has rented houses in Selden, New York; Gulfport, Mississippi, and Grand Isle, Louisiana, where he was an adopted 'grandfather' to a local family. He has also been back in Boston, phoning from there to the FBI headquarters in Quantico, Virginia, to curse his onetime FBI handler. He's travel-ling with his 20 years-younger girlfriend Catherine Greig, a dental hygienist who had a hairdresser in Grand Isle, who happened to be the daughter of the police chief, to cut and style her light platinum blonde hair. "She was nice. 'Helen' tipped well," reported the cutter. The couple was positively identified in London in 2002 and inves-tigators who have travelled to A-list places like Thailand, Brazil, Uruguay, France and Spain are again focusing closely on the UK. Phone records show a number of calls from England to Boston asso-ciates and family members of Bulger's. "A clever fugitive cuts his ties to his old haunts," said the Boston investigator. "Whitey's not stupid, so he must be confident. He was even reported at a screening of 'The Departed' in San Diego in 2006. A law officer made him, but lost him as he left the theatre. The cop called the FBI but it took them 36 days to return his calls."

Bounty hunters know that Whitey likes military history (investigators monitored the 60th anniversary memorial of the Normandy landings in hopes of spotting him there) and he reads military magazines. He doesn't drink more than a glass of wine an evening, and seeks dental care regularly. He doesn't smoke, is lactose-intolerant, takes Atenolol for a heart condition, and Xanax for depression. He loves animals and carries a bag of dog biscuits in the trunk of his car. His eyes are blue, hair is silver, he's 5ft 8 ins tall and weighs about 160 lbs. He's used the names Mark Shapeton, Tom Harris, Tom Marshall, Jimmy Bulger and Tom Baxter. Said the Boston police source: "Whitey's been seen, he's talked to his family and friends, he's not afraid, or lying low. The current FBI investigators have never seen him, never dealt with him. All his old, canny hunters have retired, and you have to wonder how much the FBI want an old can of worms re-opened. It's history to the new lot, not their problem. Maybe Whitey's beaten this rap after all. He's even the subject of an Oscar-winning film. He must be killing himself, laughing!"

ON ASSIGNMENT

Icelandic Adventures

When Michelangelo prepared his great masterpieces, he began by sketching cartoons of considerable detail, calling them his 'primo pensiere' or first thoughts, and copied them reasonably faithfully onto the walls of a fresco or onto the canvas of his next opus. In other words, he made a plan. It was yet another difference between the great artist and those who steered the Enquirer ship of editorial state. Most of the assignments I did for the tabloids had an idea that I or some editor sketched out in a wildly-inaccurate way, and the plan usually had to include a lot of seat-of-the-pants aerobatics and improvisations to keep it afloat. Such was a trip to Iceland with photographer John Miller.

I'd been busy with parapsychology stories for the Enquirer and came across Erlandur Haraldsson, a professor at the University of Iceland in Reykjavik, who had busied himself investigating reports of life after death. I put some of his cases and several other story ideas together, made an exploratory call to see if the affable academic would see us, and flew into Keflavik with Mr Miller and a case of champagne, his drink of choice. Previous visits to that green island had enlightened me enough to know that booze was extremely expensive there, so John and I had provisioned ourselves carefully. Our first stop there was to see the prime minister. Somehow, I'd learned that he lived in an ordinary house on an ordinary street in the capital and that any citizen could knock on his door to air grievances or deliver political advice. We wanted to test my half-baked story idea, and found the address. Nobody home. I made a couple of calls and established that the PM was in his office at the parliament building but he obligingly agreed to see us that afternoon. What I didn't realize was that Iceland was in the throes of another fisheries war with Britain, and the PM had the previous day announced his intent to extend Iceland's territorial waters. He gave us time, under the misapprehension that we were credible journalists on a serious political mission, not a couple of idiots wanting to prove that Iceland's leader was the most accessible in the Free World. While he was eager to encourage US intervention, we only wanted a chummy picture and a flimsy story.

Geir Hallgrimsson was certainly accessible, and very puzzled. He gave me a briefing on the new 200-mile ocean limits and the need to preserve cod breeding stocks while I nodded, uncomprehending, and Miller fretted impatiently. No, he didn't want a picture of the PM at his desk, he wanted a picture of him outside the front door, which would have to pass for his house door. Miller would really have liked the PM unshaven, in shorts and flip flops, holding a beer. We stood there, Mr Hallgrimsson in a sober suit, and Our Man in Iceland in something horribly safari that a French saleswoman had persuaded me into with blatant flattery and maybe a sense of revenge for the battle of Agincourt. "Put your arm around his shoulders!" Miller instructed me. "No way," I muttered, edging a fraction closer. "You, Mister Prime, sir. Put your arm around him. Now, grin!" I half expected Miller to pull out a Detroit baseball cap for the trapped politician, who was acting as if my leprosy was showing. Picture taken, we left, agreeing that he should have loosened up a bit. Predictably, the story of the warm, welcoming PM pictured with the stranger he was palpably shying away from never made the paper. Only now can Mr Hallgrimsson find out what we were really doing. Sorry.

However, the Icelanders had a sort of revenge almost at once.

That night, in a trendy bar, I ordered a hugely expensive Scotch and water, at roughly three times Manhattan prices, eyed the nearby table full of half-cut 20-somethings sitting around one bottle of beer and wondered at their loud merriment. After a couple of sips of my Scotch, I went to the bathroom. Back at the table, where Miller was flirting with some Dresden-china blonde beauty, my drink was missing. "Waitress must have taken it," Miller said, uncaring. I ordered another. Two sips, and a scuffle broke out at the bar. Some drunk was harassing the Dresden-china blonde. I went to interfere, came back to find my drink missing, again. Annoyed, I called over the waitress. "Oh," she said, "you don't leave drinks unattended. People steal them. They're expensive, you know." The table of young drunks, how'd they afford to get wasted at these prices? "Oh they drink a half bottle of vodka before they go out, then, in a bar, they share one beer for an hour or two. And steal."

The next day, tired and hung over, we took a flight to Akureyri, a northern town where I was to interview a psychic healer. The departure lounge was busy, but when it began to empty we were turned back. "You're on another flight," someone explained. Ten minutes later, we strolled across the rainy tarmac to a waiting 1940s DC3 workhorse, climbed the steps into the crowded plane and struggled up the steeply-slanted aisle to a front seat, where I at once fell asleep. Miller woke me as we were on final approach. "How's your Icelandic?" he asked. We were the only two regular passengers on the flight. All the others were inmates of a lunatic asylum who were being transferred to a new home. I had visions of being shackled and led to a waiting bus by people unable to understand my protestations. Wild-eyed Miller had no hope, I thought, but in the end it seemed they were unwilling to take him, so we exited unharmed.

A few days later, our lack of command of the Icelandic language was again a factor. We'd been to view Gullfoss, a giant waterfall, had picnicked on a few bottles of champagne. On the way back, Miller began berating me for being boring and recalled other adventures we'd had. On impulse, I said I'd drive through the next river. After all, the rivers are shallow, and we had rented a high-riding Chevy Blazer 4WD. We bumped across the lava field, with its four-inch covering of green moss, and began across the next creek when Miller told me: 'Under the bridge! Go under the bridge!" I turned downstream and was right under the wretched road bridge when we lurched into a hole in the creek bed and the water was suddenly five feet deep. A dashboard light that said 'Generator' came on just as I wound up the window to stop the incoming river that was soaking my elbow. We sat on the seat backs, feet on the dash, hugging Miller's camera bags. We emptied the last of the champagne, then climbed out of the window and onto the Blazer's roof. I stripped off, carried the bags to the bridge pontoon and went back to balance the photogger on my shoulders like St Christopher and the Christ child, so we both wouldn't get wet. Miller was no great help. He rocked back and forth, roaringly merry, shouting that if I fell, I was to fall forward so he could leap to safety. Somehow, we reached the bridge pontoon and scrambled out of the ice melt water. I opted to go look for help while John waited to see if a passerby could tow us out. A mile or two along, I found a farm. An old Icelandic farmer and his hefty 15 years old grand daughter understood my 'Mein Auto ist kaput' as 'He's got a flat tire' and the farm girl drove a puny Massey Ferguson tractor out of the barn. They shared the single metal seat, I stood behind, over the axle and got liberally spattered with cow dung. We found Miller lounging on the bridge parapet. The old farmer looked quizzical when I said: "Here!" "Auto? Wo ist?" he asked. When I gestured under the bridge, he about fell off the seat laughing.

Their tractor was too small to drag out the big, waterlogged Blazer, so, despite my new-found bovine fragrance, the old farmer kindly jammed us into a tiny Renault and drove us to a hamlet that was little more than wide space in the road. There, amazingly, an Anglophone young guy with a 40-seater all-wheel-drive Mercedes expedition bus was refueling. My third dip in the freezing river was most painful, as I attached a tow hawser to the submerged front wheel (Miller cheerfully volunteered to take the pictures) and we left the dripping Chevy on the bank to await repair crews. The drive back to Reykjavik was exhilarating, as the bus driver four-wheel-drifted that thing along the black lava dust roads like a full-on F1 jockey. I called the office to deceitfully complain that we'd nearly been drowned getting to the job. They told us to get a sauna and a large brandy to warm up. Needless to say, we couldn't rent from that car agency again. I don't suppose the other agency in town would rent to me again, either. I forgot to leave their car's keys at the airport when

I left, and took them to Scotland with me. It wouldn't have been so bad, but I was late for my plane, and left the rental car, locked, on a double yellow line, right outside the terminal's main door. Here and now, Icelandic car rental agents, I apologize. I know the office paid for the water damage to the Blazer, and for a duplicate set of keys for the VW. It was just incompetence, not malice. Sorry.

Air Disaster

My next assignment, in March 1977, took me to Africa. At an hour's notice, I raced to the Canary Islands to cover the world's worst air disaster. A friend called me at home in Florida to tell me there had been a terrible air crash in Tenerife, and I got some details from a BBC world news broadcast. A Dutch KLM 747 had collided in fog with a Pan Am 747 on the runway of Los Rodeos airport. The butcher's bill was horrendous: 583 dead, 60-some seriously injured. Within the hour, I was scrambling onto a flight for London, then on to Madrid and Gran Canaria, the next island from Tenerife. I arrived in Las Palmas with about $70 cash and a few credit cards to find the only way to Tenerife was by ferry, but the ship was already jammed, as all flights were cancelled and hundreds of travelers were trying to continue their journeys. Two Dutch journalists asked me if I'd share in renting a helicopter, but the brigand in charge wanted $2000 each for the trip. The Dutchmen couldn't pay that and the brigand wouldn't take my credit card, although the Enquirer would have happily paid up. We all three turned away. At the rear of the ferry, foot passengers were trickling up the car ramp and were being checked for tickets by two scruffy-looking deck hands. "We should bribe those guys and get on that way," I told the Dutchmen, who were trusting to a degree I'd never seen among English journalists. "What do you think we should give them?" asked one honest-faced Netherlander. "Don't give them too much or they'll think it's impor-tant, just give them a few dollars each," I suggested, knowing that my $70 was not going to get me very far. We all three set off up the ramp, then I paused to tie my shoelace. A woman with a large suitcase and two small children was just behind me. I offered to carry the case for her, and she smiled gratefully. The Dutchmen were in a loud alterca-tion with the seriously-offended deck hands, who were waving their arms about dramatically. They would have been happy to receive a few hundred dollars to look the other way, but they certainly wouldn't cooperate for the price of a coffee and they were doing a fine job of telling the hapless Dutchmen that. As the wrangle went on, I solicitously ushered the travelling mom up the ramp and past the ticket inspectors, handed back the suitcase and rolled under a VW camper on the vehicle deck, to hide until we pulled out to sea.

The next couple of weeks on Tenerife were a sleep-deprived blur as I interviewed survivors and looked for a sustainable angle for a magazine published a week or more after the dailies had chewed up the story. Finally, a source gave me a clue. Someone was selling a pirated tape recording of the last seven minutes of conversation between the control tower and the two jumbos. I learned that the wire services interested in buying the tape for the $24,000 asking price had stalled the negotiations. Some of their clients were radio stations and were legally unable to broadcast a stolen tape. A transcript could be used by print media, but that was all. A phone call to the office, and they wired me the goods. I walked out of a local bank with $25,000 in cash, bundled in a brown envelope, expecting to be mugged. Dazed as I was on three hours' sleep a night, I was just able to work out that someone with a connection to the control tower was the likely source of the pirated tape. One evening, I met a man who said he was acting as agent for the deal and realized that he was very eager to leave as 8pm approached. Sherlock-style, I deduced he had to be somewhere else at that time, perhaps at a night shift at the airport. He left, I drove out to Los Rodeos airport and eventually spotted him working there. It didn't take long to learn his name and find his address, as well as to learn that he'd be off shift at 6am. I saw him arrive home, gave him a minute to use the bathroom and knocked on the door. His jaw was resting on his chest as I explained that he really wanted to deal only with me, not with the Guardia Civil, but he saw the light and also lowered the asking price to $4,000.

The story made a nice page one world exclusive, and despite a brief tussle with temptation, I returned $21,000 to the Enquirer, but only after rewarding myself with a very fine seafood dinner and a couple of bottles of wine. My contact didn't feel too badly about it all, either. He called me in Florida a week later to offer more tape recordings, from the minutes after the crash.

Test Tube Trials

Back in Florida, I was busy arranging a rugby match between our Brit journos and the local Iron Horse club when news broke of the world's first 'test tube' baby. Louise Brown had been successfully conceived in a petri dish and publisher Pope wanted an exclusive. A team of nine reporters and editors was assembled, gutting the rugby XV, and scrambled to Oldham, Lancashire, where the pregnant mother was being cared for in a small hospital. We put the word around our onetime colleagues on the British newspapers that we'd pay handsomely for information. We even negotiated a daily rate for the money we spent in bars and restaurants entertaining off-duty nurses and other hospital staff as we hunted down the world's first test tube mother. It didn't take long. We monitored the visitors' parking lot, did some discreet watching and ran car license numbers through a friendly police source. Within a few days we had six likely names, and one of them was our target, from Bristol. In typical tabloid fashion, our work was wasted. The editor on the spot decided he'd negotiate directly with the doctors instead of with the family, to do a buy-up of the story. Then he settled in to spend a comfortable six months in British hotels, everything on expenses while he wined and dined them and himself, and watched as the Brit papers aced us and scored the world first.

The story had a sequel a year or so later, when my friend and colleague Joe Mullins brought John and Lesley Brown and their history-making baby to Florida. Joe secreted them away in an ocean-front hotel, away from the Enquirer's then-rivals, Star and Globe. During dinner, baby Louise started choking on her food. Her parents looked on, unmoving. It was journalist Joe who jumped around the table and started scooping mush from the infant's mouth. "I had to," he confessed. "I didn't want to be known as The Man Who Killed The Test Tube Baby." Louise's life saved, the baby handed to her mother to be calmed, Joe slumped back in his chair and looked across at the moonlike face of the baby's father. Crisis ended, John Brown sighed heavily. "Eh, Joe, fair put me off my prawns."

Back home again in Boynton Beach, Florida, I took stock. The Enquirer was ticking along, and I'd been there for more than six years. They'd paid me well, sent me to all 50 states and about 40 countries and given me nearly-unlimited rein to do the job. But I'd spent too many birthdays and anniversaries on the road, and missed too many events my tolerant wife had planned for us and our two young girls. I was a reluctant deadbeat dad who was liable to leave at a few hours' notice when some editor told me to go.

Several years' travel was fine, but after six years of it, sometimes being away for a couple of months at a stretch, I wanted more control of my own life. Jennie and I discussed it, and formed our plan. We'd move elsewhere in the states, I'd stay on staff for a year or so then I'd break with the paper and freelance for them and anyone else. Where to go? The choice to me was clear: northern California was beautiful, had scenery, seasons and facilities. The San Francisco Bay area offered access to ocean, mountains, snow and city pleasures. I knew a friend whose sons separately went skiing, surfing and riding motorcycles in semi-desert, and were all home again for dinner that day. We rented out our house, shipped our goods and took a couple of weeks to drive 4,100 miles across the southern route I-10 freeway to the Golden State itself. After going on all those assignments around the States, when I'd fly in, then drive the last 100 miles or less to reach my destination, I finally found out about America's sheer size. You don't comprehend until you start at one side and drive to the other, just how big, and often empty, is the North American continent. We found achingly open vistas, impossibly isolated settlements, skies as spacious as the anthem suggests, and an intrepid population who measure distance by hours, not miles. We were soon settled in Palo Alto, home of the university endowed by rail magnate Leland Stanford, and I carried on working for the Enquirer, but from my home office. The travel was cut drastically, the output increased, it was a happy solution.

Suicides Who Survived

From California, I did a sampling of stories, covering the eruption of Mount St Helens and the visit of Her Majesty the Queen (she slept at Yosemite Lodge, in quarters said to be haunted) and we revealed the contents of her handbag to an interested readership. (Comb, gold compact, hankie, lipstick, small camera, cough drops). I wrote about Henry Funk, a 6ft 8ins 23 year old from Vancouver who shot a bullet into his brain in a bid to end his hellish life. He hit the spot, all right. The slug cured him. Funk had spent 14 years struggling to overcome a crippling mental disorder and had tried suicide twice before. Then he shot himself in the exact part of his brain that was causing his obsessive-compulsive disorder. "Had it lodged one millimeter in any other direction, he would have died. He missed several major arteries by fractions of an inch," said his astonished doctor. "I've never felt better," said Henry, who had put his rifle barrel in his mouth and pulled the trigger. The only ill-effect of his auto-surgery by .22 bullet: he lost his sense of smell. Another would-be suicide I interviewed was 29 years old Ken Baldwin, a computer worker who lived in Tracy, California. A perfectionist who got everything right, he bungled what he intended as his ultimate task. He tried to commit suicide by throwing himself off the Golden Gate Bridge, a venue which had already claimed 1,200 lives, but he survived. Baldwin was depressed, bottled up his emotions and got worse until finally, he walked to the center of the 230 foot high span, counted to ten, and vaulted over. "My body was in midair, only my hands were still touching the red-painted rail. I was committed, about to die, and suddenly I didn't want to go," he told me. Baldwin turned in midair and hurtled towards the glittering water, feeling utterly lonely and telling himself it was the worst mistake he'd ever made. He blacked out before he impacted at 70mph, curled in a fetal position that meant he hit the stone-hard surface buttocks first. An alert bridge worker dropped down a flare to mark the spot, a Coast Guard cutter was on site in seven minutes, and the unconscious man was recovered as he floated. All he had was a bruised lung, a broken rib and a battered backside. "I have had a sense of exultation every single day since," Baldwin told me a year after his leap. "I almost threw away a wonderful life, but I got it back."

Something similar happened to another person I interviewed right around that time. Edwin Robinson was left blind and deaf after a truck crash caused him severe head injuries. "I had to learn Braille," the 73 years old Rhode Island man told me. "I had hearing aids in each ear. The doctors said I'd never hear or see again." For nine years, he didn't—until the day he went outside in a thunderstorm. A lightning bolt hit a poplar, speared Ed behind his right ear, travelled down his right arm and grounded through his aluminum cane. He was left unconscious with an egg-sized, bloody lump on his head. The lightning shattered both of Ed's hearing aids and froze his Braille wristwatch. He lay in the rain for about 20 minutes, then staggered inside the house and fell on his bed. "I woke up and realized I was looking at a plaque my grandchildren brought me. My wife came in and I said: 'You've put on a little weight.'" The bolt had left Ed with perfect vision and hearing, and his wife has gone on a diet.

The 1400 lbs Man

Eating wasn't a problem with the man I went to see in Seattle. Jon Minnoch was the world's heaviest man when he was 38 years old., weighing in at 1,400 lbs. He wasn't a huge eater, but he'd been obese all his life—around 300 lbs at age 12—because he retained fluid. In adulthood, he had an estimated 900 lbs of excess water in his body, and it finally killed him. I went to Seattle to see him when he was under hospital supervision and had dropped the equivalent of two human beings: he'd lost 400 lbs and now weighed about 1,000 lbs. Doctors at the University of Washington hospital could only guess at their patient's weight, as they didn't have the equipment to weigh him. It took six or eight people just to roll him over in his pair of strengthened hospital beds, for linen changes, a nurse told me. "A lot has been going wrong in my life," Minnoch said. "I had a taxi business, but I couldn't drive because I was too big to get behind the wheel. I spent about a month just sleeping in the cab, unable to get out. I ran a hobby business by telephone and my partner did the rest. I got so big my own body was strangling me, I couldn't even stand. Finally, I went into hospital. It was the dark side of hell."

Fire chief Don Beach told me how he moved the 1,400 lbs man from his island home in Winslow to hospital, a ferry ride away in Seattle. "He was about four feet wide, all water, like a big balloon. We handled him the way we'd handle a cow with a broken leg. We had ten guys in the truck company and we slipped an eight foot by four foot, three quarter inch plywood sheet under him, took out the whole double window frame and slid him over it." Then the firefighters loaded the helpless human bladder into a rescue vehicle and took him to the ferry, cutting the plywood down to fit through the hospital door at the other end. Minnoch spent months in hospital, on a 1200-calorie daily diet that caused him agony as his stomach shrank, but he lost weight, and was eventually released. Not long afterwards, his respiratory problems weakened him again, his weight went back up and he was returned to hospital. He died in Seattle in late 1983, a year or so after we spoke. At the end, he was 42 years old and weighed 792 lbs.

Private Lessons

Seattle was also the site of a long-running and controversial story for me, the wrenching tale of 34 years old teacher Mary Kay LeTourneau and the 12 years old pupil she took as a lover. The couple had two babies, and ultimately married. Mary Kay is 48 now, her husband Vili Fuualaau is 26. She's a homemaker, raising their two little girls. He's an art student and they're reputedly living off a six-figure paycheck they got from selling their wedding video to the media.

The LeTourneau frenzy began when the angel-faced teacher who was married with four kids was caught having sex with her sixth-grade pupil. It attracted the whole media circus, including tabloid monkey me, and I visited Seattle for the story a number of times, for various magazines, including tabloids. I became expert at tracking down Mary Kay, who stayed with friends, or in hotels and my spies held a spectrum of attitudes to her. Some called her a sexual predator, a pervert and a child rapist. Others said hers was a tender and genuine love affair, and there were no victims. Some explained she was obsessed, a woman in denial. One neighbor stopped by my car when I went to speak to a Star photographer outside the house where she was staying. "If you'd just leave her alone, it would be all right. We don't want your sort around here," he told me. I spluttered indignantly that I wasn't the convicted sex offender. He was angry. "She's a decent woman," he said. "You should leave her alone!"

I interviewed Vili, and his mother, Soona, who raised the children in the years when Mary Kay was incarcerated. Soona took the tabloids' and TV companies' money and ran through more than $150,000, taking friends on a Pacific island holiday and staying in Seattle hotels because she didn't want to have to clean her own house. When Mary Kay got out of prison, there was nothing left.

She talked of her cockeyed plans: though unemployed, she'd have a white mansion in France, and a home in Seattle. She and Vili would take one of their daughters with them to Europe for six months of the year. That way, she reasoned, she could focus more closely on each child, devote more time to her. The other child would stay with grandma Soona.

I talked to her lawyer, who said that with treatment Mary Kay was not at risk to re-offend, and I talked to her biographer, who put it succinctly. "She's not on this planet." I came away from it all thinking regretfully of the real victims: a boy who had his childhood stolen, a deceived husband, and a family abandoned by their mother. Some stories are not fun and even callous tabloid reporters can feel bad for the victims.

Creative Judges

My next tabloid job was more upbeat, and it sent me to talk to a Texas judge who was highly flexible and creative in his courtroom approach. It also inspired a good number of readers to write to us, saying "I wish we had a judge like that." The case I liked best involved the Man Who Stole The Lone Ranger's Guns. Edward Young, 45, was convicted of stealing actor Clayton Moore's silver Colt 45s while working as a baggage handler at Houston's Intercontinental Airport. Judge Ted Poe heard the case and handed down a classic, poetic punishment. He sentenced Young to spend 600 hours cleaning up after the horses at the police stables. "I had to tell him this morning what the judge was going to do to him," said defense attorney Ealy Bennett. "I told him: 'You're going to be shoveling (bleep).' You should have seen his face."

Young appealed, basing his defense on insufficient evidence and the fact that Poe let the Lone Ranger wear his sunglasses and trademark white hat while testifying. The appeal failed and the thief spent the next three years, at 20 hours a month, mucking out manure in the stables of the Houston Mounted Patrol. Said Judge Poe: "I wasn't about to be the one who revealed the identity of the Lone Ranger. Outlaws have been trying to find it out for years."

FULL CIRCLE

————•◦•————

Tabloid Turnovers

The stories in the Florida daily papers told me I'd come full circle. There was a family feud in the Pope clan. The man who turned America on its tabloid head was Generoso Paul 'Gene' Pope Jr, an Italian-American from New Jersey, the son of a quarry magnate and publisher of an Italian language daily newspaper. In 1952, GP bought the low-circulation New York Enquirer with a $75,000 loan from his Mafioso godfather, took it to Florida and built it to a five-million circulation weekly parish pump of celebrity gossip, sensation, homely tales, medical advice and stories of the occult. For almost a decade, through the 1970s and into the 1980s, National Enquirer was my employer. After I left, I worked for them as a free-lance for another 30 years. Things changed along the way.

Pope died in 1988, of a heart attack, at age 61. He collapsed at home, and expired in an ambulance he'd donated to the community, en route to the hospital on whose board he served. The shock wave was immediate, and powerful. Right after GP's death, editor Iain Calder declared that the Enquirer was 'no longer a rich man's toy,' announced cutbacks and battled with Pope's widow Lois to move at once into his old boss' office. He even contested handing over the publisher's desk to the family, arguing that it was a symbol of power. Lois sold out for $412 million, the new operators took public the Enquirer empire of magazines and distribution services, slashed staffing levels and lived off corporate and editorial reserves, using up the fat inventory of stories as they hacked down costs. When the now-lean paper went public, a handful of people became very wealthy, and about 100 of my onetime colleagues and friends were laid off.

Public confidence in the tabloids as an investment waned, the shares dropped from the teens of dollars to a couple of bucks and the conglomerate went private again, leaving employees who'd been given stock options holding nothing but some devalued bits of paper. Freelances like me knew long before the collapse that things were seriously sliding. Story payments were cut, then delayed so that what once took a couple of weeks to be paid now took three or four months. Some of my own stories went unpaid for as long as two years. It became a bitter game, guessing what excuse the editor would give for non-payment. Someone on vacation here, end of the fiscal quarter there, misplaced invoices somewhere else. At least one editor kept on-budget simply by not putting payments through at all. I had a $22,000 list of unpaid stories with the deadbeat, who kept assuring me he'd signed off on payments, and this senior editor or that accountant must be delaying them, he said. Only after the guy left did the truth come out: he'd simply ignored my invoices. Another editor, faced with months of unpaid invoices, responded by hacking down individual story fees to make the total more palatable. Freelancers who'd not only had to wait and wait to be paid now found they were getting fees well below the accepted rates, too. One longtime woman stringer, in tears, told me how she'd been forced to accept about one-tenth of the fees she'd expected. It was that or nothing, she was told as she took dimes on the dollar. After the financial straits came more disaster. In 2001, the company was hit by an anthrax attack which caused the death of photo editor Bob Stevens, injured others and shut down the building for six years. One casualty of the attack was the loss of the five million-image photo library. All that survived was a jukebox full of CD's that contained the small percentage of digital images that were just coming into currency. Five decades' worth of negatives and prints, including my original Baffling Chair of Death photographs and the million-dollar image of Elvis in his casket were all contaminated, and ordered destroyed.

American Media Inc moved the Enquirer's sister paper, Star, expensively into the realms of the glossies, shunting first Star and then Enquirer to New York. The publisher appointed a highly-paid but unregarded editor who was as effective at stemming the rising tide of fiscal woe as was Canute and the North Sea. Gossips who formed an online club to list her missteps delightedly claimed she'd returned from a stroll through the newsroom to complain that all the reporters were 'wasting time playing Google.' Desperate to improve ebbing circulation, the publisher tried to repeat history and recruited a new, British staff for the Enquirer. His error was that most of them knew little about America, and unlike Gene Pope's expatriate team, they weren't headed by veteran US newsmen who could guide them in their New World. The gossips reported next that senior Brits were noted for wandering about plaintively asking if this actor or that actress 'is famous in America?' Predictably, the Brits lasted just a year, and got their pink slips the day after their anniversary celebration. The paper was moved back to Florida, and by November 2010, American Media, publishers of Star, Globe and Enquirer, was filing for bankruptcy. The company's financial leaders had nearly doubled the debt, putting the group $855 million in the hole. Gene Pope, the portrait of a successful tabloid publisher, would have laughed at being right again. He'd specified in his will that the Enquirer was to be sold after his death because he simply didn't trust anyone but himself to run it.

Pope's widow, the former Lois Berrodin, had carried out her husband's wishes and, hundreds of millions of dollars richer, and had become a headline-attracting Palm Beach socialite and philanthropist.

The Popes might have exited the gossip business as purveyors, but they could not stay out of it as subjects. The family was split when some sensational claims were made. GP's son Paul had spent 15 years and $3 million researching his father's life for a biography, but he found more than he'd expected. He said he'd discovered that the sale of the paper when he was 20 years old had been rigged against him, and he wanted his inheritance. He claimed that a will leaving the publishing empire to him had been suppressed, and compiled a list of witnesses who could say they knew of the missing testament that GP was supposed to have kept in his briefcase. The young Pope also offered a reward for information about the way his father died because he suspected foul play there, too. He even pointed a finger at his mother, who admitted she was considering divorce before Gene died. Paul accused her of delaying help when GP was dying and criticized her refusal to allow an autopsy. Lois' attorneys called the allegations of delay 'particularly despicable.'

Pope's widow tired of her son's antics. After nearly two decades, the matriarch decided his actions showed no concern for his five siblings or her dozen grandchildren, and she declared that his lifestyle was too lavish. Tensions rose, mother and son were estranged and in 2006, Lois, then 74, sued her son for $340,000. She said it was money she'd loaned him as she tried to wean him from his spendthrift ways. Paul, who billed himself on his website as 'America's Tabloid Royalty' told his mother's lawyers he needed $71,000 a month for basic expenses, listing among them restaurant and entertainment bills ($5,000); another $5,000 for boat maintenance, $1,000 a month for a dog walker, $1,500 for dry cleaning and $7,000 for petty cash. Mama stood by her criticism of his 'profligate lifestyle' and demanded a revised budget, saying Paul had squandered $20 million since his father's death. GP's son came back with a $45,000-a-month budget, and his mother softened. She gave him a job at her charity foundation with a starting salary of $10,000 a month, plus another $20,000-a-month loan and $115,000 cash to help him downscale. The uneasy reconciliation ended when Lois sued Paul for non-payment of a $340,000 promissory note. Paul counter-sued, asking for the $5 million home, Bentley convertible and lifetime million-dollar annual income he said she'd promised him. He also attacked his mother over the performance of a family trust. "He says she's not a good steward, she's let the family fortune dwindle down and she's squandered his inheritance. She says he's a spoiled brat out to milk her of every dime," explained a former employee. "He wants everything I have," Lois said in a letter she released to the Fort Lauderdale Sun-Sentinel newspaper. "This is tough love now."

Meanwhile, Charity Navigator, a watchdog group, gave Lois' charity organisation its lowest ranking, zero out of four stars, for spending 88 cents of every dollar to raise money. The watchdog's standards: no fundraising should cost more than 10 cents on the dollar. Paul Pope said his mom's charity, which aimed to raise $65 million for a disabled veterans' memorial, had spent most of the $14 million it garnered since 1998 on salaries, lavish parties and trinkets. In 2008, the charity had more than $2 million in unpaid bills despite Lois pumping in $3.5 million of her own money. The gossips carried stories of family rows, then a dramatic mother-son reconciliation at the bedside of an ailing relative. "It's the tabloid royal family making tabloid headlines," marveled a Florida former employee of the Enquirer. "It's absolutely a full circle."

Full circle. Thirty-five years on, a second generation of British journalists had gone west to work on the Enquirer. Full circle again, in 2006, as in 1971, the paper was moved from New York to Florida, and just to complete the full circle triple, now GP's son was making headlines, just like dad. It sounded like tabloid reincarnation. All that's missing is a second Baffling Chair of Death. I'll start looking.

Lightning Source UK Ltd.
Milton Keynes UK
UKOW021406121211

183640UK00011B/33/P